Praise for *Touching All the Bases*

"If you believe you already know Dave Winfield's story, this memoir will challenge you. It is one of the most compelling leadership narratives I've encountered from the world of sports—a story of courage, discipline, faith, and vision. Dave takes us into the spaces where decisions were made and barriers were broken, and he shares lessons that apply far beyond athletics."

—Robert Smith, Chairman, Vista Equity Partners Venture Capital Firm

"As great a ballplayer and athlete as Dave was, he is an even better man. In *Touching All the Bases*, Dave shares his inspirational story. Dave's journey gives us a glimpse of all that went into making him the player and person we have come to respect and admire so much. Dave is a Hall of Famer in every way, and I am proud to call him my friend."

—Cal Ripken, Jr., National Baseball Hall of Fame Shortstop;
World Series Champion; AL MVP; and CEO, Ripken Baseball

"In the business world we define greatness by sustained excellence and the ability to thrive under pressure. For Dave Winfield, talent, strategy, and execution is what earned him a place in the Baseball Hall of Fame. His story is a master class in professional resilience and life. Dave has navigated high-stakes volatility without ever compromising his character. He's truly touched every base in sports, business, and philanthropy, and has lived his life with integrity."

—Ken Chenault, former CEO and Chairman, American Express,
and Chairman, General Catalyst

"Dave Winfield is one of the coolest people I know. He's one of the greatest athletes in American history, a legendary ballplayer, a devoted family man, and someone who strives to make the world a better place. Now, finally, he tells his story—the whole story—and it will surprise you, entertain you, and, more than anything, inspire you."

—Joe Posnanski, and *New York Times* Bestselling Author,
and 5x National Sportswriter of the Year

"In his memoir, Dave Winfield absolutely touches all the bases with his life story both on and off the field. He shares the mindset and actions it takes to become a Hall of Fame Athlete."

—Harvey Mackay, *#1 New York Times* Bestselling Author,
Swim with the Sharks Without Being Eaten Alive, and Businessman

"Dave Winfield has been an outstanding leader for players' rights, for youth, and for his community. He raised a family and became a baseball all-time great, and he set an example in philanthropy and business for generations of baseball players to come. The most amazing part of this story, though, is that he accomplished all this while battling with one of the most powerful owners in baseball history. Dave's memoir is an insightful portrait of power, race, and resilience; a great story well worth your time to read."

—Kenneth Beck, Cofounder and Chief Executive Officer, CEO Connection,
and Chairman, Wharton Club of New York

"Dave Winfield represents leadership in its fullest form—as an athlete, philanthropist, family man, and friend. Drafted in three professional sports, he chose baseball and built a Hall of Fame career, but his true impact went far beyond the field. He led with strength, dignity, generosity, and loyalty. This is more than a sports story; it's a story about character, responsibility, and using greatness to lift others."

—Dave Stewart, former MLB All Star Pitcher, World Series Champion,
AL MVP, and Baseball Executive

"I've awaited this book for 30 years. Now, it's here. Dave Winfield is a foundational figure in baseball history. In terms of talent, he was like Jackie Robinson, Bo Jackson, and Deion Sanders: world-class in multiple sports. For baseball ability, he was the five-tool heir to Mays and Aaron, the precursor to Betts and Trout. In changing the salary scale for players, he laid the groundwork for Harper and Soto and Ohtani. For those of us who saw him play, he was unforgettable. We've heard so many of the stories about Winfield, Steinbrenner, and the Bronx Zoo, but now Dave has given us the missing pieces: the story as he lived it."

—Howard Bryant, Author, Journalist, and Producer

TOUCHING ALL THE BASES

TOUCHING ALL THE BASES

A Story of Power, Purpose, and Surviving the Bronx

Dave Winfield

with Alan Maimon

MATT HOLT

Matt Holt Books
An Imprint of BenBella Books, Inc.
Dallas, TX

The events, locations, and conversations in this book, while true, are re-created from the author's memory. However, the essence of the story, and the feelings and emotions evoked, are intended to be accurate representations. In certain instances, names, persons, organizations, and places have been changed to protect an individual's privacy.

MATT HOLT BENBELLA

Matt Holt is an imprint of BenBella Books, Inc.
BenBella Books, Inc.
8080 N. Central Expressway
Suite 1700
Dallas, TX 75206
benbellabooks.com
Send feedback to feedback@benbellabooks.com

Printed in the United States of America
10 9 8 7 6 5 4 3 2 1

Library of Congress Control Number: 2026002026
ISBN 9781637748985 (hardcover)
ISBN 9781637748992 (electronic)

Editing by Lydia Choi
Copyediting by Scott Calamar
Proofreading by Marissa Wold Uhrina and Rebecca Maines
Text design and composition by Jordan Koluch
Cover design by Jason Arias
Cover image © RVR Photos-Imagn Images
Printed by Lake Book Manufacturing

To my wife, Tonya Turner Winfield,
ours has been an incredible journey of faith, forgiveness, and light

Contents

INTRODUCTION

The hour or so I spent in the clubhouse before a game was a time of intense concentration for me. Back then, there were no magic screens with every possible dataset on pitcher-batter matchups, so I had to rely on memory. What did the pitcher we were facing that day throw me the last time I saw him? What were his tendencies? What adjustments would I need to make to square up a pitch and drive it into the alley or over the wall?

But it's not easy to visualize hitting a 97-mile-per-hour fastball when you're thinking about the answers you just gave during a grilling by the team owner's attorney.

In the early 1980s, I sued George Steinbrenner for breaking his promise to donate money to my charitable foundation. Knowing he didn't have a leg to stand on, Steinbrenner had his lawyer try to wear me down with monotonous questions about the foundation's inner workings. As a result, instead of fully focusing on preparing for games, I found myself distracted by my fight against the most powerful man in baseball. The same man who had pulled out all the stops to bring me to New York had now made it his mission to take me down.

At least George had the decency on the days I was being interrogated in

Manhattan to arrange for a car service to whisk me from the Upper East Side to the Bronx in time for the ump to bark: "Play ball!"

So there I was, one warm July night in 1984, stepping to the plate in the first inning, not as clearheaded as I would've liked to be, but ready to take my aggression toward George out on a baseball. The guy on the mound for Texas threw heat. That much I knew. And his reputation for throwing up and in preceded him. But with the bases loaded, he had nowhere to put me. I didn't feel like myself, but he didn't need to know that. I strutted to the plate with a swagger that said: "You don't want to mess with me."

After taking a couple of pitches, I locked in and sat on a fastball, which came and promptly went over the center field wall at Yankee Stadium. As I stomped my foot on home plate and received congratulations from my teammates, I looked up at the owner's box and saw what appeared to be George standing alongside his protégé, a young real estate mogul named Donald Trump. *Take that, Steinbrenner, you MF!* I thought.

•

This isn't your typical baseball memoir. It's about spies and lies far more than RBIs. By sharing my experiences on and off the field, I'm giving you a front-row seat to one of the most scandalous dramas in sports history. The untold stories of my epic feud with George Steinbrenner resonate now more than ever.

Reggie Jackson once said playing in New York "can be Disneyland or it can be hell." For me, it was mostly the latter. The historic 10-year contract that I signed with the Yankees in 1980 ended up feeling more like a 10-year cold war. I came to the Bronx to help the Yankees win another World Series or two or three, never imagining I'd spend so much time sitting at mahogany tables in law offices giving depositions and chasing—or being chased by—two-bit hustlers straight out of a Scorsese movie. I can still see the cold steel of the two handguns I bought to protect myself.

I should have lived a charmed life in pinstripes. I played in baseball's greatest cathedral in front of the game's most passionate fan base. I lived in a city that never slept, with a once-in-a-lifetime chance to become a multi-hyphenate star in athletics, business, philanthropy, and media. But as much as I wanted to break new ground, I wasn't willing to sell my soul or dignity to do it.

This book is also about forgiveness, healing, and coming to terms with the past.

I learned a lot about those things from Negro Leagues legend Buck O'Neil. I remember the day the Yankees were in Kansas City playing the Royals when I noticed an older man watching me take cuts during batting practice.

"Who's that guy?" I asked Royals third baseman George Brett.

"That's Buck O'Neil," he replied. "Want me to introduce you?"

At the time, Major League Baseball hadn't made any effort to honor players like Buck who had been barred from the majors. The league office hadn't even established a formal way to celebrate Jackie Robinson's legacy. I was woefully underinformed about Buck's story and eager to learn more, especially because I'd missed my chance to meet the great Satchel Paige in Kansas City a few years earlier. Satchel and I had made plans for dinner, but before we returned to town later that season, he passed away.

A few minutes later, Buck and I were chatting in the visitors' dugout like old friends. That was the start of a beautiful bond. His experiences inspired me. We were alike in some ways, different in others. One thing was for sure: I didn't have Buck's sense of serenity. Despite constant bouts with racism from childhood onward, he never grew bitter. "Don't let anger boil up inside you," he often said. "There's too much anger out there already."

As a player, Buck didn't put up the numbers of Negro Leagues stars like Josh Gibson or Cool Papa Bell. His true gift to the game was as a historian of that era. No one held court like Buck, who was a co-founder of the Negro Leagues Baseball Museum in Kansas City. He had a lyrical way of speaking—sharp and precise at times, whispery at others. I loved listening to him, even though some of his stories from back in the day were painful to hear. I'll never forget the one about his wife touching a hat at a department store, only to be told by an employee that she had to buy it because it had been touched by Black hands.

Even as he entered his 90s, Buck and I got together as often as possible to discuss baseball and life. In 2006, when I was working as an executive vice president for the San Diego Padres, I sat with Buck to discuss an initiative I was spearheading to increase Black participation in baseball. We talked about the recent election of the inaugural class of Negro Leaguers into the Baseball Hall of Fame, a vote that inexplicably resulted in Buck being snubbed. At some point, the conversation that day rolled around to my time with the Yankees. Buck wanted to hear about how great it must have been to play at Yankee Stadium. "It would've been a whole lot greater if I was a lefty," I joked, referring to the stadium's short right-field porch.

I didn't get into the specifics of what I'd experienced in New York. It wouldn't have felt right to complain about it to a man who had experienced far, far worse than me.

If Buck could forsake bitterness, why couldn't I?

A few weeks after that meeting with Buck—which would turn out to be our last—I sat on a flight from LAX to Tampa en route to see George Steinbrenner. George's health was deteriorating following a series of mini-strokes. My wife, Tonya, echoed Buck's wisdom and encouraged me to go. "You should bury the hatchet with him before he's gone," she coaxed.

Bury the hatchet? You mean the one he used to do a hatchet job on me? I was skeptical after all the ups and downs—mostly downs—we'd been through. Still, I decided to make the trip, hoping it might help quiet some of the angry thoughts that had been pinballing around in my head for decades.

The pinball ricocheted especially hard during the six-hour flight to Tampa. As I started to nod off, I flashed back to a time 20 years earlier when George and I sat in his office, supposedly to discuss drug-testing policy. But he had come to the meeting with his own agenda. We had been at each other's throats for a few years by then, and I guess George had reached his boiling point.

"There is only one captain in this organization, and it's me!" he informed me.

We were in the workplace, but he was treating me like a disobedient child.

"I don't like you, and I can make things very hard for you!" he continued.

Now I felt like a disobedient child being disowned by a father who had learned everything he knew about leadership from reading *The Art of War* and watching the movie *Patton*.

Twenty years later, I was searching for something—I'm not sure what. Reconciliation? Closure? Validation?

I could feel the weight of people's stares when I arrived at 1 Steinbrenner Drive, home of the Yankees' spring training facility in Tampa. The younger employees there were barely out of diapers when I got to New York, but they knew enough about me to understand that Steinbrenner and I had a stormy history.

In Tampa, I saw a man who was a shell of his former brusque and menacing self. George was frail and soft-spoken and clearly slip-sliding away into the hereafter. He asked me about my family. That was a first. In all our years of combat, small talk—especially about family—had been kept to a minimum, maybe because George had tried to meddle in my personal and family life during the peak of our conflict.

I guess George was feeling nostalgic, because he soon started reminiscing about the press conference at a New York steakhouse that announced my signing in 1980.

"We were wearing matching suits, remember?" he asked.

I sure did remember. For that moment in time, it looked like we were going to make quite a team.

Unlike so many of our previous encounters, the one in Tampa was pleasant enough. It started with a handshake and ended with a hug. The 90-minute conversation never got around to the darker chapters in our personal history—the parts about George getting kicked out of baseball for hiring a huckster to dig up dirt on me, or about that same huckster going to prison for his actions. Did the meeting give me a sense of reconciliation, closure, or validation? To some extent it did. But I'll never reclaim those years of anguish.

I came to New York fully prepared to end my career there, to raise the bar for player salaries, take my place alongside all the other Yankee greats, and above all, to become a champion. Instead, I became a polarizing figure in the city and had to go elsewhere to win a championship and feel truly appreciated.

As much as I hoped it would, my time in New York didn't offer the final word on who I was as a player or person. But those years in the Bronx helped define a critical era in both baseball and American society. I didn't experience segregation, thankfully, but that didn't mean that some of the vestiges of those dark years didn't fester late into the twentieth century—and beyond. Americans like Buck O'Neil, Jack Johnson, Jackie Robinson, and Muhammad Ali belong in a class by themselves when it comes to awakening public consciousness. But my experience as a Black man who went to war with one of the most powerful owners in sports tells an essential story, not just about the triumphs and challenges of my own career, but about the dynamics of race and power in America then and now.

As I said, this isn't just another baseball memoir.

Chapter 1

•

THE TRIPLE DRAFT

Spotting a familiar face in a stadium full of people could feel like a game of Where's Waldo? If I scanned the stands looking for a friend or family member, it was always at my own peril—especially on the road. Maybe I'd meet the gaze of a child, smiling at me with wide-eyed wonder. Or maybe I'd lock eyes with a fan of the other team, who'd respond with a burst of profanity and a middle-finger salute.

As luck would have it, on the night I became the 19th player in major league history to collect 3,000 career hits, I had no trouble at all spotting my loved ones in the stadium—because they were well represented among the 14,500 people there.

That season, my Minnesota Twins were stumbling toward 91 losses, making a midweek game against the equally hapless Oakland Athletics an easy one for fans to skip. A few weeks shy of my 42nd birthday and in my second season with the Twins, I was competing against a generation of players who'd still been toddlers when I broke into the big leagues.

The sparseness of the crowd gave the evening an intimate feel. I flashed a thumbs-up to my brother, Steve, before the game. He was sitting next to our friend Bill Peterson, the man who had taught us both to play baseball on a field just a few miles away in St. Paul. It was a true community field, built by the neighborhood itself. Many of my 15 first cousins sat in the stands, escorting the elders of the family, whose old-school values dictated dressing up for a night out at the ballpark.

The person I most wanted to look up and see smiling back at me, though, wasn't there. My mother had passed away five years earlier during one of the lowest points of my career. But I could hear her voice that night, telling me how proud she was of me—and reminding me, if I got the big hit, to be eloquent and gracious in my postgame interviews.

That hit, a sharp single between third and short, came in the bottom of the ninth inning. As I glided around first base, wild cheers bounced off the walls of the cavernous Hubert H. Humphrey Metrodome. In the absence of ticker tape, fans tossed rolls of toilet paper and disposable cups onto the field. I slapped five with my first-base coach and tipped my helmet to the crowd. My teammates all gathered on the top step of the dugout to honor the moment. Even first-base umpire Rich Garcia gave me a little hug.

I came around to score, sending the game into extra innings. While my teammates returned to the field, I stayed on the bench. My days as an everyday outfielder behind me, I was now trying to contribute as a designated hitter. Sitting there in the dugout, I let it all sink in. A year earlier, I had fulfilled my career-long goal of winning a World Series. Now, through a combination of talent and perseverance, I could savor my most significant personal achievement. I was the first—and as far as I know, the only player—to notch his 3,000th hit while playing for his hometown team.

A few days later, I received a card from President Bill Clinton: "Congratulations on your 3,000th hit! What an achievement!" He'd also written to me that spring, congratulating me on my 20th big-league season.

There were still games left to play, but I could see the end was near. I had recently graced the cover of *Sports Illustrated* with a pained expression on my face as I slid into second base. The photo perfectly captured the way the body of a 40-year-old ballplayer feels. The only thing missing was another note from President Clinton: "Congratulations on getting old."

•

Reaching the 3,000-hit milestone in Minnesota meant everything to me because it's where my story began. It was a reminder of a simpler place and time. I came into the world on the same day in October 1951 when Bobby Thomson of the New York Giants hit his "Shot Heard 'Round the World" against the Brooklyn Dodgers to win the National League pennant. I grew up at 1009 Carroll Avenue on the edge of the Rondo community, a square mile of mixed-income Black neighborhoods in St. Paul that brimmed with history and pride. That pride was on full display in the Metrodome on my special night.

Time really does have a way of getting away from you. On that night in Minnesota, my major league career flashed before my eyes.

They didn't have a name for it back in the early 1970s, but today, I'd be called a "generational talent." No one had seen an athlete quite like me before. The only question when I came out of college was whether my skills would shine brightest on the baseball diamond, basketball court, or football field.

In 1973, my suitors from the respective sports started lining up. I read in the *St. Paul Pioneer Press* that the Minnesota Vikings had selected me in the 17th and final round of the NFL draft. It was flattering, since I hadn't played a down of football since I was 13 years old. Without a pedigree or position to my name, the Vikings listed me as a tight end in the paperwork they sent to the league office. Why did they draft me in the first place? Because I was big, strong, and already starring in baseball and basketball at the University of Minnesota.

The Vikings drafted me during a stretch of the hoops season when my Golden Gophers were rattling off win after win in the Big Ten. Baseball had always been my first love, but the more basketball I played, the better I got, eventually establishing myself as one of the top power forwards in the conference.

My exploits on the hardwood prompted the next round of phone calls. In late April, I was drafted by the Atlanta Hawks of the NBA and the Utah Stars of the ABA, in the fifth and sixth rounds, respectively. By this time, the college baseball schedule was already in its second month, so I decided to put off any decisions about my post-college future until after what I hoped would be a championship senior season on the diamond.

I still had a lot to prove as a baseball player. Until my senior season, I'd been exclusively a pitcher and hadn't stepped to the plate once for the Golden Gophers.

My coach, Dick Siebert, knew I could hit, but he believed my right arm needed to be protected at all costs. The last thing he wanted was for me to take an errant pitch to the hand or wrist. But he changed his tune during the 1973 season, after hearing about what I'd done during an Alaskan adventure the previous summer. In my second stint with the Goldpanners of the Alaska Baseball League, I got a chance to play the field and swing the bat after one of the team's regular outfielders went down. I ended up smashing 15 home runs. My power display became the talk of Fairbanks. Many years later, the town elders even built a statue of me near the landing spot of a 500-foot home run that I hit that summer.

With me pulling double duty on the mound and at the plate, the Golden Gophers didn't lose a game in May and early June of my senior season, earning us a trip to the College World Series in Omaha. While preparing to play our first opponent, Oklahoma, I received word that the San Diego Padres had selected me with the fourth overall pick in the MLB draft. The next day I went out and pitched a six-hit shutout. In the four games we played in Omaha, I gave up one run in 17⅓ innings and hit .467.

Sadly, our run to the championship ended in the semifinals when we blew a seven-run lead in the ninth inning against eventual champion USC. After a loss like that, it was small consolation to be named the tournament's most outstanding player.

While I was playing in Omaha, a Padres scout named Donnie Williams was tracking my every move, contract in hand. His mission was to get me to sign on the dotted line. But he kept missing me, right up until I left the state. That prompted a flurry of increasingly frantic phone messages to my family home in St. Paul.

"I'm sorry you haven't connected with David, Mr. Williams," my mom told him, "but I can assure you he'll be calling you before you wake up tomorrow."

Donnie later told me that Padres president Emil Joseph "Buzzie" Bavasi was checking in with him every hour to see if he had found me.

"Not yet," Donnie kept telling him.

"Well, if you don't find him, don't bother coming back here!" Bavasi said.

Luckily for Donnie, I always did what my mother said. I reached him by phone early the next morning, and we arranged to meet in San Diego to talk business. But I had a question that couldn't wait until then.

"Did you draft me as a hitter or a pitcher?" I asked.

"A hitter," he said. "We want you out there every day."

I still thought of myself as a pitcher, but I understood the Padres' assessment. Did I, or they, ever consider myself as a two-way player? I'll just say that no one back then could have imagined a player versatile enough to make the starting rotation and hit on non-pitching days. Even Babe Ruth gave up pitching once he established himself as a great slugger. It wasn't until Shohei Ohtani came along years later that people saw that it was in fact possible.

Looking back, I wish I'd had the chance to face even one batter in the majors. If any team should have been willing to experiment with a two-way player, it was the struggling Padres of that era. The team had yet to feature a star player or anything else to excite the fan base, and they'd averaged over 100 losses per season in their four-year existence. They had glaring holes to fill—both on the field and in their financial statements. Things were so bad that owner C. Arnholt Smith, who also ran the largest bank in San Diego, announced just a week before I was drafted that the team was moving to Washington, DC, for the 1974 season. The Padres could've used the buzz, and letting me both pitch and hit might have created it.

At the time, I wasn't too concerned about the position I would play or how unstable the Padres organization seemed. As a young ballplayer still not fully attuned to the bigger picture of my career, the only thing that mattered was becoming one of the few players in the draft era to reach the majors without playing a single game in the minors.

However, that became a point of contention. The Padres agreed I didn't need to waste time in Single-A ball in Walla Walla, Washington, but they thought I'd benefit from a stint with their Double-A affiliate in San Antonio.

Years later, I got a look at the team's scouting report on me. It said I wasn't a good hitter coming out of college because of a bad hitch in my swing. Then I reached the final sentence and did a double take: "This boy is colored."

In San Diego, I sat down to discuss my immediate future with Buzzie Bavasi, his son, Peter (the team's general manager), and Donnie Williams. Bob Fontaine, the head of scouting, stood quietly in the corner. I brought along a guy named Marvin Milkes, a former major league GM, who had agreed to sit in on my behalf. We were outnumbered, but at a time when players had virtually no leverage in the contract negotiations, I held a rare advantage. When Buzzie told me that he felt I could use some seasoning at Double-A, I hit him with a dose of reality.

"Well, Mr. Bavasi," I said, "I understand how you feel, but I also am quite interested in what the Atlanta Hawks have to offer me should I decide to pursue a career in the NBA."

Buzzie furrowed his eyebrows and scowled. Gone was the friendly, bald-headed man I'd met just a few moments earlier. I could see him sizing me up, trying to decide whether I was bluffing. I looked him straight in the eye to let him know that I wasn't.

The conversation turned to my signing bonus.

That morning, I'd read in the paper that the Padres had traded Fred Norman, one of their best pitchers, to the Cincinnati Reds for a couple of players and $150,000 in cash. It turned out to be the best thing that ever happened to Fred. He was 1–7 at the time of the trade, but after going to the

Big Red Machine, he won 12 games and earned himself Cy Young Award votes. Freed from San Diego, he got to experience postseason baseball on a regular basis in Cincinnati.

Buzzie had to realize that the Padres' brighter future was sitting right across the desk from him.

After some back and forth, Buzzie agreed to pay me a $50,000 signing bonus, more than the $35,000 their scouting report said they might get me for. That number didn't come out of thin air. It was close to the amount that David Clyde, the number one overall pick in the draft, had received from the Texas Rangers. Clyde, a pitcher just a few weeks out of high school, was going straight to the majors for two starts in front of what the Rangers hoped would be large crowds. After that, he'd be sent to the minors.

The difference between Clyde and me? I didn't plan on ever leaving the majors.

Once again, Buzzie's brows furrowed and his eyes narrowed. For the struggling Padres, $50,000 was a lot of money, but I knew I was worth every penny. The guy drafted right before me, Robin Yount, went on to have a Hall of Fame career. John Stearns, who was also selected before me, had a solid major league career after playing two sports in college. But I was the only one in that draft class—or maybe any other—who looked like he could leap tall buildings in a single bound.

As the meeting ended, I tore a page out of a small spiral notebook I'd brought with me, balled it up, and tossed it into a wastebasket by the door, feeling confident that team ownership would sign off on the bonus. Sure enough, Buzzie called the next day to say everything was set. My $50,000 signing bonus would be supplemented by an additional $15,000 in salary—the major league minimum at the time. We agreed I'd join the team in less than a week to make my big-league debut. That gave me all of three days to head home to St. Paul, see my family, and pack my bags.

Though I'd insisted on going directly to the majors, I can't say I was entirely sure I was ready. But I believed I'd figure it out quickly—just like I had on the basketball court and in the outfield at the University of Minnesota.

A famous football coach once told a young player, "When you get into the end zone, act like you've been there before." In other words, don't dance around, don't spike the ball, just let your play speak for itself. I didn't follow that advice in my early days in the majors, not because I was trying to show off, but because I was trying too hard to make a strong first impression.

Take my first major league hit in June of 1973. In stark contrast to the way I would casually round first on my 3,000th hit years later, I awkwardly dove into the bag to beat out an infield single in front of 5,000 amused fans. And as much as I would've liked to have stylishly circled the bases on my first career home run, I ended up sprinting full speed—long limbs flailing—watching to see if the ball would clear the wall. It did. After scooping up my helmet from the basepaths, I finished with a short, inelegant trot home.

The Padres were a new team in a growing city—with a young core. At 29, eight years my senior, Cito Gaston was the closest thing we had to a grizzled veteran. He'd been with the Padres since their inaugural season in 1969 and had made the All-Star team in '71. He was also one of several Black players on the roster. Most days, we'd be standing across the outfield from each other—Cito in right, me in left.

A few days after I joined the team, he came over to my locker to introduce himself.

"So, you're the one everyone's talking about," he said.

I sized Cito up. He was big, like me. I tried to read his face for clues on how to respond.

"Yeah, I'm the one," I replied, smiling.

"You're not what I expected."

"What did you expect?"

"Your name is Winfield, right?" He repeated it, dragging out the first syllable like he was doing a British accent. "And you're from Minnesota, right?"

I nodded.

"With a name like that, and all the nice things people were saying about you, I thought you were a white guy."

I looked at him. He looked at me. And we both busted out laughing.

Another of my teammates, a pitcher named Steve Arlin, noticed I had a chip in one of my front teeth—the result of a bicycle accident when I was 12. We didn't have dental insurance growing up, so I just lived with it. That meant I only occasionally smiled in photos all the way through college.

It turned out Arlin—who had led the National League in losses in both 1971 and 1972—was a graduate of the Ohio State University College of Dentistry. Maybe sensing the baseball thing wasn't quite working out, he also ran a small dental office in San Diego.

"Do you want that tooth fixed?" Steve asked me.

"Suuure," I said, a bit wary of his offer. He *was* an Ohio State man, after all—and I had a history with the Buckeyes.

Still, I decided to go ahead with it. Steve fixed me up at his practice, and I was forever grateful. From that point on, I flashed my pearly whites in every photo—even with a bit of a gap still between my front teeth.

•

I didn't know enough about being a major leaguer to realize that the Padres didn't operate like most major league teams.

When it came to equipment and just about everything else, they spared all expense. The team wore black spikes. When I arrived, I didn't own black spikes, just the white ones I'd worn in college. The solution? The equipment manager walked over with a can of leather paint and turned my spikes black.

Most other teams, from what I understood, replaced torn uniform pants with a fresh pair. Not the Padres. If I ripped my pants sliding into a base, they went to a seamstress who patched them up. If they were too far gone, they got sent down for a minor leaguer to wear.

On one of my first trips to Wrigley Field, I was finishing up signing autographs by the low brick wall along the field when I noticed my glove—my only glove—was gone. I looked around in disbelief before realizing that whoever swiped it was probably long gone. I went into the clubhouse and found a mitt that was stiff and didn't fit my hand. Out in right field, I spent the whole game praying I wouldn't give the Bleacher Bums even more of a reason to hurl insults at me. It would be years before I got my own shipment of bats. Early on, I got by using a communal one. We didn't have catered meals in the clubhouse. We had to buy our own vitamins. Our training facilities consisted of a single piece of universal equipment, the kind you might find in someone's garage.

A guy named Doc Mattei oversaw that modest operation. An old pal of Buzzie's, Doc was the Padres' first hire in 1969. A licensed podiatrist, he wore two hats with the team: trainer and traveling secretary. When he wasn't on the phone trying to book us rooms at a Holiday Inn in Houston, Doc would examine whatever bruise, bump, or scrape a player came in with.

No matter the issue, Doc's diagnosis was almost always the same: "Put some heat on it," he'd growl in his gravelly New England accent. And if heat didn't do the trick, he kept a special remedy on hand: a horse liniment called DMSO.

•

The impending move to Washington should have further tipped me off to the Padres' mounting financial problems. But the real wake-up call came when I heard the front office had recently asked players to hold off on cashing the paychecks they received every other Friday until the following week. There were newspaper stories about C. Arnholdt Smith owing tens of millions of dollars in unpaid taxes to the IRS and about his bank literally running out of money. Those headlines fueled speculation that the team might move to DC in the middle of the season.

I kept my focus on trying to hit baseballs. In college, most pitches had looked like beach balls to me. In the majors, they resembled marbles. I had never seen pitchers hit their spots with such precision. I went into survival mode, just trying to make solid contact. The strategy worked to some degree. I didn't hit for much power, but I put balls in play and didn't strike out much.

Our manager, Don Zimmer, protected me by keeping me out of the lineup if he thought I'd be overmatched. On the August night that we got no-hit by the Braves' Phil Niekro, I sat on the bench until entering as a pinch-hitter in the eighth inning. I'd never seen a knuckleball before, and though I was retired on a good play by the second baseman, it felt gratifying to have almost broken up the no-hitter.

If you'd told me then that I'd go on to have more hits against Niekro than any other pitcher I faced in my career, I wouldn't have believed it. But baseball's a funny game. The pitcher who gave me the most trouble in my career is a largely forgotten right-hander named Buzz Capra—a one-year wonder with the Braves in 1974 who had a nasty curveball. I faced him 20 times in my career and never got a hit.

I didn't yet have a permanent place in San Diego, so Doc suggested I stay at a little motel near the ballpark where a few other young players were living. It wasn't fancy, but that was no surprise.

I was also still months away from buying my first car, so transportation was a challenge. After a few weeks of seeing me scrounging for rides, one of my teammates, a utility infielder named Dwain Anderson, took pity on me and invited me to crash at his apartment in Mission Valley. It only had one bed, but Dwain insisted he was fine on the couch. He drove a Nissan 240Z, a sporty little thing I had to contort my six-foot-six frame to fit into. But it was nice to know I had a steady ride.

Dwain also helped me with my social life, though his contributions in that area would later cause me a long period of anguish. It all started innocently enough on a September road trip to Houston, where Dwain had extended family. He invited me to dinner with the group, and afterward we went back to a house that had a large party area. That evening, I met his cousin Sandra, an attractive young woman who attended Texas Southern University. We hit it off, even if our conversation never strayed beyond small talk, and agreed to stay in touch.

For the next couple of years, whenever the Padres passed through Houston, Sandra would pick me up and take me to the mall or out to eat at Frenchy's Chicken. It wasn't a torrid affair, but she was a nice girl to be around.

I had no idea the anguish that introduction would cause me over the years.

Chapter 2

•

DAVE THE RAVE

Everything about San Diego—except for the quality of baseball—was ideal. Having grown up in frigid Minnesota, I took to the near-constant sunshine and 70-degree temperatures right away.

Unlike in most major league cities, the summer ritual of rolling out the tarp during a downpour didn't really exist in San Diego. On the rare occasion it did rain, the results could be comical. I remember sitting in the dugout at San Diego Stadium during one of those rare storms, watching the grounds crew scramble to unfurl the tarp. As they ran onto the field, pieces of vinyl started coming off in their hands. It had been so long since they'd needed to use it, the tarp had rotted.

It was the perfect metaphor for baseball in San Diego, where the short-lived experiment seemed in tatters.

A grocery store magnate had agreed to buy the team for $12 million—more than the group led by a guy named George Steinbrenner had recently paid to purchase the New York Yankees. The move to DC received unanimous league approval. Even Tricky Dick Nixon weighed in with his, er, deep-throated support for bringing baseball back to the nation's capital. It all seemed like a done deal when the team posed for Topps baseball cards in Washington Stars uniforms.

But San Diego City Hall fought back, threatening to hold up the sale by suing the Padres for breaking their 20-year lease at San Diego Stadium. Things might have gotten ugly if a fast-food tycoon hadn't intervened after reading about the situation while lounging on his yacht.

Ray Kroc, an Illinois native who had recently stepped down as CEO of McDonald's, had hoped to buy the Chicago Cubs, but the Wrigley family wouldn't sell. So instead, he forked over $12 million in cash to buy the Padres. In doing so, he not only saved baseball in San Diego, but also found himself a peaceful Navy town where he could spend his twilight years.

The thought of working for a guy who had pioneered an entire industry excited me. Some of the first McDonald's in the country were in the Twin Cities, and as a kid, I'd see the golden arches whenever I traveled around playing baseball. They were always busy, never lacking for customers.

Later, when I toured the country playing college baseball and basketball, I noticed McDonald's restaurants popping up everywhere. Owning a McDonald's seemed like a license to mint money. I decided that, when the time was right, I'd talk to Kroc about acquiring a franchise of my own. But first, I was going to show the him the team had made a good investment in me.

I arrived at my first Padres spring training driving a new silver Pontiac Grand Prix with a maroon top, which I was still making payments on. To pass the time on the drive from St. Paul to Yuma, Arizona, I counted every McDonald's I noticed along the way.

Early in camp, new Padres manager John McNamara told me there were five outfielders ahead of me on the depth chart and that I'd likely start the season in Triple-A. I don't know if he thought that would light a fire under me, but the truth was I didn't need any extra motivation. After a disastrous month in Mexico playing winter ball at the Padres' request, I showed up in Yuma in top physical condition and ready to win a roster spot.

McNamara admired my athleticism enough to try me out at shortstop during the Cactus League. I enjoyed that experiment—errors and all—but there was no way I was a major league–ready shortstop. Then again, "major league–ready" didn't necessarily describe a lot of players fighting for jobs with the Padres.

A few days before we were set to pack up and head north to San Diego for the regular season, I got the chance to force my way onto the team through sheer will.

It came during a game in Tucson that we were trailing by three runs going into the final inning. I'd watched the first eight innings from the bench, but when we loaded the bases in the ninth, McNamara told me to grab a bat. My pinch-hit double cleared the bases and tied the game. The next batter slapped a single into shallow left field. I saw our third-base coach throw up his hands, signaling me to stop. But I ignored the sign and barreled toward home. The ball beat me there, but I went airborne to evade the catcher's tag. I plowed into him, jarring the ball loose.

It was a meaningless spring game, but we celebrated at home plate like we'd just won the World Series. After the game, Padres broadcaster Jerry Coleman pulled me aside and said McNamara had told him I'd made the team.

•

The first home opener of the Kroc era, played in front of nearly 40,000 hopeful fans, turned out to be one of the most memorable games I ever played as a Padre.

Down by four runs to the Astros, we loaded the bases in the fourth inning, but a baserunning gaffe killed the rally. In cities like New York or Philadelphia, a mistake like that would have drawn boos. But in mellow San Diego, it was met by a collective sigh that seemed to say, "New ownership. Same old team."

I don't know exactly what Kroc expected from the Padres, but three blowout losses on the road in Los Angeles to open the season seemed to give him an early case of buyer's remorse. Watching us bumble through the home opener was apparently more than he could handle.

After the Astros tacked on two runs in the eighth inning to put the game out of reach, Kroc left his suite and stormed into the public announcer's booth. The stadium organ's between-inning melodies came to a sudden stop as the 71-year-old owner commandeered the loudspeaker system.

A day earlier, a disgraced Tricky Dick Nixon had resigned the presidency in a nationally televised address. For all we knew, Kroc was about to deliver a similarly dramatic announcement about *his* future.

"Ladies and gentlemen," he began, his words broadcast over the radio and throughout the stadium. "I suffer with you. I've never seen such stupid ballplaying in my life."

The crowd let out a muted cheer. Kroc was about to continue, but before he could get another word out, a streaker raced onto the field.

"Get that son of a bitch off the field!" Kroc barked. "Throw him in jail!"

The evening had started with the debut of a man in a chicken costume entertaining fans. It went on to feature a team owner speaking naked truths—while a naked man ran around the field. It was one of the craziest things I ever experienced.

Looking back, Kroc's outburst was a stroke of genius. It sent the message that the owner cared . . . and maybe the fans (and players) should too.

Major League Baseball Commissioner Bowie Kuhn made Kroc apologize for calling the team stupid, but the remark didn't hurt his standing with the fans. Despite losing 102 games, the Padres drew over a million fans for the first time in franchise history—not impressive by Dodgers or Reds standards but still a vast improvement over previous seasons, when San Diego finished dead last in attendance. That level of fan support seemed to ease any doubts Kroc had about buying the Padres, which he would own until his death in 1984.

I fought my way into the starting lineup and led the Padres in most offensive categories in 1974, solidifying my status as a major leaguer. There was still room for improvement, however. Defensively, my 12 outfield errors led the National League. Once, after I flubbed a ball at Veterans Stadium in Philadelphia, the scoreboard flashed a blinking "E9" again and again, like a branding iron burning the moment into my memory.

But the Padres were willing to tolerate my misadventures in the field as long as I kept developing as a hitter. Surprisingly, it was a San Diego police officer who helped me take that part of my game to the next level.

As a young player, I was supposed to rely on the professionals in the Padres organization to analyze my approach to hitting. Unfortunately, a revolving door of hitting coaches during my early years in San Diego meant my teammates and I never had a consistent program of instruction.

That's where Bill Allen entered the picture. A former college baseball player, Bill had always dreamed of becoming a major league hitting instructor. But with most of those jobs going to former pros, he ended up on a different path, as a member of the San Diego Police Department. In his spare time, though, he preached the gospel of hitting—free of charge.

I met Bill through my teammate Johnny Grubb, who credited him with helping him hit over .300 in his rookie season. On Johnny's recommendation, I decided to pay Bill a visit at his home near San Diego State University. In his den, he had two bookshelves, one filled with baseball instructional books, including *The Science of Hitting* by Ted Williams, and the other lined with record albums like *Exile on Main St.* by the Rolling Stones.

In addition to his passion for baseball, Bill also sang lead vocals in a police department rock-and-roll band called PD5, which regularly played gigs at schools and other venues in San Diego.

The real sight to behold was in Bill's backyard, where he had a setup that rivaled what the Padres could offer in terms of machinery and equipment. Inside a full-sized batting cage that took up most of the yard was a home plate and a pitching machine. Just outside the cage were mirrors and a video camera, all positioned to capture the mechanics of a swing.

On any given afternoon, the crack of bats from Bill's backyard shattered the tranquility of his suburban neighborhood. I could imagine the conversations of the husband and wife next door:

"Honey, what's all that racket?"

"Oh, that's just Dave Winfield working on his swing."

"Dave who?"

"Dave Winfield. He plays outfield for the Padres."

"Didn't the Padres move to Washington?"

After watching me take some cuts, Bill offered a blunt assessment of my swing.

"Dave, you stand too close to the plate," he told me. "You have long arms and a long bat. Give yourself a chance to extend your arms."

It was simple and straightforward—maybe even a bit obvious—but no one had ever put it that way before. You always hear about the importance of reach in boxing, but it's just as relevant in baseball. I'm guessing I had one of the longest reaches of anyone to ever play the game. And Bill was right: I needed to use that to my advantage.

The results were almost immediate. I stopped getting jammed on inside pitches and could still reach and drive outside ones—pitches that players with shorter arms would've struggled to get to.

•

In some ways, spending three hours on a summer night trying to hit a baseball was the easiest part of my job. The real challenge came during the 21 hours between games when I sought a balance between baseball and life. As I navigated a world of new experiences and relationships, I looked within the Padres' clubhouse for guidance, aware that some teammates still saw me as a young hotshot who hadn't paid his dues.

Adding to the challenge was that I lacked the built-in peer group that comes from rising through the minors alongside future major league teammates.

Because of the hype surrounding me, I couldn't just blend in. I did my best, though. I trimmed my afro, arrived early at the ballpark, practiced hard, and mostly kept my mouth shut—a tall order for someone who'd never been the quiet type.

Back in college, my basketball teammate Robert Murphy had called me "Dave the Rave" in recognition of my personality and skills. That team, which included a pair of Top 10 NBA draft picks, had a real sense of brotherhood. As someone who never had aspirations to play college basketball, I was happy being just one of the guys.

In the major leagues, there was an expectation that I would be *the* guy. That brought a level of pressure that made me feel reserved for the first time in my life.

By the early 1970s, most major league teams had four or five Black players on their rosters. Though that was more than ever before, baseball was still very much a white-dominated sport.

I had always felt comfortable around white people—at school, at church, and on the baseball field. I had a couple of uncles who married white women. My mother's best friend, Angie, was white. My high school was about 90 percent white. I prided myself on being able to relate to anyone, whether their ancestors had come over on a slave ship or had been in the United States for eight generations.

But that didn't mean I was blind to the less tolerant side of American society.

When I played summer ball in Alaska, one of my teammates—a white kid from the Midwest—dropped the "n-word" on me while we were sitting across from each other at a restaurant. It happened just a few months after a fight between my University of Minnesota basketball team and a mostly white Ohio State team.

I started coming over the table at him before my teammates grabbed me and held me back. The next day, our manager kicked the kid off the team and sent him home.

That was the only time something like that ever happened to me. I knew people harbored ugly opinions about race, but the overt nature of being called that name—at a dinner table, no less—really shocked me.

San Diego had plenty of *sol*, but it didn't have a lot of soul, so I found myself gravitating toward the other Black players on the Padres. And there were more of us on that team than you'll find on almost any major league roster today. Dwain Anderson drove me around and gave me a place to stay.

I roomed with Cito Gaston for a while, and Nate Colbert—an original Padre and the closest thing the team had to a hitting star before my arrival—gave me advice from time to time. Those guys were all at career crossroads when I met them, and they soon moved on to other teams, leaving me once again in search of a friend and mentor.

I was fortunate to meet several amazing opponents who went out of their way to welcome me. On my first trip to Atlanta, Dusty Baker and Ralph Garr—two young guys who played alongside Hank Aaron in the Braves' outfield—called me over. I can still hear Ralph's high-pitched voice, stretching out the syllables of my last name: "Hey Winnn-field, brother, come over and say hello."

In Chicago, Billy Williams invited me to the dog track and dinner with his Cubs teammates. Bob Watson of the Astros recommended a stockbroker with whom I ended up having a long relationship. Dick Allen advised me to invest in real estate.

Of course, not all the veterans I looked up to rolled out the red carpet for me. One time, after a game in St. Louis, I ran into legendary Cardinals pitcher Bob Gibson at a downtown department store called Famous-Barr. By then, Gibson was winding down a Hall of Fame career in which he'd become one of the most dominant and feared pitchers the game had ever seen. The summer before my senior year at St. Paul Central High School, he won 22 games, threw 13 shutouts, and finished with an unbelievable 1.12 ERA. He was the guy I tried to emulate when I pitched in high school and college. Never one to be easily awestruck, I viewed Gibson as something of a superhero.

So imagine how I felt when I saw him browsing the menswear section. I walked over, introduced myself, and reached out to shake his hand. No hand came back. He just looked at me with disapproval and walked away.

A couple of weeks later, we were playing the Cardinals in San Diego when I got my first chance to hit against him. It was the seventh inning of a game we led 2–1. I dug in at the plate. Gibson didn't like it when hitters did that. He threw a fastball under my chin. But then he made a mistake and left one out over the plate. I didn't miss it, sending it over the left-field wall for a home run. Talk about a confidence booster.

I didn't want to meet my heroes during awkward encounters in department stores. I wanted to share a clubhouse with them.

On road trips to Pittsburgh, I watched with envy as a young Dave Parker of the Pirates hung out before games with the great Willie Stargell, who was halfway through a 21-season tenure in the Steel City. I wanted someone of similar stature and reputation to share his wisdom with me. To my great satisfaction, the Padres went out and acquired another Willie who gave me exactly that.

Dave had Pops. I had Stretch.

Willie McCovey was well on his way to Cooperstown by the time the Giants traded him to the Padres at the end of the 1973 season, ending his 14-year stay in San Francisco. He agreed to the trade, hoping the San Diego warmth would soothe his chronically bad knees. The Padres felt that even as his career was winding down, Willie could still deliver key hits and help boost attendance.

The Giants of the '60s and '70s had two legendary Willies—Mays and McCovey—who together inspired many inner-city Black kids to fall in love with baseball. Growing up, I admired McCovey's beautiful left-handed power swing, a thing of beauty that I would have loved to emulate if I'd batted left-handed myself.

Every National League pitcher feared Willie Mac's violent swing, but off the field, he had an easygoing disposition that made you wonder if he could ever do harm to anyone—or anything, including a baseball. With Willie Mac hitting behind me in the cleanup spot on most days, I started seeing better pitches. After games, he'd saunter over to my locker, his knees creaking with every step, and plop himself down next to me.

"Let's talk," he'd say.

Funny thing was he never came with a specific topic to discuss. I think he just sensed that I had a lot on my mind. And he was right. Most of our conversations centered on life outside the game. Willie Mac recognized that my generation of Black players had opportunities to do things in the areas of philanthropy and business that had always been out of reach for him and his peers. He encouraged me to pursue those opportunities.

That's the advice I took most to heart, because I wanted to be known for more than just hitting baseballs—an ethos I got from the community I grew up in and from my mother, who, while appreciating my athletic gifts, worked tirelessly to ensure I had a humanistic view of the world.

You can't become a philanthropist until you have money to give away. I'd kept a close eye on my finances ever since learning the hard way in my rookie season that the people who we trust with our hard-earned wages aren't always deserving of that trust.

In my case, the former Padres team owner had so badly mismanaged the bank he owned that it was declared insolvent—the same bank where I'd deposited my $50,000 bonus check. I'd never heard of the FDIC before, but I was glad to learn that there were protections in place to prevent people from losing money due to the bad acts of others.

After a few seasons in the majors, I had become financially secure enough to start thinking about ways to give back. I got a pay raise from the Padres and earned a little extra cash by doing television commercials for a company that sold recreational vehicles. By then, I felt a whole lot more comfortable in front of the camera than I had when I first broke into the majors, looking like a deer in headlights. My pitch went something like this: "Hi, this is Dave Winfield. Come see the new Winnebagos at La Mesa RV Center today. You better hurry, because when they're gone, they're gone!"

To get things started, I launched a college scholarship fund for the top student-athletes of color in my hometown of St. Paul. Over the next 50 years, I've continued to give out the Winfield Awards, which made it possible for talented young people to attend schools like Harvard, MIT, Duke, Brown, and HBCUs including Florida A&M. The success of that program motivated me to go even bigger. I just had to figure out how.

I was now living in an apartment in the same Mission Valley complex where my teammate had housed me during my rookie year. When I went out in San Diego, people recognized me. I'd swapped out my Pontiac Grand Prix for a Cadillac Eldorado with a personalized license plate that read "Mr. DMW"—Mr. David Mark Winfield—an attention-grabber I could get away with in laid-back San Diego.

I embraced my newfound status as a public figure and made every effort to be accessible. Whether grabbing a late-night prime rib at Bully's restaurant, dancing at the Jabberwocky nightclub atop the Le Baron Hotel, or pushing a shopping cart down the aisle at Safeway, I was like a real-life Ron Burgundy from the movie *Anchorman*, honoring autograph requests, posing for photos, and answering questions about how the Padres were looking that season.

One afternoon, a neighbor waved me down as I was walking to my car. She had a favor to ask.

"I have a dear friend, Dorothy, who loves the Padres more than anything. She and her husband never miss a game. She thinks you're just the greatest. It would mean the world to her if you could drop by sometime and say hello."

Believe it or not, I'd already been introduced to Dorothy by a guy I knew at a local TV station who lived on her block. San Diego was that kind of town.

I didn't generally make house calls, but the request caught me off guard, and I couldn't immediately find a polite way to say no.

"Sure, I'd be happy to," I said, thinking that I could put the visit off indefinitely.

"That's great! How about dinner on Thursday?" she asked.

Thursday was an off day before the Expos came to town. Dorothy, whoever she was, had clearly done her homework. Again, I was caught flat-footed.

"Thursday? Okay, tell her I'll see her then."

I hoped Dorothy could cook.

That Thursday, I drove out to meet my biggest fan. Heeding my mom's advice to never show up empty-handed at someone's house, I stopped at a bakery on the way and picked up a cherry pie.

"Oh, David, it is so nice to meet you!" Dorothy exclaimed as I stepped inside.

She called me "David" just like my mother did. I handed her the pie, and Dorothy escorted me onto the shag carpet in her living room. Above the sofa, the wood-paneled wall was covered with an assortment of Padres pennants. Dorothy introduced me to her longshoreman husband, Milt, and their four kids. Sensing the presence of an outsider, the family dog came over to check me out. After a few moments of invasive sniffing, he determined I wasn't a threat and trotted off.

Over dinner, we briefly touched on baseball. The Padres were 19 games out of first place at the time, so there wasn't much to say. Between forkfuls of pot roast and roasted potatoes, I talked about my other aspirations.

By the time Dorothy brought out the cherry pie, we'd already brainstormed several ideas for how I could use my status as a ballplayer to serve underprivileged youth in the San Diego area: tickets to games, health and wellness fairs, and baseball clinics.

"I'll help you do this, David," she said with a tone of confidence in her voice. "And I'll get other people to help you too."

"I've only just met you, Dorothy," I said, "but I have faith that you will."

The relationship that began that evening would go on to shape not just the rest of my time with the Padres, but later, my years with the Yankees as well.

So, too, would the strong alliance I would soon form with a man who everybody but me seemed to hate.

Chapter 3

•

AL AND ME

Dorothy Bowen cooked a mean roast, but it was Al Frohman who opened my eyes to the joys of pastrami and corned beef. The man knew his cured meats, his expertise honed over many years of running a kosher catering company in New York. For Al, catering wasn't just a job; it was a calling. As far as I could tell, he survived on a steady diet of red meat, Parliament cigarettes, and nitroglycerin pills.

One afternoon, before a Padres-Dodgers game in Los Angeles, I sat across from him in a downtown deli as he devoured his corned beef on rye, savoring every bite like it was his last. I stared at my own sandwich in awe, wondering how I was supposed to get it all in my mouth . . . and how many hours of cardio I'd need to burn it off.

A writer for *Sports Illustrated* once described Al as "10 pounds of Malt-O-Meal stuffed into a five-pound bag" and a "5-foot-4, 220-pound chunk of walking cholesterol." I can't do better than that, so I won't even try. Standing side by side, he and I made an odd pair, but despite our vastly different appearances and backgrounds, we really clicked.

After retiring from catering, Al moved west to soak up the sun and expand his side hustle of selling baseball T-shirts and advising major league players. One day, while chatting with a young teammate of mine named Jerry Turner, Al came over to introduce himself. He told me he was interested in helping me market myself. I wasn't quite sure what to make of the little man, but I took down his contact information in case I decided to reach out later.

Al told me he'd worked with a few major leaguers, including Cleon Jones and Jerry Koosman of the Mets. So the next time we played in New York, I asked around about him. Both guys sang his praises, saying he'd helped them negotiate contracts and line up personal appearances. After hearing those endorsements, I gave him a call and said I wanted to meet.

That day at the deli, we were discussing an upcoming round of contract talks with the Padres. The team had made me an offer I felt was far too low, and I wasn't sure how to respond.

"Just send it back unsigned," Al said. "It'll piss 'em off, but it'll bring 'em to the table. It's 1975, not 1955, goddammit. You need to stand up for yourself."

I took his advice—and ended up getting a significant pay bump. And just like that, Al Frohman became my agent.

Because the "a-word" was still frowned upon by baseball executives, I referred to Al in the press as "my friend and business manager." I realized early on that he could be a real pain in the ass, but in an era when major league owners still held most of the power, I needed an asshole on my side.

Al was a product of his time. Today's agents are strictly regulated and required to pass exams and earn certifications. Many of them have law degrees. Back then, no such rules existed. If they had, Al never would have made the cut.

When he wasn't negotiating or eating, he was sitting at a piano. I must admit, I was surprised by his musical talent. But what impressed me most was his problem-solving ability. I'm convinced that if you'd locked him in a vault with no way out, he'd have found a way to escape—then promptly lit a Parliament and sat down at a Steinway to play a Brandenburg Concerto.

I told Al about my idea to talk to Ray Kroc about buying a McDonald's franchise. He didn't love it, but he didn't discourage me from having the conversation, either. So I scheduled a meeting.

"You have to own and operate the restaurants, not just own them," Kroc told me. "You can either run a McDonald's or play baseball."

"I'd like to try to do both," I replied.

"You can't do both," Kroc said, standing up from his desk to signal the meeting was over.

It reminded me of one of my early contract negotiations with the Padres, when general manager Peter Bavasi told me I could accept what the team was offering or "go drive a truck."

When I told Al about my meeting with Kroc, he grew upset.

"That motherfucker!" he said, shaking his head. "You don't need to be flipping burgers anyway, David. You can do much better than that."

Indeed, Al and I were already talking about another way to make a splash in the food and hospitality industry.

Fifty years later, I still think about "Superstar Village"—our vision for a resort hotel condominium where the public could interact with professional athletes who owned units on the property.

Before long, we had a detailed plan: 700 units, a convention center, six restaurants, two coffee shops, a nine-hole golf course, hayrides and a petting zoo for the kids, and an outpatient clinic focused on preventive medicine.

Nothing like it existed, and we were optimistic about attracting investors and star athletes from across the sports world. We even scouted two possible locations: the San Diego area and Curacao.

Our work on Superstar Village coincided with the creation of the David M. Winfield Foundation for Underprivileged Youth, an idea that first took shape around Dorothy Bowen's dinner table.

Roberto Clemente had devoted his life to helping disadvantaged people in Latin America. After Jackie Robinson's death in 1972, his family established a foundation in his name. But as far as I could tell, I was the first active athlete to launch a formal charitable organization.

As promised, Dorothy, who had no previous experience in this area, assembled a team of volunteers to help me get the foundation off the ground. Joyce from the donut shop helped with accounting—and brought treats. Bob from down the street gave advice on fundraising. Mary, the pediatric nurse, shared ideas for health programs. Dorothy offered her home as the foundation's headquarters and had Pacific Telephone install a second line that became our office number. She just had to remember whether to answer the phone with "Bowen residence" or "Dave Winfield Foundation."

It was an eventful time—one that saw me sign what would turn out to be my final contract with the Padres. Team president Buzzie Bavasi had offered a three-year, $525,000 deal, but this time Al went with me to push for an extra year and a lot more money. We believed we had leverage because the Padres had just shelled out big bucks for two high-profile free agents, catcher Gene Tenace and reliever Rollie Fingers, both key players on the Oakland teams that had won three consecutive World Series earlier in the decade.

Those signings, in December 1976, showed just how badly Ray Kroc wanted to field a winning team. The question became: Would the Padres have a better chance of success with Dave Winfield or without him? They could let me play out my option and hit free agency, or they could re-sign me for what we believed I deserved: a four-year deal worth over $1 million.

A few weeks before spring training, Al paid Buzzie a visit.

"Give him his money," he said, determined to keep intact his unbroken streak of never losing a negotiation—or any conversation, for that matter. "You see what kind of player he is. And the best is yet to come. Pay the man."

"Tenace and Fingers have played in All-Star games and won championships," Buzzie shot back. "Dave is a very fine player, but be reasonable."

Buzzie had a point. I was one season away from making the first of what would become 12 straight All-Star appearances. And the teams I'd played on hadn't come anywhere near the postseason.

Al turned red in the face. He grabbed a pen out of my hand and snapped it in half. Ink streamed down his fingers.

That was just the first of several acrimonious meetings. It turned into a real battle of wills. News of the contract impasse made the papers, which led La Mesa RV Center to cut ties with me. They didn't want to be associated with a ballplayer who was being "difficult." Bavasi complained to reporters about Al's tactics, but I had his back.

"I am very happy with Mr. Frohman," I said. "He has been right by my side all along, he's been sort of a father figure to me, and we're in business together, so I know he wants what's right for me."

The talks reached a stalemate, with the Padres going as far as to lower their offer to $500,000 over three years.

Buzzie's words buzzed in my ears as the 1977 season unfolded. I went on a tear in May, hitting safely in 26 of 28 games. No longer a kid, but not quite a veteran either, I tried to stay even keeled. It was tough not having my friend and mentor, Willie McCovey, around anymore. The Padres had sold his contract to the Oakland A's the season before.

Shortly before he left, I shared a moment with him I'll never forget.

The Reds had intentionally walked Willie Mac with runners on second and third to get to me. I couldn't blame them. Earlier in his career, out of respect for his hitting prowess, he'd set a major league record for intentional passes in a season. In this case, the move gave the right-handed pitcher a chance to face a right-handed hitter.

But I never wanted to be the guy that a pitcher preferred to face. As I walked to the plate, Van McCoy's "The Hustle" played on the organ. With malice in my swing, I launched a pitch over the center field wall for a grand slam that provided us with all the runs that we needed to win that night.

As I crossed home plate, Willie Mac slapped me on the back and gave me a look that said, "This is your team now."

For a few seconds, I didn't hear the roar of the crowd. It was just me and Willie.

But was it really my team now?

In June of '77, San Diego acquired outfielder Dave Kingman in a trade with the Mets, creating a logjam in the outfield. The timing of the trade puzzled me, especially since we were already 15 games out of first place. The arrival of another six-foot-six slugger felt like a message that maybe my services weren't desired anymore. I couldn't help but feel a little on edge.

One day before a game, I was at my locker reading the Business & Finance section of *The Wall Street Journal* as my teammates filtered in around me. It was a few months after ABC aired the historic miniseries *Roots*, based on Alex Haley's book about his ancestors' forced journey to the United States as slaves. The book and series had moved me greatly, inspiring me to want to travel to Africa to trace my own family's history.

From the training room, my teammate Doug Rader saw me reading the paper.

"Whatcha reading there, Kunta?" he called out, referencing Kunta Kinte, the main character from *Roots*.

Kunta? What the hell?

I jumped up, and in two long strides, I was in his face. A couple of teammates quickly got between us as I was about to pop him.

"I don't play that shit, Rader!" I yelled.

Doug wasn't a bad guy. I just think he had a tendency to say some crazy things. Many years later, when he was my manager with the Angels, we got along really well. I think he was just trying to be funny that day in the locker room—but his timing couldn't have been worse.

That wasn't the only clubhouse hassle that summer. I don't know whose idea it was, but someone in the organization decided the team would benefit from a mental exercise focused on articulating goals. A clubhouse attendant handed out slips of paper that said:

I am . . .

I can . . .

I will . . .

Most of my teammates tossed theirs straight into the garbage. I grabbed a pen, filled mine out, and taped it to my locker.

I am BAD

I can PLAY

I will KICK YOUR ASS IF YOU MESS WITH ME

What I wrote wasn't directed at Rader—it was directed at opposing pitchers and perhaps a few local sportswriters too. It was meant to convey that each at-bat was a personal showdown, a moment when fans should be in their seats, not at the concession stand grabbing a hot dog and beer.

The idea was for others in the clubhouse to add supportive comments on what was written. I got a few—but they weren't exactly affirming. More like, "You're so full of yourself, Winfield!"

That was okay. Maybe my style wasn't for everyone.

But Kroc had to begrudgingly admit that I was a valuable asset.

As contract negotiations dragged into the summer, I posted the best statistics of my career. Center fielder George Hendrick and I were carrying the team on our shoulders. But Kroc didn't like Hendrick, because he was aloof with the press—and, even more problematically, had skipped a dinner honoring the team owner.

On July 4, 1977, the Padres blinked, and I signed a four-year, $1.4 million contract. As part of the deal, I agreed to purchase $100,000 worth of tickets at a dollar apiece to distribute to kids in the San Diego area. Those seats in the right-field stands became known as the Winfield Pavilion and helped put my foundation on the map. Years later, I learned that one of the "Winfield Kids" who sat in those seats was future major league pitcher David Wells.

Less than a week after I signed the contract, Buzzie stepped down as president of the Padres. Before leaving, he invited me to his office. I walked in to find him cleaning out his desk. He reached into a drawer and handed me a Padres necktie and a book titled *How to Negotiate Effectively*.

"Listen, Dave, you're a good kid," he said, pausing. "But the guy you have working for you doesn't do you any favors."

Al had helped me land the contract, so as far as I was concerned, he had done me 1.4 million favors. But Buzzie wouldn't be the last person to say something like that.

I intended to prove I was worth every penny the Padres were paying me. I wanted to help turn the team into a contender. But there was only so much I could do on that front. On the day I signed my deal, we got smoked by the Astros and fell even further behind the National League West–leading Dodgers.

With the tense negotiations of the past eight months finally behind me, I felt a dull sense of dread in the pit of my stomach. Had I just committed myself to staying in a losing situation?

I went home after the Astros game, opened a bottle of Cutty Sark scotch whiskey—the one with a British clipper ship on the bottle—and poured myself a drink. As my former teammate and sometimes drinking partner Nate Colbert used to say when his back problems flared up and he needed something strong, I was in the mood "to sail the ship."

I wasn't toasting the contract as much as I was drowning my fears.

•

On the national stage, I remained somewhat anonymous. My West Coast games ended too late for the East Coast papers to print the box scores, which made it tough to get noticed by anyone who wasn't already a Padres fan.

I went into the 1977 All-Star break with a .298 average, 21 home runs, and 69 RBIs—numbers that put me right up there with the best in the game. Still, I only finished 14th among National League outfielders in nationwide fan voting.

I was grateful when Sparky Anderson, the manager of the NL All-Stars, selected me as a reserve for the game in New York. I traveled east as the Padres' lone All-Star representative. Al came along with me.

With interleague play still 20 years away, it was my first-ever visit to Yankee Stadium. I had played in Wrigley Field and other National League ballparks steeped in history and mystique, but nothing prepared me for the spiritual experience of walking into "The House That Ruth Built." It felt like entering a cathedral. As I toured Monument Park and stepped onto the field, I could almost feel the presence of Ruth, Gehrig, and DiMaggio.

They gave us the royal treatment. Each All-Star received an oil painting of himself in uniform and a ring that resembled a cross between a World Series ring and the kind high school seniors used to wear.

During a closed practice session, Al made the rounds, casually asking the National League pitchers what they thought of me as a hitter. Later, he typed up the scouting report and handed it to me—a clever bit of espionage on his part.

On game day, I rubbed elbows in the clubhouse with players I had long admired, like Pete Rose and Joe Morgan, and with up-and-coming stars I had never met before, like Dave Parker. It felt like I'd gained access to an exclusive club. I couldn't help but feel starstruck by Willie Mays and Joe D himself, the honorary captains of the National and American League.

Just before the game, National League President Chub Feeney came into the clubhouse and delivered a rousing pep talk about winning for the honor of the senior circuit.

Under the lights of Yankee Stadium, I glanced over to the opposing dugout and saw Rod Carew, George Brett, and Reggie Jackson. In total, 19 future Hall of Famers played in that game.

I later heard that NBC announcer Tony Kubek called me "a strong, young giant" when I entered the game in the sixth inning as a pinch-hitter. My at-bat got off to a rough start. I took such a powerful cut at one pitch that I lost my balance and nearly did the splits. But with the count full at 3–2, I laced a ball to right field that Jim Rice couldn't handle. It went down as a double. Then in the eighth, I added a two-RBI single that helped the National League seal a 7–5 win.

On the flight back to San Diego, with Al loudly snoring next to me, I reflected on the kinship I'd felt at the All-Star Game. I wanted to keep feeling it.

That October, I watched Reggie Jackson hit three home runs in the clinching game of the World Series against the Dodgers, a legendary performance in a packed Yankee Stadium that earned him the nickname "Mr. October" and secured his place in baseball history.

I was only 26, but I couldn't help wondering what my legacy would ultimately be.

Whenever I got anxious about my future, my mother would remind me to stay grounded in the here and now. She was right, and I wanted to show her how much I appreciated everything she'd done for me.

She'd always dreamed of going to Hawaii. I think the idea of lying in a tropical paradise kept her going on all those icy Minnesota days when she rode the bus to and from work.

After the 1977 season, I had an opportunity to go to Hawaii for a Major League Baseball Players Association meeting. I called Ma to see if she wanted to come along.

"Ma, where's your favorite place you want to go in the world?"

"Hawaii," she answered quickly but a little sheepishly.

"Well, I'm going to take you there."

She didn't say anything for a few seconds.

"I don't know if my boss will give me the time off."

"Ma, if you want me to come to Minnesota and talk to him, I'll do that."

"What if he says no?"

"If he says no, I'll ask him to reconsider . . . in a nice way."

I didn't need to make that trip to Minnesota. Her boss was happy to give her the time off. And to this day, one of my most cherished memories is of Ma stretched out in a beach chair in Hawaii without a care in the world.

Looking back, that period in my life and career was one of my happiest.

On the field, the following season provided a glimmer of hope that maybe there was a future for me in San Diego. By Padres standards, it was a damn good year. Under new manager Roger Craig, we finished with a winning record for the first time in franchise history. In another first, the team drew an average of more than 20,000 fans per game. Gaylord Perry won the Cy Young Award. Our rookie shortstop, Ozzie Smith, electrified the baseball world with his fielding and speed.

I split time between right and center field and was named the first team captain in Padres history. Having switched to a longer, heavier bat after a conversation with Tony Pérez, a quintessential RBI guy I greatly admired, I drove the ball better than I ever had before. In the process, I eradicated the growing stigma that I faded in the second half of a season—an improvement I attributed to finally playing for a team that wasn't hopelessly out of contention.

A bonus of making the 1978 All-Star Game was that it was held in San Diego, which gave me the perfect opportunity to take my foundation work to the next level.

Despite another strong first half, I didn't come close to getting enough fan votes to be elected an All-Star starter. It came as a relief when Dodgers manager Tommy Lasorda selected me for the team, because, for months, Dorothy Bowen and I had been planning foundation events around All-Star week.

We were determined to go big and bold.

On the Monday before the All-Star Game, we rented an outdoor space at a hotel in Mission Valley and hosted a party with food, ice cream, and drinks. Dorothy had spent months calling major league teams to invite their likely All-Stars to attend. I followed up in person with the players when the Padres played them.

All the hard work paid off. A dozen or so All-Stars sat at a long table, signing autographs and talking with kids. We had a great turnout—even Major League Baseball Commissioner Bowie Kuhn showed up.

Dorothy beamed as she looked out at the packed lawn.

"Well, David, we did it," she said.

"Oh, this is just the start, Dorothy," I told her.

I meant that literally. The day was only just beginning for us.

After the party, we moved on to the second part of the program. Al and I had convinced the Padres to unlock the ballpark gates early so the public could attend an open All-Star practice. Around 10,000 people poured in to watch the teams take batting and infield practice.

Unbeknownst to me when the event began, the National League hitters took cuts at baseballs from an earlier celebrity game that were a little more juiced than the ones used in major league games. Our American League counterparts looked on in awe as my teammates and I rocketed balls into the walkways on the concourse and into the upper deck.

All in all, both events went spectacularly. I truly believe they helped pave the way for what All-Star week would eventually become, an extravaganza featuring a Home Run Derby and other fan-friendly festivities.

The positive vibes of 1978 didn't amount to much. In an era when only the four division winners made the postseason, we fell well short of a playoff spot. Still, I went into the next season cautiously optimistic about my future in San Diego. If the team kept improving—and if my business and philanthropic ventures thrived—I could see myself staying with the Padres for a long time to come.

But as the season wore on, my optimism started to fade.

Despite playing on a team that struggled to get runners on base ahead of me, I had the best season of my major league career, pounding 34 home runs, driving in 118 runs, and hitting .308. I finished third in National League MVP voting and won my first Gold Glove award for my work in right field. Following in my friend Willie McCovey's footsteps, I also led the league in intentional walks, cementing my status as one of the most feared hitters in the game.

But as a team we took a big step backward, losing 93 games and finishing fifth in the division. The disappointing season cost Roger Craig his job and made it feel like the Padres were back to square one. Maybe 1978 had been an aberration, and the franchise would never become a consistent winner.

At the dawn of a new decade, I needed to hear a clear vision from the organization, one that started with a manager who could stick around for more than a year or two.

A few weeks after the 1979 season ended, Padres general manager Bob Fontaine invited me down to the stadium to meet our new manager before the team made the official announcement—a gesture I appreciated.

About an hour before the scheduled press conference, I drove to the ballpark. Fontaine greeted me in the executive suite's reception area with a firm handshake. He thanked me for coming and told me the organization was really excited about the new hire.

Donnie Williams, the scout who signed me in 1973, and Jerry Coleman, the Padres' legendary announcer, were already in Fontaine's office when I arrived. Jerry, famous for his verbal mishaps behind the mic, was a local icon. One of his most memorable calls had come on a deep fly ball I chased to the outfield wall: "Winfield goes back to the wall. He hits his head on the wall and it rolls off! It's rolling all the way back to second base." I liked Jerry, and I thought it was a nice gesture for the Padres to include him in a big decision like this.

A ballplayer always has a soft spot for the scout who signed him, and I had only warm feelings toward Donnie. He was a good baseball man who knew the organization inside and out. Still, I never expected he'd be named manager—especially not at such a critical juncture in the franchise's history. But I was happy for him.

I reached out my hand to offer congratulations. Donnie pulled his back.

I froze.

What was going on?

I looked over at Jerry, who was smiling awkwardly.

"Aww, shit!" I blurted out before I could stop myself.

Fontaine quickly jumped in: "We think this is the right move for the organization, Dave," he said. Then he added, "We believe Jerry has what it takes to make us a winner."

If they'd put me in a room with Jerry and the great Ted Giannoulas—the man inside the San Diego Chicken costume—and told me that one of them was our next manager, I might have guessed it was Ted. I was totally flabbergasted. The Padres had hired a broadcaster to be my sixth manager in eight seasons.

It felt like my head was rolling all the way back to second base.

Chapter 4

•

NEW YORK STATE OF MIND

Ray Kroc hadn't become one of America's most admired businessmen by accident. He took a risk when he acquired McDonald's in 1961, but within a decade, he had turned it into a global juggernaut.

Buying the Padres in 1974 was a different kind of gamble. Baseball and hamburgers are different animals. In the fast-food world, Kroc was a pioneer. But in baseball, the equivalents of McDonald's already existed—they were called the Dodgers and Yankees. Making the Padres competitive required a different kind of vision . . . and a lot of patience.

I didn't know whether to view the hiring of Jerry Coleman as a gimmick, an act of desperation, or a sign of surrender. Kroc's blunt assessment of the team at his first home opener in 1974—"Ladies and gentlemen, I suffer with you"—had shown early on that he wouldn't hesitate to publicly air his frustrations.

My four-year contract, along with the money he spent on Gene Tenace and Rollie Fingers, further emboldened him to speak his mind. Tenace became a frequent target of his criticism for not hitting with enough power. But the truth was, Kroc seemed upset that Tenace couldn't wave a magic wand and turn the Padres into the dominant A's teams he had come from.

Kroc, who had taken over for Buzzie Bavasi as team president, set his sights high. In 1979, he had tried—and failed—to woo free-agent stars Graig Nettles and Joe Morgan to San Diego, only to be hit by a $100,000 fine for tampering by Commissioner Bowie Kuhn.

I think that his quest for respectability was also what led him to pony up $4.5 million for a team jet—more than a third of what he paid to buy the Padres. By doing so, he made us the only other club besides the Dodgers to own its own aircraft.

Ours was a Boeing 727 turboprop, trimmed in the team colors of yellow and brown, a 60-seat craft that formerly belonged to Northwest Airlines. After shelling out big bucks on the plane and hiring pilots, Kroc didn't spring for any additional crew. That meant a coach, our traveling secretary, and the equipment manager had to serve drinks and meals—and even deliver FAA-required announcements over the plane's PA system.

Kroc thought the plane would help build team morale, and in theory, it beat flying commercial. There was just one problem: It couldn't hold enough fuel to make a cross-country trek without stopping to gas up.

On one return flight from Montreal, after clearing customs, we had to touch down in St. Louis to refuel. By the time we finally reached San Diego, it was so late that FAA rules prohibited us from landing at Lindbergh Field, now known as San Diego International Airport. So we diverted to Los Angeles and took a two-hour bus ride back home.

Following the Coleman hire, Al Frohman and I met to discuss how to navigate the year ahead. First on the agenda was our Superstar Village sports resort project, which we'd been trying to launch for more than two years. Despite our best efforts to find a suitable location in Curacao, Mission Bay, or in the San Pasqual Valley, it had become clear that the project wasn't going to happen. Neither was the dairy farm I'd considered buying in Escondido.

Some city officials accused us of overpromising and underdelivering on Superstar Village. But in reality, I think we just ran out of time. By 1980, the final year of my contract with the Padres, our focus had shifted to a bigger concern: where I was going to spend the next decade.

The Padres let us know they wanted to keep me around and were ready to negotiate. Al's love of corned beef and cigarettes had started to catch up with him, so the opening round of talks took place at Scripps Clinic, where he'd been hospitalized with chest pains. Team president Ballard Smith, Kroc's son-in-law, came to Al's bedside to make a proposal.

Upon hearing the numbers in question, Al mashed the call button next to his bed. A nurse came rushing in.

"Please get this man out of my hospital room immediately!" Al roared.

On his way out the door, Smith urged us to keep the contract discussions out of the press. Al agreed, and we assumed Smith would exercise the same discretion.

His offer, a five-year contract valued at around $2.5 million, was a non-starter for us. The Astros had recently made Nolan Ryan the first player to earn a million dollars per year, and entering the prime of my career, I felt I deserved that kind of money too.

We declined the offer—and didn't wait for a second one. Once Al was out of the hospital, we took a more proactive approach by handing Kroc and Smith a list of our demands. To ensure the club's commitment to me and mine to it, we wanted a 10-year deal worth around $13 million. I also wanted written assurances that the Padres would not move from San Diego during the duration of my contract, and that no sale of the club would take place without my approval.

These requests were unprecedented at the time. Other athletes would go on to make similar demands, but I was the first. Given the circumstances, I think they were reasonable. A potential move to Washington, DC, had cast a shadow over my first year with the team, and I didn't want to be blindsided by any future backdoor deals. If I was going to stay in San Diego, I wanted to be sure the team would too.

San Diego didn't have a large corps of baseball writers, but the ones it did have enjoyed a loyal readership. The *Union*, the city's morning paper, had a columnist named Jack Murphy who wielded particular influence. The Padres held him in such high regard for writing columns that helped bring

NFL football and Major League Baseball to San Diego that they renamed the stadium after him following his death.

Though the Padres and I had agreed to keep our contract talks out of the press, Smith tipped off Murphy and a couple of Padres beat writers about the negotiations. Not long after, Murphy quoted Kroc in a column as saying that if Al and I wanted to run the team so badly, maybe he should just sell it to us.

Kroc's wife, Joan, a St. Paul native who had taken on a larger role in the team's operations, didn't hold back, either. "We'll agree to those terms over my dead body," she said.

I guess sharing a hometown with her didn't earn me any goodwill.

To show we meant business, Al came to spring training in Yuma every day wearing a different team's cap. One day it was the Dodgers, the next the Cubs, and the day after that, the Mets. He'd sit in the stands, chain-smoking Parliaments, his bedazzled pinky rings sparkling in the sun, a grin on his face that said loud and clear: *Don't mess with us.*

My local image took a hit. With the country in the throes of an economic recession and unemployment soaring, a ballplayer asking for millions of dollars struck many people as tone deaf. The boos I started hearing in Yuma didn't let up all season. In an attempt to show I could laugh at myself, I wore a pair of yellow earmuffs during pregame warmups. I thought it was funny, but I'm not sure the fans agreed.

During spring training, I invited Leon Williams, a San Diego city councilman and respected Black leader, to sit in on the negotiations as a neutral observer. As the first Black athlete asking for this kind of money, I knew there might be racial undertones to how the public viewed the situation. The Krocs had recently made some loaded comments during contract talks with my teammate Ozzie Smith. Ray had said Ozzie could sit out the season and become his yard boy. Joan added that Ozzie "could have a job carrying Dave Winfield's wallet."

We failed to reach an agreement that spring, further diminishing the chances I'd remain a Padre past 1980. Kroc all but sealed it with a string of public attacks that summer. He claimed I couldn't hit with runners on base, said I was afraid of running into the outfield wall, and argued I wasn't worth the money he was currently paying me. Finally, he declared he didn't want me around at any price.

I remained silent, letting Kroc and Frohman do the talking. As much as his comments bothered me, it wasn't the time to get in a pissing match with the hamburger king. Instead, I picked up the phone and called Al.

"Let's get me out of here," I told him.

Kroc and I didn't part on good terms, but I have to give him credit for one very important thing: Unlike another team owner I would soon get to know well, Kroc and his legal team carefully read our contract proposal. They might not have liked what was in it, but they took the time to understand every word.

I know this because when he lambasted me in the media, he singled out my request for an annual cost-of-living raise as excessive. Once I declared free agency, the escalator clause remained in our proposal so that every team would know exactly what I was asking for.

My goals for the remainder of the 1980 season were simple: Play hard and stay healthy. Maybe it was the stress of the contract talks, or maybe I was just extra aware of the need to protect my body, but there came a night in August when I lost my cool at a pitcher who threw a fastball a little too close to my head.

The pitcher in question was Nolan Ryan, one of the hardest throwers the game has ever seen. He'd spent the previous eight seasons in the American League, so I'd only recently learned the joys of facing a guy who refused to allow hitters to feel too comfortable at the plate. I loved the challenge of battling the best pitchers in the game, and I'm sure Nolan felt the same way about facing the most dangerous hitters.

So, there we were that night at the Houston Astrodome, one guy who had pioneered the million-dollar-a-year club and another who was hoping to join it soon.

In the first inning, he knocked me down with a pitch. After I grounded out, he glared at me on my way back to the dugout, a look that said, "I'm the sheriff here." In the fourth, I had to hit the dirt again to avoid another fastball. Two pitches later, he came inside yet again.

I'd had enough. I decided it was time to go and pay him a visit. Astros catcher Luis Pujols grabbed me from behind, but I tossed him aside and kept heading toward the mound. Once there, I connected with a right hook to Ryan's head before a mass of players swarmed the field and broke us up.

It was the first time I'd thrown a punch since college. I got ejected, of course. As for Ryan, he learned a valuable lesson about how to confront angry hitters. After the game, he told reporters he'd be less passive the next time a hitter came at him. And sure enough, many years later—at age 46—he famously put a mound-charging Robin Ventura into a headlock and rained down blows on his head.

You're welcome, Nolan.

•

For the only time in my career, I played all 162 games that year. As the season drew to a close, I began winding things down in San Diego.

The hardest goodbye was to Dorothy Bowen, who, in a short time, had helped me build a charitable foundation from scratch. I went over to her house, which still served as the organization's headquarters, to let her know that I'd be leaving San Diego soon.

"I know," she said. "They've been saying a lot about you in the papers . . . You and Al."

"Just wait until the other owners get a chance to meet Al," I said, laughing.

Dorothy didn't like my agent. She had too much tact to say it outright, but I knew she considered him rude and crude.

"Oh, God help them," she said with a wistful smile.

I thanked her for everything she'd done and promised her that the work we started in San Diego would continue, wherever I ended up.

As I prepared to hit the open market, I assembled a team of the smartest, toughest advocates I could find. I brought in Dick Moss, a labor lawyer whose work on behalf of Dodgers pitcher Andy Messersmith in the mid-1970s helped usher in free agency.

I met Dick during my first spring training in 1974, when he joined MLB Players Association executive director Marvin Miller for a meet and greet with the Padres. Hearing them speak inspired me to get involved in union activities, both during and after my career.

Bob Erra, whose background was in the healthcare industry, also became indispensable. I got to know Bob through his role as CEO of Scripps Clinic and Research Foundation in La Jolla. He'd read about my foundation work and introduced himself when Al came to the clinic for heart treatment. He later helped us find investors for the ill-fated Superstar Village project. In the upcoming negotiations, Bob's job was to make sure teams understood that investing in me meant investing in my foundation.

Between Dick's savvy, Bob's meticulousness, and Al's chutzpah, I knew I had a formidable team behind me.

The ridiculous rules of the day—which thankfully only lasted a few years—required players who declared free agency to enter what amounted to a reentry draft. It limited the number of teams a player could negotiate with. Our goal was simple: Identify the clubs poised to have a successful decade and sign with the one offering the best overall package. If that team happened to be in a big media market that could help elevate the work of my foundation, all the better. That narrowed the field significantly.

We got ahead of the process by sending letters to 12 teams, asking them not to select me in the draft. Based on what had already become public from my negotiations with the Padres, a few more teams knew I'd be out of their price range. The Cleveland Indians wanted a crack at me, but they didn't appear positioned to break out of the second division, so they received one of the letters. I would have loved to speak to the Dodgers, but they made it clear they weren't going to pay me the kind of money I was looking for.

Ten teams ended up selecting me in the reentry draft. From that group, four rose to the top of my list: the Astros, Mets, Braves, and Yankees.

Rather than flying around the country, we set up a war room at the

Summit Hotel on 51st and Lexington Avenue in Midtown Manhattan and invited my suitors to come to me. To mentally prepare for the road ahead, I reread my dog-eared copy of Curt Flood's memoir, which chronicled his trailblazing fight for player rights. The free agency system I was navigating was far from perfect, but without Flood's courage, it might not have existed at all.

Despite being told I wasn't interested, Cleveland picked me anyway . . . and got our attention by floating some very impressive numbers. They flew in what seemed like their entire front office to make a pitch, but the size of their offer and traveling party couldn't make up for the lack of quality on the field.

Astros owner John McMullen, who had made Nolan Ryan a million-dollar man in his first year at the helm, was the next to visit our suite. His team had just suffered a heartbreaking loss to the Phillies in the National League Championship Series, and he believed I was the missing piece that would put Houston over the top. He told us he didn't mind paying a premium for me.

"You're going to make more money than you're worth," he said.

I didn't like the sound of that. It felt like I'd just been knocked down by another Ryan fastball. Al, uncharacteristically, held his tongue as we endured the next 10 minutes of awkward conversation. I hope McMullen at least treated himself to a nice meal at Jack Dempsey's before flying back to Houston.

Being in New York energized me. With the Padres, I hadn't really had a chance to get to know the city. My trips there to play the Mets a couple of times a season usually meant red-eye flights in, a couple of baseball games, and then off to the next stop on an East Coast swing. The 1977 All-Star Game at Yankee Stadium had been similarly rushed.

My only real exposure to the Big Apple was during my senior year of college, when my basketball team played in the National Invitation Tournament at Madison Square Garden. We stayed at a hotel near Times Square, and between games, my teammates and I explored every corner of Midtown Manhattan—the flashing lights, the pizza parlors, the peep shows. The people scurried around like busy bees. A lot of baseball caps, especially Yankees caps. No Elmos, no Dora the Explorers. No kids, as far as I could tell. I liked it.

This time around, the enthusiasm for the local baseball teams left an even stronger impression on me. On our way to dinner, people stopped me on the street like we'd grown up together. I felt like John Travolta in *Saturday Night Fever*, strutting down the sidewalk like I owned the place.

"Come to New York, Dave!"

"The Mets need you, pal!"

"You'd look great in pinstripes!"

One time, a guy spotted me on Broadway. He opened his mouth to say something but walked smack into a street sign before he could get the words out.

The Mets and Yankees were starting to enjoy a home-field advantage, but I was still curious to hear what the Braves had to offer. Although Atlanta had struggled to win games for the past decade, its owner, Ted Turner, seemed to possess the three essentials for building a contender: money, vision, and smarts. It didn't hurt that Atlanta-Fulton County Stadium was a hitter's paradise.

As a businessman, Turner was doing for cable television what Ray Kroc had done for fast food. He broadcast Braves games on the WTBS cable superstation, which reached millions of households across the country, and had just launched a 24-hour news channel called CNN. In addition to the Braves, he also owned the NBA's Atlanta Hawks. It was an impressive business portfolio.

My interest level was high enough for Team Winfield to travel to Atlanta to meet Turner for dinner. He brought along a special guest, Hank Aaron, who had broken the all-time career home run record with the Braves. I'd only met Hank briefly on the field, and I must admit, I was a little awestruck.

At a downtown Atlanta steakhouse, Turner made solid eye contact with me throughout the meal. He told me I would be the centerpiece of a team he expected to compete for championships very soon.

"And if that doesn't work out, we'll make you the starting power forward for the Hawks," he joked.

He had an undeniable Southern charm, and he was clearly turning it up a notch for the two Black guys, two Jewish guys, and one Italian guy at the table.

Hank didn't say much during the meal. Before dessert, I asked him if he'd take a walk down the block with me. I wanted a chance to speak to him privately, to ask him a question that had been on my mind.

Atlanta had come to be known as the "Black Mecca of the South," but I still had misgivings about playing in a region with such a fraught racial history. I was in my first full season in the majors when Hank broke Babe Ruth's home run record. During what should have been a celebratory time, he had to contend with racist death threats and lots of harassment.

The Braves hadn't had a Black star since Hank, and I had no way of knowing if my experience would be any different. I needed reassurance from the man himself that times had changed and I would be welcomed.

I didn't get what I was hoping for.

"If you come here, Dave, you're going to be another boy," he told me.

I stopped in my tracks. So much for going back inside and trying to negotiate a financial stake in CNN over chocolate mousse. I appreciated Hank's honesty, and it meant I wasn't going to be playing for the Braves.

We returned to New York knowing that either the Mets or the Yankees would be my next team.

Mets co-owners Nelson Doubleday and Fred Wilpon made a compelling case for why their team was an ideal landing spot. While we were talking at Wilpon's home, a news report about my free agency played on the local news. They promised the Mets would do whatever it took to become a World Series contender. As Wilpon put it, I'd get all the benefits of winning in New York without the hassles of learning a new league or dealing with an owner who had a reputation for wanting to be the center of attention. Unlike with the Yankees, I could even grow a beard if I so chose.

Describing George Steinbrenner as self-centered was probably accurate, but for a few weeks in the late fall of 1980, he made me feel like I was the only person on earth who mattered. He'd flown to see me in Minnesota right after the season ended, determined to be the first owner to express interest. And in the days before we met again in New York, he made it clear just how much he coveted me.

One afternoon, I returned to the hotel suite to find a bouquet of flowers with a note that read, "Look forward to seeing you—George." Another time, the concierge tracked me down near the elevator to ask what Broadway shows I was interested in. Before I could answer, he said, "Mr. Steinbrenner can get you prime seats anyplace you like."

"Does this guy want to marry you or sign you?" Al asked, before telling me to get him and his wife a pair of tickets to *42nd Street*.

A day before we were scheduled to visit with Steinbrenner, I received a telegram from George: "We want you in New York."

By "we," he meant "he"—and he clearly didn't give a damn that another New York baseball team existed, let alone was interested in me.

Chapter 5

THE MAN WHO HIT THE JACKPOT

Steinbrenner was talking to me like he already had me.

"You're the real deal—as a person and a player," he said, as we sat in his office in early December 1980. "I know you'll represent us well."

"Dave, we just have one question," a Yankees executive chimed in.

But Steinbrenner wasn't finished. The interruption threw him off.

"Who the fuck told you to say anything?!" Steinbrenner thundered.

Al Frohman tried to stifle a snicker but couldn't, causing a chain reaction of laughter in the room—even from the executive. He never did get to ask his question.

A few minutes later, a bag of sandwiches arrived. George unwrapped his, didn't like what he saw, and hurled it against the wall.

I looked over at Bob Erra, who was there to make sure any contract I signed included annual contributions to my foundation. I whispered, "Man, if I come here, we better cross the t's and dot the i's."

I hadn't done much homework on George, but I knew one thing: He hated to lose. Under his leadership, the Yankees had ended a 15-year championship drought by winning the World Series in '77 and '78. Coming off a 103-win season to start the 1980s, they showed every sign of maintaining their status as the premier organization in baseball—if not in all of sports.

Mets co-owner Nelson Doubleday ran a famed book publishing company. Ted Turner of the Braves oversaw a cable television empire. As far as I could tell, George Steinbrenner was put on earth to run a baseball team—and he wouldn't be distracted by *New York Times* bestsellers or coverage of the Iran hostage crisis.

There was a lot I didn't know about him at the time. I had no idea he'd made his fortune in Ohio as the head of an anti-union shipbuilding company that he inherited from his father and grandfather. I didn't realize that his first foray into sports team ownership, in the early 1960s, had ended in disaster. And I certainly wasn't aware that he'd been convicted in 1974 of making illegal campaign contributions to President Richard Nixon—a conviction later pardoned by President Ronald Reagan in 1989.

During those frenzied weeks leading up to my signing, I saw his bluster, his volatility, and his gamesmanship—but I never got anything close to a full picture of the man.

In private conversations, Steinbrenner convinced Al and me that a marriage of the Yankees brand and the Winfield brand would create a revenue stream above and beyond the generous dollar figure the team was offering. But Steinbrenner couldn't express his enthusiasm without taking a swipe at one of his players—in this case, Mr. October himself, Reggie Jackson, the first Black headliner to wear a Yankees uniform.

"You're not like Reggie," George told me. "I wouldn't hesitate to take you anywhere or introduce you to anyone."

It wouldn't be the last time he compared me to Reggie.

I had waited eight seasons in San Diego for the team to win—but it never happened. I didn't want to spend another eight frustrating years someplace else.

Steinbrenner sold me on the idea that he and I could conquer the worlds of baseball, business, and philanthropy together. In several important ways we were alike: We both had business savvy, big ambitions, and impressive leather briefcases.

Of course, I was the only of us who could also hit a baseball 450 feet.

So though the Mets, Braves, and even the Indians offered more money per season, the package we negotiated with the Yankees gave me exactly what I needed in terms of years, money, and financial support for my foundation.

At 10 years, it was the longest contract in baseball history, with an annual salary of $1.3 million. In today's era, where players sign deals worth more than $700 million, that figure seems quaint. At the time, though, it was a record for any sport.

Steinbrenner pledged to donate—or arrange for others to donate—$300,000 a year to my foundation. The contract also included a cost-of-living raise each year, capped at 10 percent. The Padres had publicly balked at this type of salary adjustment earlier in the year, but my negotiating team and I felt it was especially important if I was going to play in an expensive city like New York.

Once we'd settled on the numbers, our talks shifted to forming a joint company that would secure endorsement and commercial deals for both of us.

I was happy. And George seemed happy, too, so much so that he wasted no time in getting us in front of reporters. We consummated the deal on a Sunday, and George scheduled a press conference for the following day.

Back at the hotel after signing the contract, I called my mom in St. Paul to let her know I was now a member of the New York Yankees.

"Did you get everything you wanted?" she asked.

"Everything and more," I told her.

Al motioned for me to hand him the phone.

"Hello, Mrs. Winfield," he said. "If this is the last contract your son ever signs, it's a pretty damn good one."

It had been an otherwise sorrowful week in the city. Just days earlier, a deranged gunman had shot and killed John Lennon outside his Manhattan home. I was moved by the outpouring of emotion over the death of the legendary musician.

On the day I signed, I walked through Central Park and saw tens of thousands of people standing in silence at a vigil for Lennon. Then, the crowd suddenly broke into song. I wasn't a big Beatles or Lennon fan, but I recognized the lyrics immediately. Caught up in the moment, I hummed along to the tune of "Give Peace a Chance."

I had no way of knowing that my future best friend in New York would open my eyes to Lennon's genius.

As we were finalizing the details of my contract, another piece of sad news hit, this one much closer to the Yankees organization. Elston Howard, the first Black player to suit up for the team back in 1955, passed away in New York from heart failure. I never had the chance to meet Ellie, who was only 51, but attending his memorial service was both a privilege and an education.

Steinbrenner booked the press conference at Jimmy Weston's Restaurant & Jazz Club—a spot whose regulars included Tony Bennett, Frank Sinatra, Muhammad Ali, and Steinbrenner himself. The event felt more like a cocktail party, complete with music, a cash bar, and servers carrying trays of hors d'oeuvres. In the room were 120 credentialed media members, the entire Yankees front office, a few of my new teammates, and a surprising number of curious fans who had somehow gained access.

George and I walked in a little late after making a quick stop at a Christmas party for underprivileged kids at the Waldorf-Astoria, hosted by Cardinal Terence Cooke. Steinbrenner was already making good on his promise to introduce me to his many connections around the city.

One of the first familiar faces I spotted at Jimmy Weston's was Reggie Jackson, who came dressed to impress in an eye-catching, western-themed ensemble that included a lynx coat and Stetson hat. I admired his boldness.

The lack of variety in Southern California weather had seriously limited me sartorially. Moving to a region with four seasons was going to open a whole new world of wardrobe possibilities for me. During the cold, blustery weeks I'd spent holed up in New York, I'd already gained a taste for layering—think fur—and I looked forward to showing off my fashion sense as the decade unfolded.

But on this day, I was dressed conservatively in a gray suit and red tie—an outfit nearly identical to Steinbrenner's.

With flashbulbs popping, George and I walked to a makeshift podium set up in front of an oversized Yankees logo to deliver a few remarks.

"I didn't sign Dave Winfield—the people of New York did," Steinbrenner told the crowd. "I'm just spending the fans' money, and as long as they keep coming, I'll keep spending." True to his word, he would make the Yankees by far the highest-paid team in baseball during the 1980s.

Then it was my turn to speak.

"I'm pleased and proud to be part of this organization," I said. "My job is to play baseball and do a helluva job to contribute to the team and the community."

I avoided using the kind of language that Reggie had when he signed with the Yankees after the 1976 season. Though I believed in my heart that I, too, could be the straw that stirs the drink, I didn't want to put a bullseye on my back unnecessarily.

To his credit, Reggie lived up to the hype. He'd once said that if he ever got the chance to play in New York, they'd name a candy bar after him. And sure enough, the Curtiss Candy Company did just that when it released the Reggie Bar.

Reggie, along with two of the youngest Yankees, Willie Randolph and Rick Cerone, joined me for a photo op where I held up a Yankees cap and a No. 31 jersey. It was the number I'd worn in high school and college, and it had just become available after pitcher Ed Figueroa left the team.

San Diego had a morning paper (the *Union*) and an afternoon paper (the *Tribune*), and their reporters did a thorough job covering the Padres. The New York area had the *Times*, the *Post*, the *Daily News*, *Newsday*, and the *Star-Ledger*—not to mention the headquarters of dozens of national publications. Each of these newspapers employed a small village of columnists and beat writers focused solely on the Yankees, all fighting for scoops and breaking news. Over time I'd figure out which of those journalists I could trust. But on the day of my introduction, I just marveled at the sheer number of them.

The ink was barely dry on my contract when some reporters started peddling the narrative that my new teammates resented me for signing a record-setting deal. The next day's *Daily News* featured George and me on the back cover—the most coveted real estate in New York sports journalism—alongside an article insinuating that my teammates had only shown up to the press conference because Steinbrenner made them.

The article questioned whether Reggie and I could coexist in the same city and outfield. Reggie's contract was set to expire at the end of the coming season, and he'd made it clear that he wanted a new one before spring training started.

The national media also heralded my arrival in New York. I appeared in full uniform on the cover of *Sports Illustrated* under the headline: "The Man Who Hit the Jackpot."

After the whirlwind of negotiations and my introduction, I returned home to Minnesota to gear up for the season ahead. I met up with Sid Hartman, the legendary Minneapolis sportswriter and lifelong Yankees fan I'd known since my days at the University of Minnesota. Back then, after my Gophers basketball team got into an ugly fight with Ohio State during my junior year, Sid actually called the Big Ten league office to lobby them not to suspend me.

He'd followed my professional career closely, occasionally writing columns about the local boy who made good. Whenever I met with him, he'd catch me up on the latest goings-on in the local sports scene. Sid was more than just a sportswriter. He was, in today's parlance, an influencer who shaped how Minnesota's teams conducted business. Everyone loved Sid. I was no exception.

He also counted Steinbrenner among his "close personal friends." They'd met back in the 1950s when George was an assistant football coach at Northwestern and Sid was covering college football for the *Star Tribune*.

"I love and admire George very much," Sid told me over lunch. "But I'm not sure I'd want to work for him."

It was as if he had a crystal ball.

The very next day, I got word that George had a problem with my contract. He and his lawyers apparently hadn't grasped the details of the cost-of-living adjustment and were upset that it could potentially bring the total value to $23.3 million over 10 years. George seemed to think the COLA would be paid out as a lump sum at the end of the contract, rather than added annually and recalculated each season.

It baffled me that he hadn't taken the time to understand the language before signing off on the deal. Reportedly, he didn't even realize the financial impact of the clause until he read about it in *The New York Times*.

Dick Moss, the labor lawyer advising me, encouraged me to stand firm.

"He's cheated plenty of people out of money on contracts," he told me. "You should leave it as it is."

But I didn't take his advice.

Not wanting a clash with George so early in our relationship, I asked my advisors to draft a revised cost-of-living clause that both sides could live with. That led to an agreement to split the difference between the original terms and what George thought he had agreed to.

Relieved we had reached a quick compromise, I was ready to move forward. Little did I know, the contract talks that started at 51st and Lexington would become our own personal Lexington and Concord, with my King George determined to keep me a loyal subject.

The contract dispute faded from the sports pages once camp opened. Reggie became the story. Steinbrenner fined him for showing up late and then spent the first weeks in Fort Lauderdale criticizing him, calling him a "spoiled child" who felt upstaged by me. In trashing Reggie, he built me up. I don't know if he was trying to pit us against each other or what, but I didn't like it.

I struggled to get comfortable at the plate during spring training. As a big guy with a big strike zone, it took time to get my mechanics in sync. That spring, I worked with legendary hitting instructor Charley Lau to make some adjustments—cocking my front leg more, shifting my weight back, and striding forward with my arms set further behind me. The changes improved my plate coverage, but as I got used to the new stance, I temporarily lost my power stroke.

One day before a game, George approached Al and me. Apparently, my homerless exhibition season hadn't escaped his notice.

"You better tell your boy to start hitting," he said to Al, without breaking stride.

Al ripped off his smudged sunglasses and shattered the tranquility of the Fort Lauderdale morning with a hearty "Go fuck yourself, George!"

Hank Aaron had warned me that the "boy" mentality lingered in the South, which was one of the main reasons I chose not to sign with Atlanta. But to hear that kind of racially charged language at Yankees spring training absolutely floored me.

I chose not to confront George directly. Instead, I decided to let my play and the way I carried myself do the talking.

I was no one's boy and never would be.

Chapter 6

HIGH NOTES AND LOW BLOWS

I got an apartment on the New Jersey side of the Hudson River, which, depending on bridge and Bronx traffic, was anywhere from 10 minutes to an hour from Yankee Stadium. As Opening Day approached, I burned off nervous energy by exploring my new surroundings in a loaner Cadillac Seville. I quickly got up to speed on the blaring car horns, craterlike potholes, and scarce on-street parking. On the radio, "Chief Rocker" Frankie Crocker was spinning "Funkin' for Jamaica (N.Y.)" on 88.9 WBLS.

I passed a movie marquee advertising a new Paul Newman film: *Fort Apache, the Bronx*. I saw old Italian men playing bocce on Arthur Avenue. I drove through the South Bronx, past the NYPD's 41st Precinct. I smelled the smoke from a distant fire.

As I circled back toward the George Washington Bridge, an invasive thought popped into my head: *I made it out of San Diego, but am I going to be locked up here for 10 years now?* I guess I wasn't the only one with that irrational fear. A few months later, *Escape from New York*—a movie that portrayed the city as a giant maximum-security prison—hit theaters.

For the first time since my rookie year, I was a new face in a baseball clubhouse, carrying an even heavier weight of expectations than I had when I jumped straight to the majors out of college. I was the man who'd hit the jackpot, after all. As I mused at the time: *New life. New blood. New career. New bankbook.*

My accomplishments in San Diego meant little to many Yankees fans who had never seen me play before—on TV or in person—and hadn't read about me because my West Coast games ended too late for their morning papers.

That meant I arrived in New York with a certain mythology surrounding me: I was the greatest player that people had never seen. As the season got underway, Yankees fans wanted answers to two questions: How does the team look? And—perhaps of even greater interest—is Winfield earning his money?

Adding to the tension, the threat of a strike hung over the season as the owners and Players Association debated the rules of free agency. My future was secure. But I was still ready to go to the mat for the union.

When I'd played for the Padres, the start of the season wasn't met with much excitement. It came down to tradition and geography. San Diego was still a young franchise trying to build a fan base.

That obviously wasn't the case in New York, where Yankees baseball was in the blood. On the East Coast, baseball marked the arrival of spring. In San Diego, it just meant . . . another picture-perfect 70-degree day.

A reminder that I was no longer in sleepy San Diego came when I attended the Yankees' annual "welcome home" party—a packed event at the Hilton in Midtown Manhattan, where players mingled with fans and city leaders.

Just 12 hours after posing for photos, I sat in the Yankees clubhouse, shaving down the handles of my bats in preparation for my debut. I went out and got two hits in a win.

After the final out, I drank in the moment as Frank Sinatra's "New York, New York" echoed through the stadium. I'd heard the song before, but this time it felt like it was playing just for me.

By getting off to a solid start, I kept the wolves in the bleachers, the front office, and the newsrooms at bay. It helped that the team was winning too.

The only thing still missing was my power stroke. I went the first 16 games without hitting a home run. The press hadn't jumped on me yet, but I knew that if my drought continued, I'd start hearing about what an underachiever I was.

So I decided to tempt fate by calling my own shot.

We were in Detroit at the end of April for the final game of a series against the Tigers. Jack Morris, a fellow St. Paul native and one of the best pitchers in the American League, was pitching for the Tigers.

I walked into the clubhouse that morning feeling like my rhythm and mechanics had finally kicked in. In fact, I was so confident that I posted a sheet of paper on my locker that read: "Press conference here after the game."

It was a cool and damp afternoon in the Motor City—hardly ideal conditions for hitting. In my first at-bat against Morris, I weakly grounded out. But my second time up, with a runner on base, I roped an opposite-field home run that gave us a lead we never relinquished.

Later in the game, I made a diving catch in left field with the bases loaded to help secure the win.

I don't know what would have happened if I'd struck out three times, made a fielding error, and we'd lost—but I trusted my instincts enough to risk a little bravado.

The game ended just in time for the *Live at Five* evening news broadcast on WNBC in New York. As promised, I spoke at length to reporters, who transmitted their interviews and stories back to New York.

The next day, I appeared on the back cover of the *Daily News*, all smiles as Reggie Jackson greeted me at home plate after my homer.

When manager Gene Michael asked me to play left field so that Reggie could remain in right, I accepted the assignment without complaint.

Reporters who had been looking—and maybe even hoping—for a rift between Reggie and me couldn't find a story there. The photo in the *Daily News* said it all: Reggie and I were good.

During the season, we developed a routine of brief back-and-forths. They weren't confrontational, but they carried an air of tension.

"What's thirty-one?" Reggie once asked—not really directing the question to anyone in particular—after I got a big hit to help us win a game. He was referring to my jersey number.

"I don't know what thirty-one is," I replied, "but forty-four is only important because of the short right-field fence at Yankee Stadium."

Right-handers like me, meanwhile, had to contend with Death Valley, the 430-foot stretch of left-center field that turned would-be home runs into long outs.

Another time, as I stood in the on-deck circle, he gave me a not-so-light whack on the backside with his bat as he passed by on his return to the dugout after striking out. I waited for a game where I was batting behind him in the lineup and returned the favor.

I wanted Reggie to understand that whatever he threw my way I was going to throw right back. To know Reggie was to know that he ran hot and cold. One moment, he'd be warm and affable, the next he'd look at you as if to say, *Who the hell are you, and what are you doing here?*

After sharing a clubhouse with him, I understood exactly what Steinbrenner meant when he told me he could take me places that he couldn't take Reggie. He couldn't trust that Reggie wouldn't go cold in front of the wrong people.

At some point, I realized I'd followed in Reggie's footsteps by crossing over from athlete to cultural touchstone. It hit me one morning as I flipped through the news sections of the *Times* and saw an article about NBC anchorman Tom Brokaw's contract negotiations. "Tom Brokaw is the Dave Winfield of television news," an NBC executive joked in the article. "He's the biggest free agent around."

•

By June, I led the Yankees in batting average, hits, runs scored, and RBIs. My nine-game hitting streak to start the month helped put us in first place.

But the biggest story in baseball had nothing to do with what was happening on the field. The dispute between the players and owners remained unresolved, prompting the Players Association to warn of a strike. This came after the union rejected the owners' proposal to compensate teams that lost players to free agency with a player from the signing team's roster.

In my case, that would have meant the Yankees sending a player to the Padres in exchange for signing me—essentially a trade, which defeated the whole purpose of free agency. Such an arrangement would only depress the market value of the most sought-after free agents.

As much as I hated to see the season interrupted, I wholeheartedly supported the union's efforts to protect players' rights.

After the games on June 11, 1981, with the Yankees still atop the American League East, we went on strike.

The only upside of being out of work was that it gave me time to continue setting up my foundation in New York. A New York version of the Winfield Pavilion ticket program was already up and running. I'd also rented office space in Fort Lee, New Jersey, not far from the high-rise apartment I'd leased. I was excited about taking a modest organization that had operated out of a three-bedroom house in San Diego and turning it into a major force.

With the help of the money that George Steinbrenner was going to donate, I was assembling a team of staff and volunteers to ramp up the foundation's health and wellness offerings.

After a short vacation in Aruba, I returned to the Big Apple and put the finishing touches on my first event—a picnic and baseball clinic at Randall's Island, a city-owned piece of land beneath what is now known as the Robert F. Kennedy Bridge. Like the party my foundation threw during the 1978 All-Star Game in San Diego, I invited local community groups to come out and enjoy food, drinks, and hands-on batting and infield practice with me and 10 of my Yankees teammates.

It was a fantastic day that drew a few thousand people—including my mom and brother, Steve, who flew in for the occasion. When the event wrapped, I led the folks who stayed behind in a spontaneous cleanup effort, which ended up saving the foundation thousands of dollars in sanitation costs.

A few days later, the 50-day strike came to an end, with both sides agreeing to create a free-agent compensation draft in which major league teams were required to make a certain number of rostered players available. I won't get started on that—it was a flawed system that didn't last more than a few years anyway.

To make up for the large chunk of the season lost to the strike, Major League Baseball split the season into two halves. As the first-half winners of the American League East, the Yankees were guaranteed a spot in the post-season—regardless of our performance in the second half. If we ended up winning that half, too, we'd face the second-place team from the final two months in a divisional playoff.

The post-strike season resumed with the All-Star Game, played in front of 72,000 fans at Cleveland Stadium. As a Padre, I'd never cracked the Top 10 in fan voting and always had to rely on making the team as a reserve. But with the increased exposure of playing in New York, I was elected as a starter for the first time.

This time, I also had plenty of company among my teammates. Reggie, Bucky Dent, and Willie Randolph got voted in, while Ron Davis and Goose Gossage made the team as reserves—giving the American League squad a distinct Yankees flair.

In early September, I experienced another first: my first opportunity to play in my hometown as a major leaguer. Having spent my career up to that point in the National League, I'd never had a chance to face the Twins. To mark the occasion, I hosted a small get-together at my condo in Minneapolis.

"You gonna bring the Yankees?!" my childhood friend JD asked. "Is Reggie gonna be there?"

I got variations of the same question from other loved ones. So I explained the situation: All my teammates were cool, I said, but when it came to Reggie—who I expected to be there—I urged them to stay calm and not make any sudden movements.

"Tell him you appreciate his body of work, but don't fawn," I said. "And if he gets a look in his eye that says he doesn't want to talk to you anymore, go grab another cup of punch."

Everyone followed my instructions, and the party turned out great.

Already in the postseason, we played average baseball over the final months, prompting George to fire Gene Michael. Proving what a weird season it was, we didn't make our first visit to Boston until mid-September. But the moment I stepped onto the field at Fenway Park, I was initiated into the long-standing feud between the two teams.

Echoes of "Hey, Winfield, you suck!" rang out from the stands, probably from people seeing me play for the first time. It felt good to make my mark on the rivalry with a game-winning, three-run homer in my first game at Fenway—though, funnily enough, it only seemed to convince them I sucked even more the rest of the series.

It was a good warmup for the postseason.

•

We got by the Brewers in the divisional round to advance to the American League Championship Series against the A's. I loved getting my first taste of playoff baseball, where the crowds are electric and every pitch matters that much more.

After winning three straight games in the ALCS, we were World Series bound.

The offseason contract dispute and the unpleasant spring training incident with Steinbrenner had left a bad taste, but I'd successfully adjusted to a new city, position, and league and had played well enough during the season to enter the MVP conversation. Things were still tense between George and me, but if the Yankees won four more games, they were hopefully going to get a whole lot better.

Our World Series opponent was the Los Angeles Dodgers, whose National League Championship Series against the Expos had come down to the last inning of the deciding game. Not that I needed extra motivation, but I hadn't forgotten that the Dodgers had shunned me in free agency.

For fans of both teams, it was another showdown between two iconic franchises that had met in the 1977 and 1978 World Series, with the Yankees winning both times.

Excitement swelled inside me.

I hadn't exactly knocked the cover off the ball in the opening rounds of the playoffs, but I was looking forward to facing a group of pitchers I knew well from my National League days. I was ready to go . . . I just needed to make sure I didn't end up taking the field in half a uniform.

As the season went on, I noticed I was running low on pants and other pieces of my uniform. I just assumed things were getting misplaced in the summer-long shuffle of packing, unpacking, and washing. By the time we reached the playoffs, it had gotten so bad that I had to borrow a pair of pants from my teammate Tommy John just to have a complete uniform for one of the games.

When I told my agent, Al, about the situation, he laughed and told me that everything used or worn by Yankees players—bats, jerseys, pants, caps, batting gloves—had incredible value.

"Your pants aren't missing," he told me. "They're in a frame on somebody's fucking wall."

Thankfully, I was able to get the pants situation sorted out in time for the opening World Series games at Yankee Stadium.

My only contributions in the first two games were a bases-loaded walk and an outfield assist that killed a potential Dodgers rally in Game 1. But we didn't need much offense. Thanks to a couple of pitching gems from Ron Guidry and my pants godfather, Tommy John—combined with outstanding bullpen work from Goose Gossage—we jumped out to a 2–0 lead in the series.

With momentum on our side, we switched coasts for the middle part of the series, needing to win two out of three games in Los Angeles to seal the deal.

After falling behind early in Game 3, we had Dodgers pitcher Fernando Valenzuela on the ropes but couldn't land the knockout blow that might've given us a nearly insurmountable series lead. In a performance that would be unheard of today, Valenzuela threw 147 pitches in a complete-game effort. The National League Rookie of the Year and Cy Young Award–winner held us scoreless over the final six innings, and the Dodgers held on for a 5–4 win. I drew two of Valenzuela's seven walks, but once again, I went hitless.

The next night, I came up in the sixth inning of a game we led 4–3 and lifted a high fly ball that Dodgers left fielder Dusty Baker squeezed into his glove at the wall. Two innings later, I crushed a ball to the deepest part of the ballpark in center, but my former Padres teammate Derrel Thomas made the catch on the warning track. We ended up losing an 8–7 heartbreaker, and just like that, the series was tied at two games apiece.

The "s" word started to rear its ugly head in the New York media, so I decided to address it head-on in my postgame comments.

"I never did like the word 'slump,'" I told the writers gathered around my locker. "I call it a period of adjustment."

It's true what they say about baseball being a game of inches. If the balls I hit in my final two at-bats of Game 4 had traveled just another 120 inches farther, I would have been answering a whole other set of questions. I was hitting the ball hard, just not getting results. And the team was in a nosedive.

Game 5 was another tightly fought battle. I finally got my first hit of the series, a fifth-inning single. For a split second, I thought about asking for the ball as a souvenir, but I quickly dismissed the idea. It didn't feel like the right moment for dark humor. We had a game we desperately needed to win.

Guidry was pitching another gem, cruising with a shutout into the seventh inning. But then, Pedro Guerrero and Steve Yeager hit back-to-back home runs, giving the Dodgers a 2–1 lead. That ended up being the final score.

For the third day in a row, we lost a one-run game.

We'd flown to Los Angeles in high spirits and returned to New York feeling somber. But there was still hope. Despite the nightmarish results out west, all we had to do back home was win two straight games—something we'd done plenty of times during the season.

As if I didn't have enough on my mind already, Al phoned me on the off day between games and said he had something important to discuss. I'd hoped to spend the day clearing my head before Game 6, but by the tone of his voice, I could tell this couldn't wait.

"Meet you at the Bagel Nosh?" I asked, referencing one of our favorite places in Fort Lee.

"Nah, I want to talk in private," he replied.

Fifteen minutes later, he was sitting in my apartment, telling me about a disturbing phone call he'd answered in my room at the Wilshire Hyatt Hotel the night before the previous game.

"The guy said he was going to kill you the next time you played," Al said nonchalantly. "But you played and you're fine, so I wouldn't worry too much about it. Just wanted to let you know it happened."

I'd read in the papers that two of my teammates, Rick Cerone and Graig Nettles, had received threatening letters in recent weeks. Maybe it was just the price of fame. Still, Al's news hit me hard. Earlier that year, President Ronald Reagan had Secret Service protection when a man, trying to get the attention of actress Jodie Foster, shot and wounded him. What chance did a ballplayer with just a few security officers have if someone truly wanted to harm him?

Before I could fully process what Al had just told me, he dropped another bombshell: He knew about two letters and three other phone calls that had made similar threats against me.

"The *Daily News* is doing a story," he said.

"What? How'd they find out about it?" I asked.

"How do they find out about anything? They're a bunch of jackals."

It was a variation on his usual line about reporters not knowing their ass from their elbow.

I shot him a look to show I wasn't buying it.

"I might have mentioned it to a few people," he admitted. "Lousy jackals."

The story was scheduled to run the day after our next game, but rain in New York pushed the series back a day. On the morning of Game 6, I woke up to see this headline on the back cover of the *Daily News*: "Threat to Winfield: 'Bang . . . you die!'"

The article revealed details about the threats that Al hadn't shared with me. It printed the contents of the letters, one of which referred to me as the "n-word" and warned that I would be harmed during the playoffs. Al was quoted in the story as saying that he hadn't reported the threats to law enforcement, the Yankees, or Major League Baseball because he didn't think it would help.

"We didn't want people to think we were using this as an excuse for Dave being 1-for-18 during the World Series," Al said. "Besides, what could the police or FBI have done? If a guy wants to pop you, baby, he's going to pop you."

The individual—or individuals—behind the calls and letters clearly wanted to scare me and break my focus. But I wasn't about to let that happen. The Yankees promised to increase security for the rest of the series, which gave me some peace of mind.

When we finally took the field for Game 6, I felt ready to channel all the adrenaline coursing through my veins. But once again, my best efforts ended in disappointment.

As with every other game of the series, we took a lead. But with everything on the line, we just couldn't find our power or footing—both literally and figuratively. A bank of lights in the stadium went out in the third inning, forcing a brief delay. And with the Yankee Stadium grass still damp from the previous day's rain, I slipped and fell both in the field and at the plate. I took an 0-for-4, and after three close losses in Los Angeles, Game 6 ended in a 9–2 rout.

I switched my brain to autopilot as reporters streamed into the clubhouse after the game. The reasons we lost were clear: Our ability to hit with runners in scoring position had failed us, and our bullpen had sprung leaks. The pressure hadn't gotten to me—I'd simply had a bad week. And it stung to see my boyhood dream of winning a World Series slip through my fingers.

Someone asked Reggie about his future, and he shot back playfully that he hoped to live at least another 35 years. Out of the corner of my eye, I caught a glimpse of Steinbrenner going into manager Bob Lemon's office for what I could imagine was a very depressing conversation.

Faced with questions about my performance, I avoided excuses and spoke optimistically about what lay ahead. In my heart, I believed I'd have the chance to play in many more World Series with the Yankees.

It was Steinbrenner, of course, who would deliver the final verdict on the season. He held back his criticism, praising the team for winning the American League pennant and blaming the World Series loss on a few bad days at the ballpark. Contrary to popular belief, he didn't call me "Mr. May"—that would come a few years later.

In a private meeting later that week, George and I focused on the future rather than dwelling on the past. At a time when I was feeling pretty low, I appreciated that he didn't pile on.

•

When life knocks you down, you have to get back on the horse. In my case, the horse was a parade float.

I still question how I got talked into it, but less than a month after losing the World Series, I found myself perched atop a *Daily News* float at the Macy's Thanksgiving Day Parade, singing my heart out to America.

When John Campi, the newspaper's head of promotion, pitched the idea of me belting out a song at the event, I was of two minds. I'd always loved watching the parade on TV and was flattered by the invitation to take part. But I worried about the optics of putting myself out there so soon after the disappointment against the Dodgers.

There was also the not-so-small matter that I couldn't carry a tune. I had no problem singing in the bathroom, the shower, or the car. But doing it in public, by myself, in front of millions of people watching on TV? That was another story.

"Have any other players ever done this?" I asked Campi.

"No, but we had Diana Ross one year," he replied.

Campi had a reputation as a marketing genius, so I let him convince me to follow in Diana's footsteps—even though I'd be singing a song I'd never heard before, an old American standard called "Manhattan."

On the Monday before Thanksgiving, I went to Radio City Music Hall to rehearse and pre-record my performance. After hearing the song a few times, I started to get a feel for it. On Thanksgiving Day, I'd be doing what later became known as "a Milli Vanilli," named after the pop duo that got caught lip-syncing their hits. In my case, not performing live wasn't a scandal. I was a baseball player, after all.

It was cold and blustery on Thanksgiving morning. The wind howled through the streets as I bopped around atop a "Big Apple" float in full Yankees uniform, mouthing along to the lyrics we'd recorded earlier in the week.

Even though it took me out of my comfort zone, I'm glad I did it. My friends and family watching in Minnesota got a kick out of it, and, in a strange way, it helped me clear my head and start moving on from the World Series loss.

Before heading home to Minnesota for the December holidays, I had one last important piece of business: putting the finishing touches on my largest foundation event to date—a Christmas party for Bronx kids and their families at Yankee Stadium. We'd booked the field, arranged for a Santa, and bought hundreds of bags of groceries and toys to distribute to our guests. I was excited to ring in the holidays early with the Bronx community.

The day before the event, one of Steinbrenner's assistants called the foundation with a message from George.

"Mr. Steinbrenner has decided you can't have your party at the stadium."

It was probably for the best that a foundation volunteer answered the phone instead of me. I would've grilled the assistant until she either put George on the phone or hung up on me.

For the next few hours, I tried repeatedly to reach George to understand why he'd canceled the event. But—surprise, surprise—I couldn't get through.

Seeing no other options, I drove over to the stadium. On the way, I passed a billboard near the George Washington Bridge—a giant image of me, smiling in a Bill Blass designer suit.

When I got to the stadium, I was told George had already left for the day.

With just over 24 hours until the event, my foundation team and I scrambled to find a new venue. We called a dozen or more places—hotels, churches, community centers—only to be told every time that they couldn't accommodate us on such short notice.

Then, one of our volunteers reached out to someone she knew at the New York City Department of Education, who suggested we ask if a Bronx school could host us. So I drove a few blocks to Public School 114. A few jaws dropped when I walked into the main office. After I explained the situation to the principal, she walked me to the auditorium.

"How does this look?" she asked.

"This looks just about perfect," I replied.

"We'll see you tomorrow, then."

It was a Christmas miracle.

I was disappointed that the kids didn't get to celebrate on the field at Yankee Stadium, but the party turned out great.

Still, it didn't take away the anger or the hurt of what Steinbrenner had done. Was he bitter about my contract situation? Mad that I sang in the Thanksgiving parade? Upset about my World Series performance? All I could do was guess, because he never offered an explanation.

I could've just chalked it up to George being George. I could've just shut up, hit the ball, smiled for the cameras, flattered him, and put up with his unpredictability. Life probably would've been a lot easier that way.

But my mom didn't raise me to back down or let people walk all over me.

Chapter 7

•

ORIGINS

Yankee Stadium was the "House That Ruth Built." The Oxford Playground in St. Paul, Minnesota, was the House That Winfield Built. I don't say that to boast—I mean it literally. I helped build the baseball field there with my own two hands.

In the early 1950s, the playground down the street from my house in the community of Rondo was something of an eyesore. Because it was mostly used by Black kids, it wasn't much of a priority for the city's parks department. Hockey was the only sport my friends and I could really play there during my early childhood, because all you needed to make a rink was an open field, water, and the frigid Minnesota weather.

That changed one summer day when a former University of Minnesota student named Bill Peterson showed up. At first glance, all I saw was a white guy with a military buzz cut, scribbling notes on a pad. He didn't exactly blend in, but in his new role as park supervisor, he was about to open a whole new world of athletic possibilities for Rondo.

Bill had grown up in a nearby community with an abundance of playing fields, and he believed the youth of Rondo deserved the same. One of his first projects was to enlist the neighborhood's help in building a baseball field.

Armed with shovels, chalk, and measuring tape, that's exactly what we did, young and old all pitching in throughout the summer.

By winter, Bill had organized the city's first all-Black youth hockey team and booked them games at indoor rinks. I wasn't on the team myself, but I watched as they went on to win the city championship.

I skated but wasn't much of a hockey player, so I couldn't wait for spring and my first chance to play baseball on the field I'd helped create.

From a young age, I was tall, lean, and athletic—traits that would serve me well as I got older. Thanks to Bill Peterson and my other youth coaches, I learned to harness my talent and developed a deep passion and appreciation for baseball.

No team hustled more than Peterson's. If you didn't run on and off the field, you didn't play. Our devotion to fundamentals gave us an edge before games even started. Opposing teams would see us whipping the ball around the infield and outfield with perfect execution in warmups and realize we were a cut above.

I remember one game, when I was 12 or 13, where we didn't display our usual sharpness. It was a cold and drizzly day, and the gloom seemed to seep into our dugout. Worst of all, we got outhustled, which resulted in a rare loss.

Bill wasn't a yeller or screamer, but he wanted us to know that lackadaisical play wouldn't fly. So, as the rain started coming down harder, he took us back to Oxford Playground and ran us through a series of bunting drills. We got soaked to the bone, but after that, we were the best bunting youth team in the Twin Cities. Even after I became a major leaguer, I started every batting practice with a round of bunting.

My older brother, Steve, also gravitated toward baseball. When the Washington Senators moved to Minnesota in 1960, we found heroes in players like Harmon Killebrew and Tony Oliva. We'd read about their exploits in the *Minneapolis Tribune*, listen to them on the radio, and dream of a day when we might get paid to play the game ourselves.

•

For most of my childhood, it was me, my mom, and Steve at home. My mom, Arline Winfield, encouraged us to play sports—as long as they never got in the way of what really mattered to her: education and learning to be well-rounded people.

Ma worked for the St. Paul School District's audiovisual department and rode the bus to and from work, sometimes hauling a film projector and reels with her—not an easy task for a petite woman who stood just five foot two.

Before bedtime, she'd feed a scholastic film into the projector and give us lessons on things like the early space race between the United States and the Soviet Union—or on something far more routine, like how to answer a telephone.

As Steve and I got older, we graduated to films about nature and history, along with stacks of *National Geographic*. It mattered to Ma that her sons presented themselves well, so she made it a point to teach us a new vocabulary word every day.

In the summer, my brother and I were outside from the midmorning hours all the way until the streetlights came on. We played baseball and other sports, of course, but we also created additional forms of entertainment: catching bees in a jar, Hula-Hooping, tossing Slinkies around, playing board games, performing sock-puppet shows, even using the plastic lid of a coffee can as a Frisbee. On rainy days, we'd race boats made out of Popsicle sticks down the street, cheering them on like they were racehorses.

Then there were the experiences that you carry with you your whole life, like the time I fell down and got a shard of rock embedded in my arm, which led to a severe case of blood poisoning. Or in fourth grade, when I was crossing Selby Avenue on the way to school and a milk truck came barreling through the crosswalk and hit me, fracturing my leg. Or the time lightning struck a tree we were playing under, blowing its branches to smithereens.

All of it became neighborhood legend.

It was the three of us at home, because my father, Frank, went his own way when I was four. As a young man, he served in the European Theater during World War II before going to work for the Great Northern Railway as a Pullman porter—a job performed almost exclusively by Black men for many years. At six foot three, he must have cut a striking figure in his uniform as he traveled the rails on overnight trips from St. Paul to cities all over the country. For reasons unknown to me at the time, Seattle was his favorite. The job suited his wandering spirit, but seeing a lot of the country came at the expense of seeing much of his wife and kids. I guess that took a toll on his marriage.

When commercial air travel took off in the late 1960s, my father moved to Seattle and was hired by Western Airlines as a skycap. He used some of the free tickets he received as a job perk to fly my brother and me out for visits. By this point, he'd remarried and built a new life for himself. My mom, on the other hand, never remarried.

Even without my father as a consistent presence in my life, I never lacked affection or attention as a child. Our street was within walking distance of my Grandma Jessie and the rest of Ma's family, so I was always surrounded by aunts, uncles, and cousins from the Allison side of the family. We all met up on Sundays at the African Methodist Episcopal St. James Church.

During the week, Grandma Jessie would help out our working mothers by lining up brown-bag lunches in the vestibule of her house for my cousins and me to pick up on our way to school. Each bag, holding a peanut butter and jelly, bologna, or tuna fish sandwich, was labeled with one of our names: Steve, David, Kathy, Tommy, and Carol.

On my tree-lined block and the surrounding streets, we knew our neighbors because they were the ones who sold us groceries, cut our hair, and taught us in school. It felt kind of like a "Black Mayberry"—a small town within a big city.

Those shiny new McDonald's restaurants I admired as a kid? I never actually ate at them—and I never asked to. I knew we couldn't afford to eat out, so I happily lived on a steady diet of fish sticks and Swanson TV dinners, looking forward to the occasional trip to Dairy Queen for ice cream.

I would later learn that Rondo wasn't immune from the social upheaval gripping the country in the 1960s. During that decade, Uncle Sam built new highways running straight through urban communities like Rondo. Ma and her siblings half-jokingly said the Federal-Aid Highway Act made it easier for the government to roll in tanks if uprisings broke out in Black neighborhoods. But there was a more calculated reason: These projects were designed to isolate and segregate Black communities within the larger urban framework. Despite vocal opposition from the community, more than 600 Black families in Rondo lost their homes to the Interstate 94 project, which ran from 1956 to 1968—or the entirety of my childhood. Similar scenarios played out in cities across the country under the pretense of better "connecting" communities with highways. Even after Rondo was cut in half, the community's pride lived on. But the forced displacement of people and businesses marked the end of Rondo as it had been.

•

At St. Paul Central High School, my brother and I both starred in baseball. I even earned all-city and all-state honors. While Steve went on to the University of Minnesota, I stayed behind to finish up my senior year.

Coming out of high school, I was considered one of the top baseball prospects in the Twin Cities. The Baltimore Orioles drafted me as a pitcher in the 40th round, offering me $500 to sign, but I decided to pass. I knew I could improve my draft stock in college—and I couldn't picture myself riding buses in the minors, especially not around a southern town like Bluefield, West Virginia, where the Orioles had their rookie-league team.

More importantly, Ma had instilled in us the value of education. It made sense for me to follow Steve to the U of M—unless another college opportunity came along.

Out-of-state recruiters weren't exactly breaking down my door, but I do remember getting a letter from a recruiter during spring practice of my senior year. He said the university he represented had reached the College World Series quarterfinals the year before—and that a player like me could keep them in the national conversation.

That night at dinner, I told Ma about the letter.

"Where's the school?" she asked.

"Massachusetts."

"That's pretty far away, David."

My uncle Jimmy had attended Cornell, but I had to agree with Ma—so my courtship by Harvard ended there. Even without me, they made it back to the College World Series three times in the 1970s. Who knew those brainy guys had game?

I enrolled at the University of Minnesota, becoming the first Black athlete to receive a baseball scholarship in school history. Back then, collegiate baseball programs didn't offer full scholarships, but since I'd be living at home my first year anyway, I was happy to receive a half scholarship that covered my tuition.

The NCAA was a few years away from allowing freshmen to play Division I sports, so I experienced my first year of college as a "regular" student, with plenty of free time on my hands outside of playing freshman baseball and basketball.

Even though the campus was just five miles from my house, the distinguished buildings and the crowd of young people hurrying across the green made it feel like a different world. I commuted either by bus or with my childhood friend Jerry Douglas. Jerry—or JD, as he was known—was an improbable six-foot-four, 150 pounds, yet somehow he avoided nicknames like "Slim" or "Stretch." He and I made a good team: JD had a driver's license and a car, and I had the sports cred that opened doors socially. In a student body of around 40,000, there were maybe a couple hundred Black students at the U of M. The white girls on campus—usually with incense burning and Joni Mitchell albums playing—were especially curious about us, wanting to hear all about the Black experience and what it was like to live "in the ghetto."

Being a college student in the late 1960s came with plenty of opportunities to meet women, but I did my best to exercise self-control, not always an easy task on a college campus during the peak of the sexual revolution.

JD was a loyal friend with a sense of humor that made everyone around him laugh, but he also had an impulsive streak—one that got us in trouble one afternoon while driving around. It involved the most Minnesota of crimes: stealing a snow blower from a display outside a campus hardware store.

The compact vehicle caught JD's eye. I think he thought it'd be fun to take it for a spin. He looked at me, flashed a wide grin, jumped out of the car, and grabbed it.

"Help me get it in the car," he called out.

Against my better judgment, I did.

Minutes later, with the blower crammed into the back of JD's green Ford Galaxy, we noticed a black-and-white with two men inside tailing us. JD tried to lose them in traffic, but it didn't work. The car pulled up next to us, and one of the men ordered us to pull over.

The next thing we knew, there were cops at each door, guns drawn.

Since we'd both just turned 18, they took us downtown, fingerprinted us, and charged us with felony theft. It was a Friday, which meant no court appearance until Monday morning. So instead of being surrounded by inviting young women at college parties, we spent the weekend in jail, locked up with some of the rudest and smelliest guys in the Twin Cities.

At first, the jailer put us in the same cell, but when he found out we'd been arrested together, he moved JD into a cell with a guy accused of murdering his family.

It was a long few days—especially for JD.

To put the situation behind us, our attorneys entered guilty pleas on our behalf, and we each received three years' probation. I stayed out of trouble the entire time, and partly in recognition of the work I later did with my charitable foundation, the charge was eventually expunged from my record.

But the incident was a major wake-up call. I had let down my mother, who had put everything into setting me on the right path. And I had embarrassed myself.

As I transitioned into adulthood, I made a promise to myself to do better—and to make a positive impact on an ever-changing world.

•

Growing up, I lived day-to-day—going to school and playing sports, first with just Black kids, and, after the passage of the Civil Rights Act of 1964, with white kids too. I was never made to feel inferior or less than because of the color of my skin. But to steer clear of trouble, my friends and I knew which parts of St. Paul to avoid.

As a kid, I remember seeing images on TV of water hoses and dogs turned on civil rights protesters, but I didn't fully grasp how tense things were racially and socially in America until the assassinations of Martin Luther King Jr. and Robert F. Kennedy in 1968, and Black Panther Fred Hampton in 1969.

The end of the '60s was a time of mixed messages. On one hand, you had the peace and love of Woodstock and the celebratory news of the moon landing. On the other, you had the assassinations, the Manson Family murders, and the Vietnam War—a conflict that hit many communities close to home.

There was an older kid in my neighborhood I looked up to named Dickie Sharpe. One day, we all waved goodbye as he left for Army basic training. A couple of months later, when Dickie was shipped off to Southeast Asia, I remember Ma talking in hushed tones with his parents. And I remember the tears in the neighborhood when word came that he'd been killed in Long An province in 1968, the deadliest year of the Vietnam War.

In my late adolescence and early adulthood, music helped me make sense of the world around me. A few months after the assassinations of MLK and RFK, James Brown released "Say It Loud—I'm Black and I'm Proud," a song that became a Black Power anthem. All these years later, the lyrics about empowerment and dignity still resonate.

In college, Stevie Wonder and Gil Scott-Heron provided the soundtrack of my life. Their music sounded good and carried weight. When Stevie sang about living for the city, or Gil warned that the revolution will not be televised, I listened and understood.

America's college campuses buzzed with political energy. My brother, Steve, who loved baseball as much as I did, made the bold choice of choosing campus activism over sports. The year I arrived at the University of Minnesota, Steve was one of several dozen Black students who staged a 24-hour sit-in at the university's main administration building to protest what they saw as an unwelcoming environment for Black students. The Afro-American Action Committee, as they called themselves, demanded that the university establish an African American studies department and major.

Aside from some damaged office equipment during the Morrill Hall sit-in, the protest remained peaceful. Still, three students who took part in the occupation were indicted for aggravated criminal damage to property, unlawful assembly, and rioting. That heavy-handed response sparked a much larger outdoor protest involving thousands of students.

As a result, the University of Minnesota became one of the first schools in the country to create a department dedicated to teaching the history, culture, and politics of African Americans and Africa.

All these years later, it angers me to see this type of instruction under attack in our country.

As a freshman in the fall of 1969, I was among the first students to benefit from the university's new commitment to offering a broader view of race and racism. I had the privilege of studying under Professor Mahmoud El-Kati, who had made a name for himself as a community activist in Rondo. Through his classes, I became more aware of who I am and where I come from.

My name was Winfield, but that didn't mean I descended from British aristocracy. From Professor El-Kati's teachings, I learned that the oppression of Black people in America was preceded by a long history of honor and achievement in Africa—the true beginning of my origin story. I also took to heart his message about the hypocrisy of a country that touts "all men are created equal" while allowing human beings to be treated as property.

Five years before Alex Haley's *Roots* brought genealogical awareness into the mainstream, my eyes were opened. It inspired me to trace my maternal roots back to Guinea, on the west coast of the continent, where my ancestors lived and thrived before being brought against their will to the American South.

Professor El-Kati helped make my college experience about more than just sports, and I've kept in touch with him over the years. As a tribute to him, I used the undercover name "Mahmoud El-Kati" when checking into hotels during my major league career. Don't worry, Professor El-Kati, I always paid my minibar charges.

I declared a double major in Black studies and political science, also studying under the venerable Professor Mulford Q. Sibley, a legend in Minnesota state politics who vocally opposed the Vietnam War and spoke of "the obligation to disobey" injustice—peacefully, of course.

Based on my classroom experiences, I was convinced that if baseball didn't work out, I could become mayor of St. Paul or Minneapolis.

A lot of what my professors taught came rushing back to me in the wake of the murder of George Floyd in 2020, a tragedy that impacted me even more because it happened in Minneapolis. Afterward, Professor El-Kati was out there with everyone else, protesting for racial justice. And if he were still alive, I have no doubt Professor Sibley would have been right by his side.

I fell a few credits short of completing my degree, but after my baseball career, I returned to school and began an independent study program that would have allowed me to finally graduate. Unfortunately, the professor I was working with suffered a stroke, and I never completed the program.

•

It goes without saying that my college years were also a formative time for me on the baseball field. Over three seasons, culminating with a deep run in the College World Series during my senior year, I reaffirmed both my love for the game and my potential to play at the major league level.

Playing baseball for the Golden Gophers shaped my future, but it was my time on the basketball team—specifically, one infamous moment during a game—that led to my first national headlines.

I started playing intramural basketball just to stay in shape. JD assembled a talented team called "the Soulful Strutters" that scrimmaged against the junior varsity squad. My play caught the eye of an assistant to newly hired varsity coach Bill Musselman, who had come from a small college in Ohio with the goal of turning Minnesota into a national power.

I turned down the assistant's advances until the start of my junior year, when Musselman himself said the magic words: "full scholarship," which meant I could live on campus and no longer had to sneak food from the university cafeteria. I quickly warmed up to the idea of seeing what I could do as a power forward in the Big Ten. I was excited at the prospect of playing in front of 15,000 fans in packed arenas, instead of a few hundred people in rickety baseball bleachers.

I just didn't expect the experience to be so intense.

Musselman's leadership style combined physical toughness with relentless mental pressure. We practiced in 20-pound weight jackets and ran until we almost dropped.

In the locker room, he posted a sign that read, "Defeat is worse than Death, because you have to live with Defeat!"

He also liked to blare classical music by the German composer Wagner before games.

His defense-first style emphasized nonstop movement, hard-nosed play, and aggressive boxing out under the boards.

Oh, he let us have fun—just not during games. In his view, fun was reserved for pregame warmups. So, before home games, we'd run onto the court to the sounds of "Sweet Georgia Brown," thrilling the early arrivals with a series of Harlem Globetrotters–inspired ball-handling drills that got the crowd buzzing.

Once the ball was tipped, however, the fun was over.

Before Musselman arrived, the team routinely put up scores in the 80s and 90s. But he preferred physical, low-scoring battles, even if that meant stifling his team's athletic ability.

In my first months on the team, I was happy to chip in a few points and rebounds off the bench to support our formidable starting five of Clyde Turner, Jim Brewer, Keith Young, Ron Behagen, and Bob Nix.

Like many teams in the Big Ten, Minnesota's roster had become increasingly Black in the 1960s. Ohio State, however, remained an outlier, maintaining a predominantly white lineup that led some to speculate that Buckeyes coach Fred Taylor was in no rush to recruit a more diverse team.

With Ohio State starting only one Black player and Minnesota starting only one white player (Nix), the racial optics of our January 25, 1972, game against the Buckeyes were striking.

Williams Arena—our home gym, known as "The Barn"—was a sea of maroon and gold for the nationally televised game against our sixth-ranked opponent. We came in riding a six-game winning streak, ranked 16th in the AP poll, and confident after a recent win over Indiana and its new coach, Bobby Knight. We viewed this game as another test of where we stood among the Big Ten's best.

The Barn was even more electric than usual that afternoon, as the game turned into a classic Musselman-style defensive slog, featuring a level of physicality that referees today would never allow. From the bench, I admired it all, waiting for my chance to get on the floor.

Right before halftime, things got even more heated. Brewer and Ohio State center Luke Witte, a seven-footer with a mop of blond hair, got tangled up and exchanged shoves. But only Brewer was whistled for a foul.

Then, as we headed to the locker room, Witte—apparently frustrated by our tight defense—threw an elbow at Nix. Behagen saw it happen and had to be physically restrained from going after Witte.

At the start of the second half, I could feel the tension in the air. With points at a premium and elbows flying, the refs swallowed their whistles. We trailed 50–44 with less than a minute left when everything blew up.

After a game-clinching steal, Witte was cruising down the court on a fast break when two of our guys converged on him, blocking his shot but fouling him hard in the process. Witte went down in a heap. Corky Taylor, a bench player who was in the game, later claimed that as he helped Witte to his feet, Witte spat on him, prompting Corky to knee him in the groin.

After that, it was just bedlam. Both benches cleared. Behagen, who had already fouled out, ran onto the floor and landed a couple of kicks to Witte's head, knocking him unconscious. I saw an Ohio State player about to clock Brewer, so I rushed off the bench and decked him.

The scene, memorialized in grainy TV footage, turned even uglier when fans came down from the bleachers, eager to join the fight.

Though time remained on the clock, security quickly ushered the players off the court, and the game was officially ruled a victory for Ohio State. Afterward, three Ohio State players—including Witte—were hospitalized with injuries.

The popular version of events holds that we started the fight. I've never seen it that way. But we did finish it—and I don't say that with pride. What happened that day was ugly. So was everything that followed.

Behagen and Taylor were suspended for the rest of the season. Ohio State's coach publicly argued they deserved even stiffer punishments. The governor of Ohio called the incident "a public mugging." A writer for *Sports Illustrated* described it as "a cold, brutal attack governed by the law of the jungle."

In *SI* and elsewhere, the fight was reduced to a group of Black guys with afros viciously attacking a clean-cut group of white kids.

At a time when George Wallace—"I say segregation now, segregation tomorrow, segregation forever"—was making a serious bid for the White

House, the Minnesota–Ohio State brawl became another referendum on how the public viewed Black men in America.

With Behagen and Taylor out, I was thrust into the starting lineup. In every arena we visited, the fans made sure we knew exactly how they felt about the Ohio State incident. But shorthanded and playing with a chip on our shoulder, we banded together. We became known as the "Iron Five," and together we went on a roll, winning the Big Ten title for the first time in decades.

Years later, Corky Taylor and Luke Witte met up in Minnesota. Over the course of a couple of days, they talked about the incident and the impact it had on their lives. They reconciled and became close friends, bringing a sense of closure to the story. Still, for people of a certain age—especially in Ohio—the fight and my role in it still gets resurrected from time to time.

If growing up in Rondo and attending the University of Minnesota taught me anything, it was to keep learning, stay strong, and, when necessary, fight back—lessons that benefited me almost every day during my time in New York.

Chapter 8

FRIENDS, LOVERS, AND LOSERS

My first year with the Yankees was an intense experience that demanded every bit of my focus. After the season, my personal life finally got the attention it had been missing. I'd left San Diego single and unattached, but now I was open to the idea of steady companionship—and maybe even finding "the one." But I still wanted to have fun too.

That winter, I rekindled a relationship with Sandra Renfro, the woman from Houston I'd dated while playing for the Padres. We'd drifted apart after she married a professional basketball player and moved to the Philippines. But after I signed with the Yankees, she reached out to let me know her marriage had ended and that she was working as a flight attendant for Braniff Airways.

We met once in Boston during the season. Then, in January, Sandra was taking a flight to Rio de Janeiro and invited me to come along. So I did. We had a nice time, and when we parted ways, we agreed to stay in touch—no pressure, no commitment.

I had mixed feelings about making the trip to Brazil, as there was another woman whose company I was starting to enjoy.

Her name was Tonya Turner, and I'd first met her at a luncheon in Los Angeles during the World Series. I admired her from across the table and later found out she was a friend of my teammate George Frazier's college roommate. I couldn't take my eyes off her. We only exchanged hellos that day, but I later got her number from Frazier and asked her out.

Our whirlwind romance really took off after I returned from Brazil. Tonya joined me in Las Vegas for a Major League Baseball Players Association meeting.

"I knew you were gonna be here," Al Frohman said when he laid eyes on her.

It was an improvement over the grunt he'd offered when they first met.

After Vegas, Tonya and I flew to Hawaii and spent a blissful week together at a condo I'd bought on Kauai.

Tonya, who graduated from Louisiana State University with a political science degree at just 20, didn't know much about baseball, so we talked about the other things in my life that inspired me. In return, she shared stories about her upbringing in New Orleans and the trail she was blazing in corporate America, working for Control Data Corporation, one of the pioneering companies in the computer industry, where she helped CEOs quickly access and utilize market data.

Tonya had a friend in Los Angeles she'd met back in college when he was visiting New Orleans. By the time she moved to LA for work, he was already living there, so he showed her around and helped her find a place to live.

One day, she brought me up in conversation.

"Earvin," she asked, "do you know a guy named Dave Winfield?"

"I've never met him," he said, "but I know who he is."

"Well, I'm dating him. Would you like to meet him?"

"I'd love to."

And that's how I met—and began a beautiful friendship with—Earvin "Magic" Johnson.

I didn't want to say goodbye to Tonya, but as February approached, I knew it was time to gather my gear and my thoughts and report for spring training. I arrived in Fort Lauderdale feeling healthy and rested. To satisfy the team rules of the day, I shaved off my winter beard and prepared to get down to business. But my relaxed state of mind didn't last long.

Sandra called me on Valentine's Day with news I hadn't expected: She was pregnant. The news hit me like a sledgehammer. In our past encounters, she'd always been on contraceptives, but I shouldn't have assumed that was still the case in Brazil. It was my responsibility to protect myself.

I struggled to find the words to respond to what she had just told me. But finally, I composed myself long enough to ask the questions I needed to.

"Are you sure?"

"Yes."

"Are you sure it's mine?"

"Yes."

"What do you want to do?"

She sounded hurt.

"What do I want to do? I want to keep it . . . I thought you'd be happier."

"I'm just . . . surprised, that's all."

I took questions from reporters about the upcoming season and Reggie Jackson's signing with the Angels, but my mind was elsewhere. The situation with Sandra was causing me a great deal of anxiety. I never saw myself as someone who would father a child out of wedlock, especially with a woman I didn't know all that well.

The media wanted to know why I was off to a slow start at spring training. They didn't need to know the truth, but in a moment of deep introspection brought on by my personal struggles, I opened up to a *Times* reporter about my baseball journey.

"Maybe I cheat myself a little bit," I said. "Maybe I could have been a Joe DiMaggio or a Willie Mays. Maybe I could be that good if I was willing to give up the rest, the other things in my mind, but I'm not an ordinary ballplayer. Do you think people would understand that?"

Maybe I was walking a thin line between selflessness and selfishness, but I wasn't willing to give up everything else.

I tried to clear my head and focus on two goals for the season ahead: getting back to the World Series and positioning my foundation for long-term success in New York. The community event at Randall's Island during the '81 strike and the anxiety-inducing but ultimately successful Christmas party in the Bronx had gotten things off to a strong start. I sat down to talk with Al about the next step: potential partnerships with New York–area hospitals. But before we could get into that, Al said he had something else we needed to discuss.

"Steinbrenner hasn't paid up," he said, referring to the $300,000 a year—$75,000 per quarter—that George had pledged to my foundation as part of my contract. "He only gave about half last year, and this year, nothing so far. And he isn't returning my calls."

I'd suspected that George was behind, because he'd joked before that I'd have to take him to court to get the money he owed.

As if I didn't have enough on my plate already, I was now facing spring training drama with Steinbrenner for the second year in a row.

Al reached out to a New York lawyer he knew, Gerald Blumberg, and we scheduled a meeting with Steinbrenner. Blumberg arrived at Yankees spring training prepared, legal papers in hand, just in case.

The four of us crammed into a trailer that doubled as Steinbrenner's office. We exchanged pleasantries and shared our mutual belief that the Yankees were in store for another winning season. But we weren't there to make small talk.

"So, to what do I owe this pleasure?" he asked, flashing an insincere smile.

I didn't need an agent or lawyer to speak for me, so I got right to the point.

"Where's the money for my foundation?" I asked. "You're late on the payments."

Any trace of even a smile disappeared from George's face.

"Listen, fellas, I've been thinking a lot about this, and I've decided I'm not going to give you the money. And if you don't like it, sue me."

He hadn't been joking.

Without missing a beat, Blumberg handed him the papers. George's face twisted in anger.

"Get the hell out of my office!" he yelled.

We did as he asked, his yelling and cussing trailing behind us as we stepped into the Florida sunshine, which, despite its warmth, couldn't thaw the growing cold war between Steinbrenner and me.

The deep freeze and foot of snow that fell on the New York area on Opening Day seemed fitting.

The weather-delayed start of the season gave me a few extra days to settle into a house I'd bought in Teaneck, New Jersey. Moving there meant I was a little farther from the places I spent the most time—Yankee Stadium and my foundation in Fort Lee—but getting out of a high-rise into a spacious home with a well-manicured lawn made the extra commute worth it, especially because New York City wasn't the most inviting place to live in the 1980s.

Steinbrenner had said during the offseason that he would give manager Bob Lemon a full season to prove himself. But after just 14 games—six of them wins—he backtracked and hit the panic button. Lemon was out, and Gene Michael—who'd been fired the previous season—was back in, at least temporarily.

Despite posting a winning record, Michael was also relieved of his duties in August. Between the constant leadership changes and a series of injuries, the team never found its rhythm. I'd been playing well until a hamstring injury sidelined me in late May, landing me on the disabled list with several teammates.

While out of action, I filed a lawsuit against Steinbrenner in US District Court in Manhattan, formally accusing him of failing to make payments to the foundation. This came only after our attempts to resolve the matter out of court had fizzled when Steinbrenner requested a full audit of the foundation's activities. That was a nonstarter—not because we had anything to hide, but because his pledge to help fund the foundation didn't entitle him to oversee its operations.

He'd also raised concerns about the makeup of the foundation's board of directors, a group that included my agent and my brother, Steve. Steinbrenner felt there should be fewer people with direct ties to me on the board. On that point, we agreed. As we grew, I planned for the board to evolve.

Still, George's attempt to micromanage my foundation rubbed me the wrong way. It was his prerogative to critique my on-the-field performance—though that would have been tough to do in a season where I far outpaced everyone on the team in home runs and RBIs. But when he questioned the foundation's work, he was questioning my integrity as well.

It didn't take me long to realize that most of my teammates were afraid of Steinbrenner. He couldn't fire them as easily as he could managers, but they still feared the cutting remarks that came every time they fell short of his expectations.

I wasn't the only Yankees player at odds with Steinbrenner. Goose Gossage and I were very different. He didn't care much about what others thought of him, while I considered myself more of a people person. I loved dressing up for public events, whereas Goose preferred jeans—even when the occasion called for something more formal.

But that season, I had to admire Goose for speaking his mind in a room full of reporters, accusing Steinbrenner of treating his players like animals instead of people. What he said took some of the heat off me, and more importantly, every word of it was true.

"All you guys with pens and tape recorders, you can turn them on and take it upstairs to the fat man, because I'm sick of this negative stuff!" Goose bellowed.

George laughed off the insult, claiming Goose couldn't possibly be talking about him since he'd recently lost a few pounds. Then he fired back, "If I were thirty-one [years old] and couldn't run any faster than him, I wouldn't call anyone else fat."

That season, I developed a strategy I tried to stick to throughout my time with the Yankees: I'd only strike back if provoked—and I wouldn't let myself be bullied by Steinbrenner or anyone else. The incident with Goose came at a time when George was whispering to his media contacts that I wasn't a leader and a winner like Reggie Jackson, because I didn't have a World Series ring.

"When I lost Reggie, it left a void," he said.

If that kind of talk continued, I wasn't going to let it go unchecked.

•

As Sandra's due date neared, I took steps to make sure she and the baby had everything they needed. I bought a condo in a safe south-central Houston neighborhood, far removed from the Fourth Ward, where she had been living. I sent money to cover prenatal medical bills and to help with all the things the baby would need.

When Sandra gave birth to a daughter in late September, I was in Cleveland finishing out what would be the Yankees' first losing season in a decade.

By mutual agreement, we decided to name her Lauren Shanel Winfield. A few days later, I flew to Houston to meet my daughter and sign her birth certificate. I stayed in the condo for a couple of days and met some of Sandra's friends. It reassured me to see that she had a strong support network around her.

Still, the whole situation continued to unsettle me. I had helped bring a new life into the world, and even though I wasn't in love with Sandra, I intended to fulfill my responsibilities as a father. I just needed her to understand that we didn't have a future together as a couple. But Sandra struggled to accept that reality, which only added to the stress.

My head was spinning. I felt drawn to Tonya's intelligence, beauty, and thoughtful outlook on life, but I wasn't sure I was ready to settle down yet. She had her life in Los Angeles, and I had mine in New York.

So I kept playing the field, romantically. Shortly after returning to New York, I geared up for my first-ever trip to Africa, a *Roots* tour that included a stop in Gambia, the ancestral homeland of author Alex Haley. And I invited a female friend—not Tonya—to join me.

As we sat at the gate at JFK Airport waiting for our flight to board, I heard my name over the intercom, along with instructions to pick up a red courtesy phone. Heads turned as I stood up.

When I answered, a voice said, "Stand by for your call." The next thing I heard was Sandra screaming in my ear.

"I just had our baby, and you're taking a trip to Africa with another woman?!"

I was speechless. How did she know where I was going or who I was going with? Then it hit me—one of her colleagues at Braniff Airways must have tipped her off.

"Yes, I am taking a trip," I said, trying to keep my voice calm.

She started going off on me again, but I wasn't about to have that confrontation in the middle of JFK.

"I have to go now, Sandra," I said, cutting her off.

And with that, I hung up the phone.

The Africa trip turned out to be one of the most personal, uplifting, and inspiring experiences of my life. It put my personal and professional challenges in perspective.

But I still couldn't avoid confronting them. I just needed to be careful about who I trusted.

During this time, I mostly withdrew from my teammates, probably out of fear of revealing too much about the Steinbrenner and Sandra situations. One of the few guys I felt comfortable around was veteran pitcher Rudy May, who lived just a block away from me in Teaneck. Rudy had been in the majors for 15 seasons and was winding down his career in the Bronx. He called me "Big Blood," and I called him "Dude."

While many of our teammates were out at exclusive clubs or chasing women, Rudy had a different way of spending his downtime. After most home games, he'd drive home and spend hours tinkering with his ham radio—the pre-internet version of an online chat room.

Feeling like a homebody myself during that time, I found it oddly relaxing to sit in his living room while he fiddled with the knobs, trying to connect with other ham operators from across the globe.

"Hey, Big Blood," he'd exclaim, "I got someone from New Zealand on here! Can you believe it?!"

After retiring, Rudy planned to scuba dive in New Zealand—one of many activities that major league players were contractually prohibited from doing. The list also included bicycle races, speed skating, and fencing duels.

Unlike most of our teammates who fished, hunted, or golfed closer to home once the season ended, Rudy and I shared a wanderlust that set us apart. While waiting for his chance at deep-sea diving, he spent his offseasons fishing in Tasmania.

Some of the guys on the team had another nickname for Rudy—"E.T."—because of his resemblance to the extraterrestrial from that summer's biggest hit movie. I'm glad they never found out about his ham radio hobby, or he would've been serenaded with "E.T., phone home!" every time he walked into the clubhouse.

That nickname might've bothered him, but I wore it as a badge of honor that Rudy and I were brothers from another planet.

•

Away from Yankee Stadium and Rudy's living room, my foundation's office became a sanctuary.

In San Diego, I'd relied on Dorothy Bowen to oversee operations. She worked tirelessly to ensure everything ran smoothly, never asking for anything in return—other than the satisfaction of seeing her favorite Padre helping the community.

The plan for New York was to build a more professional organization, with an executive director and other paid staff to manage a team of volunteers and help create program partnerships. But not receiving the money Steinbrenner promised had put a serious dent in my ability to plan for the future or even to continue hosting kids in Winfield Pavilion at Yankee Stadium.

Until I could sort all of that out, I needed someone to keep an eye on things when I wasn't around. Enter Mario Casciano.

Mario first heard about the foundation when he read an article about our Christmas party. As a native New Yorker from a working-class background, he was impressed by my desire to give back to the community. For several years, he had been a personal assistant to John Lennon, and Lennon's tragic death had left a gaping hole in his heart. When Mario came by to meet me, he was seeking something to help restore his faith in the world.

Only in his early 20s when he started volunteering at the foundation, Mario quickly impressed me with his instincts and encyclopedic knowledge of New York. I realized he could be far more helpful as my assistant than as a volunteer stuck behind a clunky IBM computer, taking messages and typing event invitations. I was still new to the city, and I soon came to rely on him for street-smart advice about what to say—and what not to say—in uniquely New York situations.

We also broadened each other's musical and culinary tastes. Mario turned me on to Lennon and the Beatles, and I introduced him to the classic R&B and hip-hop I was listening to. He brought me to Wo Hop, a basement joint in Chinatown that lacked the polish of Mr Chow in Midtown but served the best egg foo young I've ever had. He also introduced me to egg creams—making me the latest to discover that the classic drink has neither eggs nor cream.

I got a kick out of taking the kid from Brooklyn to soul food spots around town. But probably the most fun we had was sneaking out for late-night sliders at White Castle.

As lucky as I was to find a friend like Mario, I was just as unlucky to have someone like Howie Spira enter my world.

To this day, it still blows my mind that Spira became such a major player in my story. I guess it all started when my agent Al took a liking to him. Howie presented himself as a freelance sports reporter, and for reasons I still don't fully understand, Al let him in.

A weasel has a way of slipping through even the smallest cracks, but Al gave this weasel an opening wide enough to drive a truck through.

I only met Howie once or twice before realizing that he wasn't the type of person I wanted anywhere near me or my foundation. But by then, it was already too late.

I had no idea until years later how close Al and Howie had become. When I'd signed my contract with the Yankees, we'd talked about forming a company to help Steinbrenner and me secure endorsement deals. That company became Top Hat, with Al and Steinbrenner as its signatories—and, inexplicably, Howie as its vice president for public relations.

For a college dropout in his early 20s, it was a big step up—especially considering Howie's other activities, which Al either knew about and didn't tell me or never knew about at all.

I later learned that Howie had been working as an FBI informant against members of the New York Mafia. It also came out that he was a degenerate gambler—the last person a professional athlete wants to be associated with.

If I'd known any of this, I never would have let Al talk me into loaning Howie $15,000. I had no idea he needed the money to help pay off gambling debts to organized crime—or that he might be dropping my name in order to get bookies to extend his line of credit. I also didn't know that a chauffeur Al hired for Top Hat had spent time in prison for bookmaking. And if Al was gambling on sports, I wasn't aware of it, aside from watching him once lay down a few bucks at a jai alai fronton in Tijuana. But all of it put me in dangerous territory.

In my first two years in New York, my interactions with Howie were few and far between. But guys like him always have an angle. It quickly became clear that he wasn't reporting on sports for the love of the game—he was doing it to cozy up to athletes and their handlers. And I'd soon find out exactly what he wanted from me.

My life was getting more complicated by the day. I never imagined that signing with the Yankees would pull me into entanglements with a woman, a spiteful owner, and a small-time hustler—three people united by their vendettas against me.

But here I was.

Chapter 9

DAVE VS. GOLIATH

I give credit to the many managers the Yankees went through for not making a bad situation worse. They knew about the bad blood between Steinbrenner and me, but rather than piling on to win favor with George, they treated me with the respect I deserved. Without their support, there would've been no guardrails.

That doesn't mean they necessarily had the courage to praise me openly. Doing so might only have alienated an impulsive owner known for hiring and firing managers over lesser things. Gene Michael was a case in point. He was hired in 1981, fired later that season, rehired in 1982, and then fired again before that season ended. I'm not sure George himself could have told you why he fired him each time.

In private, Gene would tell me how much he appreciated my contributions to the team. Blessed with an eye for talent that would later serve him well as a general manager, Gene told me I was his idea of a complete player. But with TV cameras rolling or tape recorders on, Gene kept his superlatives to himself.

Gene and the other two managers I played for during my first two seasons in New York—Bob Lemon and Clyde King—were company men who seemed to accept that they served at George's pleasure. But George had a way of pushing the buttons of even his most loyal subjects. In 1981, Gene refused to apologize for daring George to fire him, as George was threatening to do—so George did just that.

The game of musical chairs never stopped.

In 1983, George hired Billy Martin for a third time as Yankees manager. The first time Billy had been forced out, in 1978, the Yankees were defending World Series champs and a few months away from winning back-to-back titles—accomplishments that would normally guarantee job security. But this was the Bronx Zoo. Billy wasn't getting along with George or his superstar player, Reggie Jackson. And all it took was one quote in the newspaper to do him in.

"One's a born liar, the other's convicted," Martin said, the "convicted" part referring to Steinbrenner's 1974 guilty plea for making illegal campaign contributions to President Richard Nixon.

Martin touched a nerve with that one, and it was bye-bye, Billy. He was put in time-out for a year before being brought back. Then he was fired again—this time for a very clear reason: He punched out a marshmallow salesman at a Minnesota bar.

Now he was back again. I liked the idea of playing for a guy who had won five World Series as a not-so-great player on the great Yankees teams of the 1950s—and another as a manager. Everywhere he went, Billy seemed to have the magic touch.

I was more than a little intrigued by his on-again, off-again relationship with George. I remembered the beer commercial they had starred in—one of those "Tastes Great, Less Filling" ads that spoofed how stubborn and outspoken each was. At Billy's introductory press conference, they performed a little comedy skit that felt like a sequel to the commercial. They'd later appear together on the David Letterman show, again playing up the drama between them in a comedic manner. They even looked the part—the heavyset owner with the booming voice and the wiry manager with the loose tongue. Though only two years apart in age, they looked like a principal and mischievous student.

George let Billy get his licks in, but he never let him forget who was calling the shots. I think that was the secret sauce in their relationship.

When Billy signed a five-year contract to manage the team in 1983, I don't think anyone believed he and George could peacefully coexist for that long. Five human years was something like 50 Steinbrenner-Martin years, after all.

I wondered how George having his favorite sparring partner back would affect his relationship with me. Goose Gossage had been his chief antagonist the previous season, but I knew it was only a matter of time before George came back around to me.

And I was ready. As I told reporters during spring training: "I'm prepared for everything on the field and away from the field. You come to spring training, you get your legs ready, your arm loose, your agent ready, your lawyer lined up."

A few months earlier, I had reached an out-of-court settlement with Steinbrenner, which required him to bring his payments to my foundation up to date. In exchange, I agreed to changes to the board of directors that included Al Frohman's resignation. Al had recently suffered a stroke and was scaling back a lot of his activities. He'd gotten into a habit of saying things he didn't remember later.

Billy brought along his best friend, Art Fowler, as pitching coach—a tradition that had started at Billy's first managerial stop in Minnesota and continued when he was hired as skipper in Detroit, Texas, Oakland, and New York. During spring training, my teammate Graig Nettles shared a bit of Yankees wisdom with me.

"Keep an eye on Fowler," he told me. "If George gets pissed at Billy, he'll fire Fowler. And if Billy doesn't quit over that, George will fire him too."

When Art wasn't working with a talented pitching staff that included Ron Guidry and Dave Righetti—who threw a no-hitter that season, on Steinbrenner's July 4 birthday, no less—he could often be found knocking back a few mugs of beer with Billy. As the season wore on, their drink of choice switched to whiskey.

Back when Billy played, he and his teammates—Whitey Ford and Mickey Mantle—had such a fondness for the hard liquor that manager Casey Stengel nicknamed them "Whiskey Slicks." It seemed Billy was trying to initiate a new generation of Yankees into the club.

"Hey, Winny, come have a drink with us," he'd implore me.

I appreciated the invitation, but the last thing I needed was a reporter seeing me drinking whiskey with the manager. Billy doing shots wasn't a story—Winfield doing shots was, especially now that I was the Yankees' union rep.

"Thanks, Billy, I'll take a raincheck on that," I replied.

My image was important to me—and that's why what happened in Toronto that August caused me a lot of grief.

We were up in Canada playing the last game of an important three-game series against the Blue Jays—one of five teams, including the Yankees, who were within five games of first place in the American League East. Back then, the Jays played in Exhibition Stadium, an outdoor multipurpose park that was also home to the Toronto Argonauts of the Canadian Football League. Located on the shores of Lake Ontario, the stadium was a popular gathering spot for the area's seagulls, who knew it was a place to find scraps of discarded food. If you played in Exhibition Stadium, you got used to the birds landing and sitting on the field for innings at a time.

That evening, I was in center field, playing catch between innings with right fielder Ken Griffey Sr. As the inning was about to start, I tossed the practice ball back in. On its way to a ball boy who was standing on the first-base line, the ball short hopped and struck a seagull on the field. Feathers flew everywhere, and the bird dropped to the bright green turf, motionless.

"Pow! Right in the head! The bird went pffft," a Yankees coach who saw the whole thing from the bullpen later recounted.

The Blue Jays ball boy rushed out and gathered the bird up into a large white towel. The Toronto fans instinctively started booing and throwing cups and other items at me. They probably thought I'd hit the bird on purpose, when in fact, it had simply landed in the wrong place at the wrong time.

Each time I came to the plate or took the field for the remainder of the game, the fans continued to heckle me. We won 3–1, thanks in part to an RBI double I hit before the incident. As a result, I was named "Player of the Game" and got wired up for a postgame interview with WPIX back in New York.

I was in the dugout talking to announcer Phil Rizzuto when Billy rushed in and told me to hurry it up.

"There are police officers in the clubhouse," he said. "They want to talk to you."

I thought he was joking, but he wasn't.

The Royal Canadian Mounted Police were responding to a complaint that I had committed an act that met the legal definition of cruelty to animals. They took me downtown—the first time I had stepped foot in a police station since the unfortunate snowblower incident in Minnesota. As I was being processed, the officers brought in the deceased bird and placed it on a table, its feet sticking straight up in the air.

I flashed back to the first college summer I spent in Fairbanks, playing for the Alaska Goldpanners. It was team picture day, and my host mom, Patsy, had offered to give me a lift to the stadium. On the way, her car struck a squirrel. By the sound of it, you could tell the squirrel wasn't going to be darting across any more streets. Patsy was rattled, so I told her to pull over and take a moment to collect herself. For the next 10 minutes, we stood on the side of the road and gave the squirrel its last rites. By the time we got to the field, I had missed the team photo.

I wondered if Patsy would be available to testify to my better nature.

My bail was set at $500. I only had $339 on me, but the Blue Jays were nice enough to pay the rest. I left the station still facing charges and with instructions to return for a hearing the following week. Because my case had an aggravating circumstance—the seagull was a protected species in Canada—I faced up to six months in jail.

When I finally returned to the team plane, everyone was in high spirits—especially Billy. "Winfield, that's the first time all year you hit the cutoff man," he joked, a glass of whiskey in his hand.

It was late. No one was watching. And it had been quite a night. I laughed and told Billy to grab me a beer.

Steinbrenner's unpredictability was becoming almost predictable, but he was still good for the occasional surprise. The day after the seagull incident, he came out and defended me in no uncertain terms, demanding an apology from Toronto police for charging me with a crime. In the next breath, he actually paid me a compliment. "We know that Dave Winfield is perhaps one of the most caring players in baseball today," George said. "I can assure you that I personally, and I am sure that our players as well, care about wildlife in our country just as much as the Canadians do in their country."

It didn't take long—maybe a day or two—for the Crown Attorney in Canada to drop the charges against me. Maybe if George had told them to go ahead and lock me up, they would have continued with the prosecution—so, for that, I have to thank him, even if he was just doing what an owner should do by protecting his investment and defending his organization's name.

A few months later, I was invited—not extradited—to take part in a charity event in Toronto benefiting the Easter Seals society. I commissioned an artist I worked with at a gallery I owned in Minnesota to create a painting of a seagull standing in front of a maple leaf. It sold at auction for $32,000. From that point on, Canada and I were good.

Was it possible that the same could be said for George and me?

The Toronto incident was the second time that season that George had gone to bat for me. After I was kicked out of a May game against the A's for my part in a benches-clearing fight that started after a Mike Norris pitch buzzed my neck, he blasted the umps for not ejecting the A's catcher who helped instigate the fight. That drew a threat of disciplinary action from American League President Lee MacPhail, causing George to get on his high horse.

"This is a free country and we are all free to express our opinion as far as I know, unless Lee MacPhail has authored a new Constitution and Bill of Rights for the US," George said.

I can't remember a more eventful season. Along with the bird and George evoking the founding fathers, there was also the "pine-tar game," where an irate George Brett of the Royals created an iconic moment by rushing onto the field at Yankee Stadium to protest his home run being overturned for having too much pine tar on his bat. There was also Billy Martin angrily accusing *New York Post* reporter Henry Hecht of spreading fake news about his relationships with George and players on the team. One day, Billy ordered every reporter except Hecht out of the clubhouse and laid into him in front of all the players.

"I don't know where you come up with your information, you little shit, but I oughta put you in the dumpster!" Billy ranted.

I didn't mind Billy ripping into a reporter from the *Post*, whose journalistic standards I'd found questionable ever since my name showed up in a bogus Page Six gossip item. It came after I bought an airline ticket for Tonya Turner, who I was continuing to date. The name on the envelope in the clubhouse said "T. Turner." Someone saw it, got carried away, and called in a tip to the *Post*. The next day, Page Six claimed I was secretly dating pop star Tina Turner, who happened to be performing in New York at the time.

Some of Billy's other conduct rubbed me the wrong way—like when he banned Griffey's 13-year-old son, Junior, from sitting in the dugout with his dad before games. Acting on George's orders, I assume, Billy claimed the dugout was for players only.

As someone who didn't have a dad in his life as a teenager, I thought it was nice for the Griffeys to get to spend that kind of quality time together. I remember young Griff throwing a ball off the wall outside the clubhouse, just a kid having a good time and soaking up the experience of being around big leaguers.

Billy's edict really pissed off Griffey Sr., and I didn't blame him. It was a clear double standard.

"You see Nettles's son out there taking infield practice, and they're going to ban my son?" Ken said to me. "That's bullshit. Fuck the Yankees."

Griffey Jr. never forgot the slight, either, refusing to ever consider playing for the Yankees after becoming a superstar himself.

We won 91 games that season, but Baltimore won 98 to claim the American League East title—and eventually the World Series. Art Fowler didn't make it through the season as pitching coach. Steinbrenner fired him in June. As Nettles correctly predicted, Billy wasn't far behind. After the season, George replaced him with Yogi Berra. But George kept Billy close by giving him a front-office job—one that should have come with the tag: "In case of managerial emergency, break glass."

The relative harmony between George and me proved fragile. I knew by then that he had it out for my foundation. He thought it distracted me from my job. But it was more than just that. I heard through the grapevine that he complained about the publicity I was getting for my off-the-field works. "I give money to good causes too," he'd say. "I just don't make a big show of doing it."

For a few months, Steinbrenner stuck to the terms of our settlement from the year before, but then he stopped making payments to the foundation again. He said he still had concerns about its operations and that the money was safely in the hands of his attorney, Roy Cohn—a man I would soon have the displeasure of meeting.

This couldn't have come at a worse time. The foundation had just announced a $6 million partnership with Hackensack University Medical Center to create an exercise center and nutrition program for kids, seniors, and the special-needs community. If our revenue fell short of projections, we risked being unable to complete the project.

I would have loved to be on the evening news talking about winning our division and preparing for the playoffs—and I'm sure George saw red when he instead saw me at a ribbon-cutting ceremony for the Hackensack partnership. If he could produce a shred of evidence that I was distracted by my foundation work, that would have been a different matter. But, in 1983, I again led the Yankees in every offensive category—including games played. I was an All-Star, Gold Glove winner, Silver Slugger recipient, and came in seventh in American League MVP voting.

Three days after the season ended, I again sued Steinbrenner for failing to meet his financial obligations to my foundation.

Aside from the headlines my conflict with Steinbrenner made, my experience wasn't all that different from the millions of people in America who clashed with their bosses. The concept of a "toxic workplace" wouldn't gain popularity for another couple of decades, but that's exactly what Yankee Stadium was for me.

My workplace had all the elements: high turnover, bullying, and lack of trust. Eventually, I even started to feel the physical effects of the stress I was carrying around every day.

I'm not looking for sympathy, however. Unlike your average Joe from Parsippany, I had the resources to fight back.

If Steinbrenner was going to put my foundation under a microscope, I needed to make sure there was nothing he could use against me. I had begun assembling a board of directors that soon included executives from Xerox, New York Life, and Equitable.

I asked my trusted assistant, Mario Casciano, to report any day-to-day issues he observed directly to me.

"The only issue I see is Howie Spira," he told me. "He keeps calling, wanting to talk to you. And he comes by the office a lot. He's becoming a nuisance."

"Talk to me about what?"

"He wants a job."

Not surprisingly, because of the strained relationship between Steinbrenner and me, the company that was formed to secure endorsement deals for us—the one that had Howie as its vice president of public relations—hadn't produced any results. So, now, according to Mario, Howie was angling for a position at the foundation.

"What did you tell him?" I asked.

"That you're not hiring right now . . . but he said he knows you're looking for an executive director."

"Okay. Thanks, Mario, I'll handle it."

The next day, I called Howie with a straightforward message.

"Quit calling and asking for things," I told him. "I want you to leave me alone. I want you to leave everyone at the foundation alone. I don't want to see or hear from you again."

"But Dave, what about Top Hat?" Howie asked.

"What about Top Hat, Howie? What has Top Hat done for me?"

"Listen, Dave, if you just—"

"No, Howie," I cut him off. "That's how it's going to be. Understand? If you don't, there's going to be a big problem."

I guess I got my message across, because Howie stopped calling and dropping by the foundation. I felt a sense of relief at having one less thing to worry about. But I should have known that guys like Howie never truly go away—they just lie in wait.

Chapter 10

THE RACE

The best weeks of any season were the ones when Ma and Steve came to visit me in New York. Being around family nourished my soul. Like most mothers, mine brimmed with pride at what I had become, especially because she never forgot what my father had told her when he left her alone to raise two sons—something to the effect of: "You think you're so smart. Let's see you make it on your own."

Sitting beside her older son, who was a community leader in St. Paul, and watching her younger son roam the outfield on a sunny day at Yankee Stadium filled her with warmth.

I'm sure Ma would have preferred that I had a steady relationship before having a child, but she'd been around the block enough times to know that life doesn't always go as planned. After the 1982 season, I'd flown Sandra and the baby to Minnesota from Texas to meet her. They stayed at a hotel near the University of Minnesota campus, just a short drive from the building where I'd bought two condominiums—one for Ma and one for myself.

She understood that the circumstances would prevent her from having a close relationship with her granddaughter, but she made it clear that she expected me to be a good father.

"Be sure you take care of that baby," she told me.

"I will, Ma," I said.

She put a high value on parenting. It was what she had devoted her life to. And even though she raised her sons entirely on her own, she never badmouthed my father—at least not in front of us. She didn't object to Steve and me visiting him in Seattle as teenagers, and she didn't stand in the way when he came back into my life as an adult.

In 1980, when he was still living in Seattle, my father called to share some exciting news: He was moving to San Diego. We hadn't seen much of each other since I got to the big leagues, mainly because he lived in an American League city and I played in a National League one.

He'd followed my baseball career—just not closely enough to know about my impending free agency.

"You can move to San Diego, but I won't be there much longer," I told him. "You can move anywhere you want. You had the Winfield name first, but I'm the one who made something of that name."

And that's how it went.

He moved to San Diego, and word got back to me that he dropped my name a few times to get in places. I went to New York. Our paths crossed only when the Yankees traveled to Anaheim to play the Angels. He'd usually ask me to get tickets for him and a couple of friends. We'd say a brief hello before the game, and that was it. This went on for a year or two before I asked to speak to him alone, away from his friends.

"Look," I said, "it's nice that you've been coming to my games, but I feel like you're not really coming to see me. It's just a night out for you and your friends. I understand. We're not that close. We don't have that kind of relationship."

I hadn't planned this kind of speech, but there was no turning back now.

"You're my dad, but you had nothing really to do with raising me. You never bought me a bike. You didn't pay child support on time. I'm thirty years old, and we still don't know each other that well."

From that point on, things were different. Whenever I played in Anaheim, he showed up to the ballpark early, and we sat down and talked—like a real father and son. We talked about where we came from, who we are, and life in general. He only came to New York to see me once, and I rarely saw him in the offseason, but for those couple of hours before games in Anaheim, we found the closest thing we had to a father-son relationship. It didn't fix everything—not by a long shot—but it was a start.

Rebuilding that relationship—and leaning on other family ties—helped distract me from everything else that was going on. But it was just a temporary escape.

One morning, I got a call from Sid Hartman, the Minneapolis sportswriter who was friends with both Steinbrenner and me.

"What's going on with you and George?" Sid asked.

I wasn't sure how to answer—not because I didn't trust Sid with the truth, but because I really didn't know how to describe how things had gotten so bad so quickly.

"Well, I'm not really sure, to be honest," I replied.

"Let me talk to George," Sid said. "He'll listen to me. Whatever it is between you two, I'll get it straightened out."

Sid had a long and successful track record of bringing people together, but I didn't think his intervention would do much good in our case.

"Thanks for the offer, Sid," I told him, "but you could be Henry fucking Kissinger, and I still don't think you'd be able to solve this mess."

If Sid did end up speaking to Steinbrenner, it didn't do any good.

•

This is my book, which means you're hearing my side of the story. But it's important to me that George doesn't come across as a cartoon villain. He wasn't that—nor was he the comedically buffoonish character that people loved watching on *Seinfeld*.

He was a living, breathing human being—full of thoughts, feelings, desires, and complexities, just like the rest of us. He craved personal and professional success. Nothing wrong with that. We all strive to be the best we can be at work and at home. He seemed to love his family—always a good thing. He contributed generously to charities and institutions including Grambling State University, a prominent HBCU in Louisiana. He also spoke out about his anger over the living conditions of poor people in America.

But he set himself apart with a drive that made it clear to everyone around him that his thoughts, his feelings, and his desires took precedence over everyone else's. And he used bluster and intimidation to get his way—an approach that won him many admirers.

Above all, he hated to lose—something he'd remind the team of during an annual spring training speech.

In all these senses, he was as American as apple pie, continuing and helping to shape a long tradition in this country of privileged men building business empires by whatever means necessary.

He liked to say that he wanted to prepare his players for success in life after baseball. But his actions didn't always reflect that.

I sometimes think about his treatment of Bo Jackson, who the Yankees took in the second round of the 1982 draft. George recognized his enormous athletic ability and pushed hard to sign him. But Bo chose instead to become the first in his family to attend college.

George didn't take the rejection well and said things to Bo and his mother that Bo never forgot—or forgave.

Years later, Bo made a point of reminding people how much he enjoyed hitting three home runs in a game at Yankee Stadium in 1990—as a member of the Royals. The performance came just a couple of weeks before George was banned from baseball for reasons that will become clear. Now that's poetic justice.

George could turn his charisma on and off like a light switch, depending on what he hoped to gain from any given interaction. When he flicked the switch on, he became someone you wanted to align yourself with. I experienced this firsthand when George wooed me to the Yankees, and I saw it time and again as he turned on the charm to sell himself to the public.

Like most of us, he liked to be liked—but never at the expense of compromising with adversaries. He was an immovable force. But guess what? So was I. I didn't have it in my DNA to bend, bow, retreat, or cower.

There's one word you won't find anywhere in this book: *victim*. Quite simply, I don't view myself that way. While I don't believe I was treated fairly, I've never allowed myself to succumb to feelings of victimization. In fact, I actively resisted that label by fighting back against George at every turn by putting myself on full display—to sell myself, my abilities, and my causes.

•

A day after hitting a 10th-inning, walk-off home run to beat the A's in a May game at Yankee Stadium, I stood in the White House Rose Garden, talking with President Ronald Reagan about my role in the Summer Jobs '84 program in New York. The goal of the program was to find private-sector employment for at least 25,000 underprivileged youth and young adults—a target that was far surpassed.

When he introduced me, Reagan shouted out my game-winning homer from the previous day. It was a real thrill to know that the president of the United States—or at least one of his speechwriters—was following my performance.

Following my White House visit, my play attracted even more attention. I started June with a solid .293 batting average, but just a week later—thanks in large part to two five-hit games—I'd raised my average 42 points, positioning myself to compete for the American League batting crown.

By that point in my career, I'd racked up plenty of individual honors, but the chance to capture a batting title had added appeal to me. Defying expectations was part of it. A player with my size and power didn't typically compete for the highest batting average—an accomplishment that meant more in the 1980s than it does in today's era of advanced statistics.

I'd always rejected the all-or-nothing approach to hitting in favor of consistency. There were times when I knew I could have led the league in home runs, but I didn't want hitting for power to come at the expense of striking out a lot and hitting for a low average. In some ways, that was a business decision. Playing in New York, especially, I knew I'd only invite further scrutiny of my performance if I became known as a streaky player. That's why I worked on hitting line drives and creating havoc on the basepaths. I didn't set out to be a guy who hit 500 home runs, but thanks to many seasons of steady hitting, I ended up with 465.

A competition within the clubhouse raised the stakes of the 1984 batting race. On June 5, my teammate Don Mattingly and I had identical .335 batting averages—a fact that didn't escape the notice of the Yankees beat writers. And who could blame them? Other than Yankee legend Yogi Berra coming back to manage the team for the first time in 20 years, there wasn't much else worth writing about. By summer, the division race was already over. The Tigers won their first nine games of the season and never looked back. Even though we played great baseball in the second half of the season, the Tigers had already left us and everyone else in the dust.

The batting race didn't have the allure of the historic Roger Maris–Mickey Mantle home run duel that captivated New York in 1961, but it provided enough drama to spice up an otherwise forgettable season.

Mattingly was in his first full season with the Yankees. He would later become "Donnie" to me, but back then, he was just Don—an aw-shucks kid from Indiana who played ping-pong with clubhouse attendants, because he didn't know his teammates well enough yet to ask them to play.

But he quickly grew on the fans—and Steinbrenner. George called him the best young talent in baseball and said he preferred him over a tall, athletic player who could run and hit for power. Sound like anyone you know? George was supposedly making a direct comparison between Mattingly and Darryl Strawberry of the Mets, but I'm sure I wasn't the only one who interpreted it as a dig at me.

I couldn't escape the feeling that the Yankees were trying to downplay my significance. Mattingly was the darling. I was the guy they tried to impugn. I wanted to show Steinbrenner that I was every bit the ballplayer that he thought I was when he signed me. If I won the batting title, I figured he'd have to say something positive about me—especially after spending most of the season making my life as difficult as possible.

Behind every man with an agenda are tacticians who help him ram it through. I was told that Steinbrenner had one of the best and most ruthless tacticians around in Roy Cohn, whose name meant nothing to me before our paths first crossed at his law office.

Al Frohman was eager to continue serving as my field general, but with his health in steady decline, I realized it was time to find someone else who could go toe-to-toe with my adversaries. I hired Jeff Klein, an attorney whose firm Weil, Gotshal & Manges represented the Major League Baseball Players Association. He seemed up to the task of serving as my agent—and handling everything else I was dealing with.

Before my first meeting at Cohn's office, Al brought me up to speed on the man I would be sitting across from. Listening to his profane history lesson about Cohn helped put my situation with Steinbrenner in perspective.

He was a man who seemed to take pleasure in ruining people, using whatever dirty tricks were necessary to win a case. As a prosecutor, he'd sent a husband and wife—Ethel and Julius Rosenberg—to the death chamber for spying for the Soviet Union. From there, he moved on to a cause that I remembered learning about in school: McCarthyism—a 1950s political campaign aimed at exposing alleged communist sympathizers in the United States.

As an aide to Senator Joseph McCarthy, Cohn hauled dozens of prominent Americans before Congress and interrogated them on their political allegiances. If they said the wrong thing—or refused to testify—they were blacklisted. He helped destroy a lot of lives that way. One of my professors at the University of Minnesota, Mulford Q. Sibley, taught us that McCarthyism was particularly aggressive against prominent Black writers and artists, including Paul Robeson and W. E. B. DuBois.

Al wanted to come to the meeting with Cohn. I wasn't so sure that was a good idea. Because of his health issues, he was speaking with less of a filter than ever. But he really wanted to see Cohn up close, so I said I'd think about it.

"If you come, you can't say a word. Understand?" I told him. "Jeff can handle it."

"I just want to ask him, 'Are you now or have you ever been a putz?'"

"What's a putz?" I asked.

"Cohn is," Al replied. "He hates Blacks, gays, and Jews—even though he's two of the three."

Al's health took a further turn for the worse, so he couldn't make it to the meeting—which was probably for the best.

Jeff and I went to Cohn's four-story townhouse on East 68th Street, between Madison and Park avenues. He lived upstairs and operated his law office out of the lower floors. I would have loved a tour of the place, but Cohn didn't offer one.

Steinbrenner was already there when we arrived. He and Cohn were talking about a party that Cohn had recently hosted. The first thing that struck me about Cohn was how he looked and how he dressed—tired, and wearing a silk smoking jacket, white shirt, colorful ascot, and slippers. He also had pale-blue eyes and a deep scar running down his nose. He looked like someone—not anyone in particular, just someone important, someone with influence, someone who held grudges.

I was sure I'd seen his picture in the papers, but back then, you couldn't simply Google someone to learn more about them. I really had no idea what Cohn was up to in the 1980s—other than representing Steinbrenner in our legal battle. I didn't see the photos of him hanging out at Studio 54, surrounded by young male friends who were, of course, nothing more than friends.

The proceeding felt more like a negotiation than a deposition. For all the back and forth over the years, the case never actually went to trial. We all sat at a long desk as Cohn, speaking in a monotone voice, tried to put me on the defensive.

"Mr. Steinbrenner would like access to the following records," Cohn said, listing a series of documents pertaining to the foundation's activities.

"Mr. Winfield would be happy to provide Mr. Steinbrenner with those records as soon as a judge orders him to do so," Jeff responded. "Until then, Mr. Steinbrenner isn't entitled to them."

And so it went for over an hour. As much fun as I was having, I eventually had to snap my briefcase shut and head out to get ready for a game.

With the batting title—and my pride—on the line, I turned the final months of the 1984 season into a rigorous mental exercise. As Yogi once famously said, "Baseball is ninety percent mental. The other half is physical." With that in mind, I heightened my concentration and refused to give away any at-bats. In a way I'd never done before, I willed myself to experience the game pitch by pitch, out by out, inning by inning, series by series, week by week, month by month. I don't know a whole lot about Eastern philosophy, but I think I found a sense of zen during that time.

It helped playing for Yogi, a man I loved as both a player and a person. If you look it up, you might be interested to see that Yogi—all five feet seven inches of him—and I, standing nearly a foot taller, had similar career statistics. How could you not admire a little fireplug of a guy who, after serving in World War II, made the absolute most of his abilities, winning three MVP awards and 10 World Series—a record that will probably never be broken.

Yogi was a kind and gentle soul—something rare in Yankeeland—whose presence put me at ease. I credit him for helping me accomplish some of what I did that season.

That summer, I saw Steinbrenner sitting in the owner's suite with another of Cohn's clients: Donald Trump. I'd been reading about Trump's growing real estate empire and his move to become a powerful figure in the sports world. He'd recently bought the New Jersey Generals of the USFL, a league that was luring some of the best young talent away from the NFL. Cohn was representing the upstart league in an ultimately unsuccessful antitrust lawsuit against the NFL.

Trump had already taken over the Manhattan skyline and now seemed determined to leave an equally large footprint on New York sports. At one point, he was even talking about building a domed football stadium in Queens.

Trump would later claim in his book *The Art of the Deal* that he had declined an invitation to chair a dinner benefiting my foundation because he didn't feel comfortable asking his wealthy friends to donate to yet another cause. But I don't recall ever asking Trump to help my foundation in any way. I didn't like what I'd read about him refusing to rent apartments to Black people early in his career.

Even though he loved being photographed with famous athletes, I passed on the opportunity. There are ample photos of Trump with Herschel Walker, Hulk Hogan, Mike Tyson, and other big names in sports from the 1980s, but none with me, even after my foundation work was featured in a cover story in his short-lived *Trump* magazine in 1991.

Years later, we were seated together at my friend Star Jones's wedding, but we didn't have much to say to each other. (Full disclosure: I did call Trump after his TV show, *The Apprentice*, became a hit. He asked me if I wanted to go golfing. I passed.)

I would have thought that George viewed Trump as a rival, if for no other reason than that Trump was trying to solidify football's status as the new national pastime. It wasn't until later that I realized the two men shared a kind of cosmic bond—one that allowed them to set aside egotism, narcissism, and their transactional natures to form something rare in both their worlds: a real friendship. Trump bestowed a double honor on Steinbrenner, referring to him as both his mentor and best friend.

Over the years, I've come to realize just how much the two men have in common.

Both thrived on high-profile feuds in the 1980s—Trump with New York City Mayor Ed Koch and Steinbrenner with me. In 2025, when President Donald Trump demanded that an unflattering photo of him be removed from the Colorado state capitol, I flashed back to the time that Steinbrenner ordered the Yankees to pull 50,000 yearbooks from concession stands because he didn't like a photo of himself.

Trump's angry late-night phone calls to cabinet secretaries may or may not have been inspired by George's wee-hour tirades at his managers. Of course, there was also Trump's signature line—"You're fired!"—on *The Apprentice*, a clear nod to his mentor's habit of firing managers at will.

But perhaps their greatest shared trait was their instinct to define their opponents before their opponents could define them. George and Trump viewed themselves as part of a small circle of elite New Yorkers who steamrolled obstacles and valued winning above all else.

I could imagine Steinbrenner and Trump half watching a game together, each swapping stories about the people they'd ridiculed or bullied into submission with lawsuits.

Throughout the summer, I stepped to the plate, picturing their heads as baseballs. Maybe that wasn't exactly "zen," but it helped motivate me. And sometimes it worked.

There was the game against Texas, played a few hours after my meeting at Cohn's office. And there was the game a week later, which came after a federal judge ordered Steinbrenner to pay my foundation's legal fees. Both times, I spotted the mentors and their mentee in the box and dug in. I would've liked to send them scurrying for cover with a scorching foul ball, but I had to settle for hitting home runs both times.

I was hitting fewer home runs than usual that season, but I was driving the ball into both gaps like never before. By the All-Star break, my average had climbed all the way up to .370—40 points higher than Mattingly's.

There was no way I could maintain that pace, and I inevitably fell back to earth during the second half of the season. On most nights, Mattingly hit third in the lineup and I hit behind him, which gave me the chance to admire his compact, left-handed swing from the on-deck circle.

Our competition turned into a seesaw battle. For the benefit of reporters, we exchanged playful banter in the clubhouse after games.

"Guess I'm chasing you now," I said to Mattingly one day when he pulled ahead of me.

"Looks like you're back out in front, Dave," he quipped after another game.

There's a photo of us from that summer, horsing around in the clubhouse. He's got me in a playful headlock, pretending he's about to punch me. It all felt very performative. I didn't dislike Mattingly, but I wasn't ready to be his friend, either. I couldn't shake the feeling that the Steinbrenners, Cohns—and all the Joes from Parsippany—of the world were rooting for Mattingly to beat me. My ears became attuned to the volume of cheers each of us received when we reached base—and his were definitely louder.

With all the attention being paid to the batting race, it was a welcome break to take part in a true team activity—even if the activity was a fight between the Yankees and the Angels.

For some reason, the Angels had it out for our rookie shortstop, Bobby Meacham. A day after an Angels baserunner plowed into him at second base, he got beaned on the top of his helmet. When one of our pitchers retaliated, both benches cleared, and I found myself right in the middle of it, throwing punches—mostly air punches—at anybody in my path. I was proud our pitcher stuck up for Meacham, and when things escalated, I wasn't about to hang back.

When the dust settled from that game, I was hitting .352, and Mattingly was at .351.

I tried to keep things as loose as possible as we entered the final week of play. Yogi and I agreed to appear in a *Saturday Night Live* sketch that was filmed before the live show—a "pre-tape," as they call it.

In our part of the sketch, shot at Yankee Stadium, Yogi and I reminisce about the legendary exploits of two fictional Negro Leagues ballplayers. One of my lines was, "The Rooster was so fast, he hit a line drive up the middle, and he got hit in the head sliding into second base."

The Rooster and King Carl were played by two *SNL* cast members in blackface—something I wasn't aware of until the sketch aired. The show didn't have a Black cast member at the time. That obviously wouldn't fly today—and rightly so. But at the time, the sketch made me laugh.

Going into the final game of the season against the Tigers at Yankee Stadium, I was ahead of Mattingly, .341 to .339.

Trying to stay healthy and rested for the playoffs, Detroit fielded a B-team that included a young pitcher named Randy O'Neal, who was making his fourth career start.

Mattingly hit a soft single to left field in the first inning. I grounded out. He doubled in the third and fourth innings. I walked and hit a single. There wasn't a calculator nearby, but the math suggested the race would come down to our final plate appearances.

Nobody in the dugout spoke to us, as if we were pitchers working on no-hitters. We both made outs in our next at-bats. Then, in the eighth inning, after Mattingly picked up his fourth hit of the game, I grounded into a fielder's choice.

After the inning ended, Yogi removed us both from the game. The crowd cheered as Mattingly joined me on the field, and we shook hands before walking into the dugout together.

Mattingly finished at .343, compared to my .340. He spoke humbly after the game: "Someone said if I didn't get a hit the last time up and Winfield did, he would've won by two-thousandths of a point. Right then I knew there was no way I could be a loser. Neither of us could be a loser. But I guess it's the American way—someone has to win and someone has to lose."

But I wasn't around to hear it. Knowing what the topic of conversation would be, I gathered up my stuff and made a quick exit before reporters could find me. I didn't feel up to playacting a final scene in the drama. I felt like our heartfelt, on-the-field moment had sufficed.

The next day's papers didn't say the Yankees had won. They said Mattingly had won.

The World Series that season pitted the Tigers against the Padres. In the four seasons since I'd left, San Diego had put together a strong team, led by rising star Tony Gwynn and seasoned veterans like Steve Garvey and two of my former Yankees teammates, Goose Gossage and Graig Nettles. The Padres had never finished higher than fourth in the National League West, making their run to the World Series all the more surprising.

The Padres came up short against the Tigers, but they made it clear that season that they could be successful without me. That only added to my desire to win with the team I was with.

Chapter 11

MR. WHAT?

Following another successful Winfield Foundation holiday party, I was getting ready to head home to Minnesota for the holidays when I experienced my first full-blown New York City tabloid circus. Thankfully, it had nothing to do with me—but the frenzy of news gave me a much deeper understanding of the city I now called home.

The story centered on a subway shooting, in which a white man claimed he shot and wounded four young Black men because he thought they were trying to mug him. The tabloids quickly dubbed Bernhard Goetz the "Subway Vigilante," and his actions set off a vigorous debate about public safety, race, and criminal justice in New York during the mid-1980s.

Some headlines portrayed Goetz as a hero, defending himself against a group of screwdriver-wielding thugs. Others painted him as a racist who fired shots not because they threatened him, but because they were Black.

It was far from the last story that decade to spotlight race relations in New York. In 1986, there was the deadly, racially motivated attack on 23-year-old Michael Griffith, a Black man who had wandered into a predominantly white neighborhood in Howard Beach, Queens. Then, in 1989, two more incidents dominated the headlines. In Brooklyn, a group of young white men attacked a Black teenager named Yusef Hawkins with baseball bats before fatally shooting him. And, in Central Park, a group of young Black men were arrested for raping a white jogger. They were convicted—but later exonerated—of the crime.

In response to these incidents, civil rights leaders—including Reverend Al Sharpton—organized demonstrations that helped ignite a renewed racial justice movement. With each high-profile case, the movement became louder and stronger.

I was carving my own path when it came to political activism.

Rather than aligning myself with a political party or taking sides in every debate, I sought support for my foundation from all camps. That doesn't mean I lacked strong opinions about what was happening in New York and across the country—I certainly did.

If people wanted to read into my 1984 meeting in the Yankees clubhouse with presidential candidate Jesse Jackson, they were free to do so. I wasn't going to pass up the opportunity to meet the first Black man to make a serious bid for the presidency.

But I felt just as comfortable attending a state dinner at the White House for German Chancellor Helmut Kohl. I brought my mother as my date. It was a thrill for us both to have gone all the way from 1009 Carroll Avenue in St. Paul to 1600 Pennsylvania Avenue in Washington. Neither of us mentioned to President Ronald Reagan that we'd recently voted for Minnesota's own Walter Mondale in the 1984 election that Reagan won by a landslide. It was a lovely evening. I can still taste the trout mousse with aurora sauce.

The opportunity to play baseball for a living opened extraordinary doors for me. It got me invitations to fancy dinners, provided me with resources to travel the world—and enabled me to give back in a meaningful way. Yet right outside the walls of Yankee Stadium, tens of thousands of people were struggling. On my very first drive through the Bronx, I could feel the hopelessness in many neighborhoods. Then I saw the numbers: Nearly half of all families in the South Bronx lived in poverty, trying to scrape by from one day to the next.

There was a lot to love about New York—as the ads of the time liked to remind people—but there was another, less privileged side of the city that deserved attention.

One of the main goals of my foundation was to reach kids in underserved communities—many of them Black and Hispanic—and offer them two things: a sense of hope and some of the tools they needed to create opportunities for themselves.

At the holiday celebration we hosted at the *Daily News* building in 1984, I met a woman named Dorothy Ford, whose four-year-old son, John Nathan Ford, had fallen to his death from a sixth-floor fire escape of a tenement building earlier that year. John Nathan's heart was successfully transplanted into the body of a Colorado boy born with a serious heart condition.

Dorothy came to the party with her four surviving children. There was nothing I could say to ease the heartbreak she had experienced, but I hoped that the time we spent together let her know she wasn't alone—that there was a community of people who cared about her and her family.

That day was especially meaningful because of the presence of another Dorothy—Dorothy Bowen, my first foundation director in San Diego. She and her husband, Milt, had never been to New York before and were making a week of it, visiting Rockefeller Center and Radio City Music Hall to see the Rockettes. Having them at the Christmas party made it even more special.

As we posed for photos in front of a Christmas tree, Dorothy's eyes welled up at the scene around her.

"I'm so proud of you, David," she whispered in my ear.

"Well, I couldn't have done it without you, Dorothy," I said.

A few years later, when she passed away, she was laid to rest in a No. 31 Padres jersey—my biggest fan to the very end.

I was proud of the team I'd assembled in New York. Mario Casciano did a little bit of everything for me—so much so that I eventually had business cards printed for him that read "The Expert." Rick Scott, our volunteer coordinator, was a human Rolodex because of his work with the South Bronx Community Action Theatre. And in 1985, after cycling through a few executive directors, I brought in Gary Rivers, who had helped raise millions of dollars for the Congressional Black Caucus. He was young, energetic, and a skilled fundraiser—exactly the combination I was looking for.

Together, we organized an event called "Home Run for Kids" at the Borough of Manhattan Community College. Bill Cosby—who still had his good name at the time—headlined, and we booked George Benson, Ashford & Simpson, Chaka Khan, Phoebe Snow, Chita Rivera, and Bobbi Humphrey as musical guests.

Gary also helped me implement a program aimed at confronting a new problem just starting to afflict urban America: crack cocaine. My eyes were opened to the issue during a 1985 trip to DC, where Gary and I met with Jack Lawn, head of the Drug Enforcement Administration—who would later become vice president and chief of operations for the Yankees.

During our meeting, Lawn pulled a small vial from his desk containing what looked like a crystal rock. This was before the high-profile, crack-related deaths of two first-round draft picks—Len Bias in basketball and Don Rogers in football. I had no idea what it was.

I listened as Lawn laid out statistics about the toll crack was already taking on inner cities. On our way back to New York, I tasked Gary with creating an antidrug initiative to address it. He ran with it, and together we developed the "Turn It Around" program, which became one of the foundation's most successful ventures.

•

My other team—the one that played at Yankee Stadium—could have used that kind of leadership.

After a third-place finish in 1984, Steinbrenner promised Yogi Berra another full season to show what he could do. But just 16 games into the '85 season, he fired him—and in classic George fashion, he brought back Billy Martin for a fourth time.

Thank goodness for Rickey Henderson.

Earlier in my career, I'd sought mentorship from veterans like Willie

McCovey. When Rickey came to New York in a trade with the A's, I found myself on the other side of that dynamic. I was still in my prime, and at 26, Rickey was no kid—but I saw him as someone I could take under my wing, even if he exuded the supreme confidence of someone who wasn't looking for a big brother.

Rickey became my guy. Of all the players I called teammates, he and Kirby Puckett stand out as my absolute favorites. I loved everything about Rickey—his talent, his focus, his flair, his audacity. I'd gotten to know him a little when we were opponents, and I was thrilled to have him as a teammate. He added swagger to the clubhouse.

I remember one time we were by our lockers after a game when a few reporters approached Rickey—who hadn't exactly made himself available since arriving—about being more accessible.

"I don't have time for interviews," Rickey said.

One of the reporters—evidently speaking for the group—tried to throw his weight around.

"Rickey, you *need* to talk to us," he said in a mildly threatening tone. "It's important."

Rickey stared at the guy and laughed.

"Nah, I don't need y'all. Y'all need Rickey."

That was the only season I got to play alongside two of my closest friends, Rickey and Don Baylor. Rickey kind of stayed to himself, but Don and I enjoyed a lot of good meals together. One stands out in particular—but not because of the meal.

After our game was rained out in the second inning, we went to Hell's Kitchen for a late dinner at a soul food restaurant called Jezebel to celebrate Willie Randolph's birthday. Willie and Don brought their wives, and I came with my girlfriend, Tonya.

As we were enjoying appetizers and drinks, the maître d' rushed over to our table.

"Mr. Randolph, can you come with me, please? There's been an accident," he said.

We all looked at each other, confused. Whatever was happening, it sounded serious, so we all followed him out to Ninth Avenue.

There, parked on the street, was Willie's Jaguar four-seater. The windshield was shattered, and the hood had a massive dent—as if someone had dropped a bowling ball from a fourth-story window and then stomped on the car for good measure. Oddly, there were clumps of animal hair stuck to the hood and roof.

Apparently, a passing car had clipped a horse pulling a carriage, causing the animal to rear up, break loose from its harness, and stomp on the car. The horse was still on the loose.

To this day, every time I see one of those auto insurance ads on TV where mayhem strikes cars, I think of that night—and Willie's poor Jaguar getting pummeled by a frightened horse.

Baylor understood what I was going through in New York as well as anyone. He, too, had joined the team as a free agent—effusively praised by Steinbrenner . . . until he started wearing pinstripes. Then he had to read all about his supposed shortcomings in the newspaper.

Don was a tough dude who did whatever it took to win. One season, he was hit by pitches 35 times. To put that number in perspective, I got plunked 25 times in my entire career.

I also respected him for his charitable work on behalf of cystic fibrosis, which earned him the 1985 Roberto Clemente Award—given annually to the player who best represents the game both on and off the field.

•

Up until the 1985 season, my teammates hadn't seen my feud with Steinbrenner up close. But that season, an open clash in the Yankees' clubhouse pushed our relationship further down a path of no return.

The issue centered on how drugs were affecting baseball.

In response to high-profile amphetamine and cocaine scandals that had rocked the sport in the early '80s, Commissioner Peter Ueberroth was pushing for league-wide drug testing. I think he believed that if Steinbrenner and the Yankees got on board with the idea, the rest of the league would follow.

I'll admit I had no idea what—if any—impact drugs were having on the game. I wasn't a user—plain and simple. Whenever I hosted a party, I kicked anybody out if I thought they were doing drugs—at least any heavy stuff. As far as I could tell, the drugs of that era were more about a reckless lifestyle than about enhancing performance. That, of course, would soon change.

There was one problem with Ueberroth's plan: Owners couldn't implement drug testing unilaterally. As the union representative for the Yankees, I knew that any such proposal had to be collectively bargained. So, I was blindsided when Steinbrenner marched into the clubhouse one day—flanked by several Yankees executives—and pulled a stack of papers out of his briefcase.

"I'd like all of you to sign these consent forms," Steinbrenner announced.

Half-dressed, I approached Steinbrenner and the other men in suits.

"Consent for what?" I asked.

"Drug testing," Steinbrenner said.

In the words of Yankees broadcaster Phil Rizzuto, "Holy cow!" I couldn't help but smile. What Steinbrenner was trying to do was—using another Rizzuto catchphrase—unbelievable.

"You know this isn't how it works," I told him. "If you'd like to talk about this with me in private tomorrow, I'd be happy to set a time."

George grew red in the face. Everyone waited to see whether he was going to have it out with me in front of the team. If so, I was ready. But, instead, he slammed the papers down on the clubhouse picnic table and stormed away—past Billy Martin's office and out toward a pool of TV cameras, all waiting for a scoop George had promised but wasn't going to deliver.

The next day, I got a message: Steinbrenner wanted to see me in his office. We never got around to talking about drug testing. He was more interested in delivering a lecture.

"I don't like what happened yesterday," he told me. "There's only one captain of this organization—and it's me. I can't have you kicking me out of my own locker room."

He paused, then added, "You and I are never going to get along, are we? Pick a team that you want to be traded to, and I'll make it happen. I don't like you, and if you stay, I can make life very hard for you."

"What are you going to do—bench me?"

"I can do more than that. I can release you."

I scoffed at that comment, knowing he'd never do that.

Then I saw his eyes, and a cold chill ran over me. The look on his face told me he was capable of anything. In mid-September, right after we lost to the first-place Blue Jays and fell three and a half games behind Toronto, George started to deliver on his promise. Looking over a sheet of statistics showing that Ken Griffey, Don Baylor, and I had been struggling of late, Steinbrenner muttered into an open mic:

"Where is Reggie Jackson? We need a Mr. October or a Mr. September. Winfield is Mr. May . . . He gets his numbers when it doesn't count."

That's the part of the quote that people remember. But he also admitted he'd been "out-ownered."

Part of me didn't want to dignify George's words with a response. I was having another solid season, and the team was 31 games over .500—more than enough wins to be a lock for the playoffs in today's game. It wasn't the right time for George to open his mouth, especially not to bring up how I'd struggled in the postseason four years earlier. That was a cheap shot.

I kept my rebuttal short and sweet.

"You wonder why guys don't want to talk to the press," I said into the dozens of microphones shoved in my face. "You have the man upstairs who had nothing to do with the first 130 games getting the press and the fans on us . . . It's like rattling a stick across the cage—like at some animals."

The stick rattling didn't work. We lost six more in a row after his rant, ending any shot we had at winning the division.

That's when a couple of the caged animals got loose—and nearly tore each other apart.

The Billy Martin–Ed Whitson cage match at the Cross Keys hotel in Baltimore spoke volumes about the Yankees in the mid-1980s.

Whitson was in his first year with the team, having signed a lucrative five-year deal that Steinbrenner hoped would make him the ace of the starting rotation for the rest of the decade. But Whitson, a journeyman coming off a strong season in San Diego, didn't adjust well to playing in New York. He started the season 1–6 and never fully found his form.

The 1985 team had a ton of offensive firepower. Don Mattingly and Rickey Henderson finished first and third in American League MVP voting. Willie Randolph, Don Baylor, and I hit in the middle of a lineup that was dangerous from top to bottom. On the mound, Ron Guidry won 22 games, and Phil Niekro chipped in with 16. A better season from Whitson probably would've put us over the top.

Whitson had expected to pitch a Friday night game in Baltimore in late September, but Billy gave the ball instead to a reliever named Rich Bordi for a spot start. That didn't sit well with Whitson, a big guy from Appalachia who drank firewater and wasn't shy about airing his feelings about Billy.

"If I ever get my hands on that guy, I'm gonna kick his ass," I once heard Whitson say, to no one in particular.

I wasn't in the habit of hanging out in hotel bars, so I was one of the few players and beat writers who *didn't* see what happened the next night—and early morning—in Baltimore.

Billy had nearly got into a fight with a wedding party at the hotel after Friday's game, and that set the stage for the main event on Saturday. Eddie was pounding drinks in the bar when he got into an argument with a Yankees fan who'd come down from New Jersey to watch the series. Billy stepped in—supposedly to break it up—and that's when all hell broke loose.

With fists and feet flying, Billy and Eddie went at each other. The fight spilled into the lobby. Eddie landed a kick to Billy's groin, dropping him to the floor. A few players and coaches grabbed Eddie and ushered him outside. But when Billy got to his feet, he followed, and the fight continued out on the cobblestones in front of the hotel.

Eventually, the combatants were herded into elevators and taken to their rooms—but not before they crossed paths again in the hallway, where they lunged at each other one more time.

Billy came away from the fight with a broken arm and a black eye but was sitting in the dugout a few hours later like nothing had happened. Eddie emerged with a cut lip and an assortment of other bruises and scrapes.

At least the weekend ended on a high note—for Rickey and me, at any rate.

Whenever possible, Billy preferred to travel by limousine rather than take the team bus—not just to and from the Newark airport, but also on road trips to Boston and Baltimore. Thanks to Steinbrenner's pal, the limousine tycoon Bill Fugazy, Billy always had a car at his disposal.

After the eventful weekend, Billy wasn't quite ready to return to New York, so with an off day on Monday, he decided to stay behind in Baltimore. The only problem was that his limo driver needed to be back in New York the next morning. So Billy made me an offer.

"Hey, Winny, do you and Rickey want the car?" he asked.

"Yeah, we can do that," I said, playing it cool—like that was a routine question managers asked me all the time.

Rickey and I loaded up the limo with friends who had come down to Baltimore. Billy had equipped it with a nice little bar—soft drinks and an assortment of miniature liquor bottles. The driver cranked up the hits station, and Rickey did a nice sing-along to Stevie Wonder's "Part-Time Lover." We cruised up I-95, enjoying every moment of riding in the manager's limousine.

Someone asked me to make a toast. I raised my tiny bottle of booze and kept it simple.

"To the fighting spirit of the New York Yankees!" I said.

We passed through Philadelphia and stopped at an Italian restaurant in South Philly for Sunday dinner. The other customers looked like extras from *The Godfather*. They eyed us warily—we were Yankees in Phillies country, after all—as we enjoyed a wonderful meal.

In addition to being generous with his limo, Billy posted the best winning percentage of his managerial career that season—but that still wasn't enough to save his job. Whitson, too, wasn't long for a Yankees uniform. The following July, he was traded back to San Diego, where he started winning again. His story just goes to show: Playing in New York isn't for everyone. But with cracks beginning to show in my armor, I was still determined to prove it was for me.

Chapter 12

•

HOLDING IT TOGETHER

As a bit player in the so-called "War on Drugs," I preached prevention, logging thousands of miles traveling to schools, malls, and youth centers to talk with kids about the dangers of drugs. But the agency I partnered with wasn't called the Drug Prevention Administration—it had "enforcement" in its name for a reason. I didn't love how the DEA was trying to arrest its way out of the crack epidemic, filling prisons with addicts while the crisis kept growing—but I still believed there was value in working with them.

"I'm Dave Winfield of the New York Yankees. Getting to first base in baseball means playing up to your potential every time you're at-bat. Be a winner. Team up against drugs."

Those might sound like easy lines to deliver, but in the world of public service announcements—where young directors treat the material like it's *Citizen Kane*—they can take a few tries.

Shooting that PSA for the DEA/FBI Sports Drug Awareness Program lasted most of a late February day. As a result, I missed the Yankees' first voluntary spring workout in Florida.

When asked for his reaction to my absence, my former Yankees teammate and new manager, Lou Piniella, said he wasn't fazed.

But guess who was?

"It just tells you something about the man," Steinbrenner told reporters.

I'd argue that criticizing a player for filming an antidrug PSA on a day when a team is holding an *optional* workout really tells you something about *that* man.

But as the 1986 season approached, I had even more than just drugs, baseball, and Steinbrenner on my mind.

I'd done my best to give Sandra Renfro the financial support she needed to raise our daughter. They were living rent-free—along with Sandra's son from a previous relationship with a professional basketball player—in a Houston condo I'd bought, until she went back to work. In addition, I was sending her $1,400 a month to help cover expenses.

Could I have provided more? Yes, I could have—but I didn't want Sandra to become dependent on me. I wanted her to go back to work. I wanted her to move on with her life—to find someone who loved her and wanted to be with her. That, I believed, was what would bring long-term happiness to her and our daughter.

Instead, Sandra became threatening and hostile.

The first warning sign came when I flew her to Minnesota in the winter of 1982 so my mother could meet little Lauren Shanel. On the day they were leaving for home, I went to the hotel to take Sandra and the baby to the airport. I came up behind her, unnoticed, as she was asking the woman at the front desk to change the room registration from "Sandra Renfro" to "Mr. and Mrs. Winfield." When I sidled up next to her, she looked like she'd just seen a ghost.

"What are you doing, Sandra?" I asked quietly, not wanting to make a scene in the lobby of the Marriott.

She picked up the baby carrier. I grabbed her suitcase. And we found a quiet corner to talk.

"I have a lawyer," she told me. "I want one hundred thousand dollars a year. Or I'll sue you."

"Sue me for what?" I asked incredulously.

"My lawyer says we have a common-law marriage, and I should get alimony and more child support."

That hit me like a Louisville Slugger to the solar plexus. I was all in favor of formalizing an agreement on child support and visitation. But now she was talking about a common-law marriage? Even at the peak of our interactions, we'd never spent more than a few days together—let alone lived under the same roof.

We drove to the airport in silence. I was stunned that she'd try to blackmail me, but I decided it was better to say nothing—and to avoid any contact with her—until I could get my ducks in a row. Every now and then, she'd call and renew her demand for $100,000 a year but a couple of years passed without her following through on her threat to take me to court.

Then, in January 1985, she filed a case against me in family court in Harris County, Texas, claiming our relationship met the conditions of a common-law marriage: that we'd agreed to be married, had presented ourselves as husband and wife, and had lived together.

If that were true—which it wasn't—I'd owe her half of what I'd earned since 1982 in a divorce.

She and her lawyer didn't run to the media with the lawsuit. For a year and a half, the case just sat there. I could see what was happening: With the threat of her going public hanging over me, Sandra was trying to pressure me into a settlement. But I wasn't going to participate in a shakedown, so I braced myself for the inevitable day when the story leaked.

Shortly after returning from a trip to Hong Kong with Tonya, I began experiencing a burning sensation in my stomach—especially before and after meals. I popped antacids, hoping it was just a case of severe indigestion. The pain would last for weeks, disappear on its own, and then return with a vengeance. I wasn't used to my body acting up like that, and I took it as a sign.

•

With Steinbrenner—and now Sandra—taking aim at me, I decided it was time to take control of my own story. I couldn't advocate for myself on a podcast or social media—because they didn't exist yet. And I could only get so far by going to the papers. There were reporters I trusted—some who even liked me—but at the end of the day, they were journalists, not publicists. No, I needed to take matters into my own hands by writing a book—not a tell-all, but a narrative focused on my experiences and motivations as a player. My new agent, Jeff Klein, supported the idea, and, in short order, we had interest from publishers.

That story, of course, was still very much a work in progress—much more so than I ever could have realized at the time.

At the age of 34, I was approaching career milestones—2,000 hits and 300 home runs—that most players dream of. I was on a Hall of Fame trajectory. But I still wasn't fulfilled.

My focus on baseball was intense, but it wasn't singular. I wanted to save the Yankees, but I also wanted to help make the world a better place. And somewhere along the way, I started to feel a little adrift.

So I did the only thing I knew to do: I kept going.

I had come to New York intending to make a splash in four areas: athletics, philanthropy, media, and business. By 1986, I'd checked the first three boxes, leaving only an entrepreneurial itch left to scratch.

My interest in the food and hospitality industry dated back to my time in San Diego, when Al Frohman and I developed an ambitious concept for the resort hotel condominium, Superstar Village. The project ultimately hit a dead end, but instead of discouraging me, it motivated me to stay alert for future opportunities in the industry.

Before Superstar Village, I had asked Padres owner Ray Kroc for advice on how to become a McDonald's franchisee. He barely gave me the time of day—scoffing at the idea that a ballplayer could also run fast-food restaurants. I guess I never forgot that slight.

My lawyers told me it wasn't feasible to buy a McDonald's franchise, so I did the next best thing: I started acquiring Burger King restaurants on the East Coast. Within a few years, I owned 17 locations, including a very successful one at Dulles International Airport, just outside Washington, DC.

I also got involved in the New York culinary scene as a co-owner of a

Tex-Mex restaurant on the Upper West Side of Manhattan called the U.S.A. Border Cafe, which opened its doors in 1986. Through that experience, I received a crash course in the realities of running a restaurant in the city's ultracompetitive dining market. Our first challenge? Shedding the restaurant's early reputation for having restrooms that doubled as drug dens.

Al still had dreams of Superstar Village dancing in his head. The idea of me "slinging burgers" or "owning a taco joint" wasn't part of the grand New York vision he had for me—for us.

But by then, Al was a shadow of his former self. A series of strokes had dulled his once-sharp tongue and left him unable to advise me on my business affairs. He'd moved back to Los Angeles, getting around with the help of two canes.

Once we chased off the dealers, the U.S.A. Border Cafe became my favorite place to host out-of-town guests. Sometimes those invitations were extended on the spur of the moment. During a game against his Twins, after Kirby Puckett made a great running catch in the outfield to end an inning, I intercepted him on his way to the dugout and asked him to dinner that night.

"Okay, Mr. Winfield, that sounds great," he said with a grin.

I knew Kirby was joking, but the fact was that we represented different generations. That didn't prevent us from becoming close friends—and eventually part of baseball history together.

•

Once again, the Yankees stayed in the thick of the division race for much of the 1986 season—but both the team and I hit the skids during a rough stretch in June, when we fell from three games behind the first-place Red Sox to eight back. As was the case the year before, we just didn't have the pitching to stay in the race.

For the first time since my rookie year, I got benched—a decision I didn't agree with, obviously. My average had dipped below its usual level, but I was still hitting for power. It was clear to me that Piniella was getting his orders from the man upstairs.

I tried to remain zen at the ballpark, realizing that anger wasn't the best fuel, but if that was the emotion I was feeling, I figured I might as well put it to use—like when I imagined Steinbrenner's head as the baseball.

One July night against the Rangers, I sat on the bench, visualizing what I was going to do if I got into the game. Occasionally, I'd look over at Lou and scowl.

Rather than have me shoot daggers at him all night, he put me in as a pinch-hitter in the third.

By the end of the night, I'd driven in five runs with a double and a triple—the triple being my 2,000th career hit.

Like I had from day one, I still busted it out of the batter's box to stretch a single into a double, a double into a triple, or to go from first to third on a single like "a pursued cheetah," as one columnist aptly put it.

I think Lou got the message that keeping me on the bench wouldn't sit well with the fans, so he stopped doing it. But he continued to irritate me by occasionally dropping me to the sixth spot in the lineup.

The 1986 season delivered a double gut punch. First, the rival Red Sox beat us out for the division. Then, our "little brother," the New York Mets, went all the way and won the World Series.

In the years that followed, that Mets team became the stuff of legend, remembered as much for their talent as for their personal excesses.

I guess there's always a place in fans' hearts for "bad boys" in sports. At a time when the NFL was asserting dominance, the '86 Mets gave baseball a much-needed jolt. Darryl Strawberry and Dwight "Doc" Gooden made the national pastime feel cool again. The public couldn't seem to get enough of the late-night and clubhouse antics of Darryl, Doc, and the rest of the crew. I know because, when I began working on my book back then, my publisher pushed hard for similarly juicy material.

It's all fun and games until someone gets hurt—or hooked. By the start of the next season, Doc, just 22 years old and fresh off a dominant 24-win year, had checked himself into drug rehab. The New York papers devoted full pages to the story, packed with fan reaction. Doc had become a hero to Mets fans, and they took his struggles personally.

I didn't know Doc—or Straw, who would later get busted for drugs too—but I knew enough secondhand about the struggles of addiction not to pass judgment. It didn't escape my notice that the young Black stars on that Mets team got most of the bad press, while several of their white teammates with documented or later-revealed drug problems escaped scrutiny.

I wasn't a teetotaler—I liked to have my fun. But as a high-profile athlete, it was important to me to set a positive example for young people. Whether we liked it or not, and despite Charles Barkley's famous words in that 1990s Nike ad, those of us who played professional sports *were* role models to millions of kids.

That's why I hoped that dads and moms reading the newspaper would tell their kids about how Dave Winfield received an honorary degree from Syracuse University—alongside a Nobel Prize winner and a future cabinet member—even if attending the ceremony did almost make him late for a game.

My desire to lead by example prompted me to turn down an endorsement deal from Seagram's to promote one of their adult beverages. Considering how much time I spent in schools educating kids about substance abuse, I just didn't think it would be a good look for me. Instead, I did a splashy ad for Nature's Milk Treat, a healthier alternative to sugary drinks like Yoo-hoo. Despite the campaign, the product never really took off.

But looking back, whatever I was doing seems to have made an impression on young people.

Around this time, I'm told, I met a young Yankees fan, living a couple of hours from Detroit, who drove with his father to see us play the Tigers. I was the kid's favorite player—he even had a poster of me on his wall. As he got older, he learned more about the things I'd been doing off the field.

I don't remember having met Derek Jeter that day—back then, I met a lot of young people. But for Derek, it became a moment he never forgot.

During his rookie year with the Yankees in 1996, he started the Turn 2 Foundation, a charitable organization he said I had helped inspire.

•

The Mets winning the World Series should have pushed Steinbrenner to go all in on keeping the Yankees on top in New York. He was very competitive in this regard. When the Mets once handed out strawberry sundaes for "Darryl Strawberry Day" at the ballpark, George countered by giving away digital watches at the Yankees game that same day. Afterward, he proudly pointed out that the Yankees had drawn 20,000 more fans.

But staying the city's top baseball team wasn't his only concern. When the New York Giants hoisted their first Lombardi Trophy in January 1987, it knocked the Yankees another rung down on the city's sports ladder.

But even the almighty George was no match for forces in baseball that discouraged him from signing a star pitcher—one who might have helped bring another championship to the Bronx.

We had a glaring need for a top-line starting pitcher. In 1986, our only pitcher to win more than 10 games was Dennis Rasmussen, who was a nice addition to the rotation but not exactly what you'd call ace material.

There were several top players on the free-agent market that offseason—but the funny thing was, no one seemed the least bit interested in them. Behind the scenes, the owners had come together and agreed not to get into bidding wars. This practice had a name: collusion. The goal was to drive salaries down by pressuring free agents to stay with their current teams. It would later result in some big-name players receiving restitution.

Donald Fehr, the executive director of the players' union, singled out Steinbrenner for his role in the scheme.

"Could you have believed you'd have a year in which the Red Sox win the division and the pennant, and the Mets win the World Series, and Steinbrenner abandons the division and the town?" Fehr said. "Steinbrenner as much as announced that his team will be a second-class citizen."

In response, George called Fehr "stupid" and warned that he'd "rue the day" he made such an insulting comment.

We could've used free agents like Tim Raines, Andre Dawson, or Lance Parrish. But what we *really* needed was a star pitcher—someone like Jack Morris of the Tigers, who put the Yankees at the top of his list of prospective teams. Proving Fehr right, Steinbrenner—along with the other owners and general managers whose teams Morris expressed interest in—gave him the silent treatment. So, with no other offers, he re-signed with Detroit.

This wasn't right. And it made me question the integrity of the people calling the shots in baseball—especially after what happened on Opening Day in 1987. That night, during an episode of the news program *Nightline*, Dodgers general manager Al Campanis responded to a question about the scarcity of Black people in baseball leadership by saying, "I truly believe that they may not have some of the necessities to be, let's say, a field manager or perhaps a general manager."

Necessities like the ability to come together and stiff players out of the money they deserve?

Campanis's words were all the more shocking because he had once been a teammate and close friend of Jackie Robinson. If someone like Campanis felt that way, what chance did we have?

His words stuck with me long after my playing career ended.

•

We were in first place when we made a late-July trip to play the Twins. As was always the case when I returned home to Minnesota, I used the three days there to spend time with my mother and Steve. On the day the series ended, Ma invited me over to her condo for lunch—just me and her.

"David, there's something I've been wanting to tell you," she said.

To my ears, that didn't sound good. I braced for bad news—and I got it.

"I went to a doctor, and they found a lump in my breast," she continued.

I got up from my chair, walked over to where she was sitting, and put my arms around her.

"I'm scared, David."

She'd known for a few months that she was sick and had been waiting for the chance to tell me in person.

"I know you'll beat this, Ma," I said, holding her.

That night, I played a baseball game—but my mind was elsewhere. And my stomach was burning again.

Over the next two months, we slipped from first to fourth place in the division. And I went from believing my mother was invincible to realizing that she wasn't.

It wasn't just pitching that caused us to come up short again in 1987. Don Mattingly and Willie Randolph had standout seasons, but we got very little from the bottom of the lineup. For the first time since joining the Yankees—aside from the strike-shortened 1981 season—I failed to drive in a hundred runs, even though I hit for a higher average with runners in scoring position than in any other season with the team.

Our pitching rotation featuring Rasmussen, 44-year-old Tommy John, and an injury-plagued Ron Guidry helped keep us in first place for a while. But things started to come apart in August, right around the time that Steinbrenner publicly blew up at Piniella for not returning a phone call.

With Morris leading the way, the Tigers won the division.

Behind my calm exterior, disappointment ate at me as I faced reporters' questions about another season of unmet expectations. I knew the narrative Steinbrenner had helped shape: Winfield isn't a leader and lacks commitment.

Proving a negative is impossible, so I didn't waste time trying. I just played.

The most fun I had that season was at the All-Star Game in Oakland, which ended up going into extra innings. I had a chance to win the game for the American League in the ninth, but I was tagged out in a home-plate collision with the National League catcher to end the inning. The play reminded me of the 1982 All-Star Game, when I slid into second baseman Steve Sax to break up a double play, sending Sax and the ball hurtling through the air in a cloud of dirt and flying limbs. Good, clean baseball, but not something you'd see in an All-Star Game today.

By the time the Oakland game ended in the 13th, every player on both sides had subbed out—except me. It was a meaningless game, but I was honored to be playing in another one, and I wanted to see it through to the end.

I was also ready to show that kind of commitment in my personal life.

Having Tonya Turner by my side on a more regular basis helped my state of mind immensely. She had left her job at Control Data Corporation to spend more time with me in New York. We were starting to build a life together. Tonya had seen her fair share of obnoxious behavior in corporate America, but even she was stunned by what I was experiencing.

One day, she came into my home office in Teaneck and found me staring off into space. She could tell I was agonizing over everything.

"You know you don't have to stay here, David," she told me. "The Yankees didn't make you. You aren't who you are because of the Yankees."

Her words—calm and soothing, yet forceful—jolted me back to reality.

"Nobody is going to run me out of this town," I said.

After the season ended, I chartered a small yacht, and Tonya and I set sail for the US Virgin Islands. There was a captain, a first mate, and the two of us—out on the open sea, with no distractions and no stress, just amazing food, wine, and company.

As we made our way south, I tuned in to a radio broadcast of the World Series. Normally, it would have pained me to hear other teams competing for the championship. But in this case, I felt genuine happiness for my friend Kirby and the Twins when they beat the Cardinals.

I didn't propose to Tonya on the yacht, but the trip brought me a step closer. We had talked about marriage—it was always just a question of finding the right time and place to tie the knot.

A few weeks after we got back, I proposed over the phone—not the most romantic way to do it, but the only real option, because I was in New York, and she was back in LA.

"You'll have to ask my parents," she said, laughing.

So I got Robert and Louise Turner on the line from New Orleans, and they heard their daughter say "I do" on a three-way call. I'd grown close to the Turners. Whenever they drove up to New York for visits, Louise brought cauldrons of gumbo with her. I could almost smell it over the phone.

No one was more thrilled about my proposal than Ma—the next person we called.

"David's a big chicken," she told Tonya. "He's always been scared of settling down. I'm so happy he's finally ready."

A few weeks later, I flew to LA for three very different purposes: to give Tonya her engagement ring, to put the finishing touches on a segment of *Lifestyles of the Rich and Famous*—and to attend Al Frohman's funeral.

Al had suffered another stroke at age 61, this one leading to cardiac arrest. It felt strange to see him lying still and quiet in the casket. I almost expected him to pop up, mop off his brow, and request a corned beef sandwich.

In my eulogy, I spoke about how deeply I appreciated Al's friendship and everything he had taught me about the art of negotiation.

"Al spent more time with me than any other grown man ever did," I said. "Under him—and with him—I grew in wisdom, ability, and stature. We have shared our last meal, our last journey, our last negotiation, our last battle. Anyone who knew you knows you lived for the challenge of it all. I loved you, Al. I'll miss you. Rest in peace, my man."

Some of Al's old friends came up to me and told me how much he loved me—how he used to refer to me as "my boy, David," like a father would a son. When Steinbrenner had told Al, "You better tell *your boy* to start hitting" at my first spring training, he was parroting Al's own language.

As it turned out, Al got out just in time to avoid witnessing the consequences of the worst decision he ever made concerning me. Smart guy—to the very end.

From the end of one life to the beginning of another, I visited Tonya, ring in hand. Instead of putting it on, she hid it in her apartment—someplace no one would ever find it. Her way of saying: There's no backing out now.

As an early wedding gift to ourselves, I bought us a condo in Beverly Hills.

We didn't want to have to wait another year to get married, so we set a date of February 18—just three months away. Part of the reason was that my mother's cancer had advanced to Stage 4.

That offseason began on calm seas. Little did I know a hurricane was coming.

Chapter 13

THE GLOVES COME OFF

I'd barely walked in the door after returning from Los Angeles when I got a call from a *Daily News* reporter. He knew about Sandra Renfro's lawsuit and wanted a quote. He didn't say how he found out about it, but that didn't matter. I knew the day would come when it leaked to the press. And now that it had, I was ready.

"I can't think of another word but extortion or blackmail," I said. "She's cooking up the idea of a marriage—and we never have been, not even by common law."

In return for talking to him, I made the reporter promise that he'd make it clear in the story that I had every intention of supporting my daughter, Lauren Shanel—both financially and emotionally.

That was my side of the story. Renfro's was much different, of course.

She claimed we'd agreed to a common-law marriage before Lauren Shanel was born, that we'd honeymooned in Dallas afterward, that we often referred to ourselves as "Mr. and Mrs. David Winfield" when traveling, and that we'd been planning a formal wedding—until I got romantically involved with other women.

None of this was true, and I was prepared to prove it in court.

It felt like Steinbrenner seized on the lawsuit to put me further on the defensive. Maybe it was just a coincidence, but suddenly, my name started popping up in trade rumors—even though, with 10 years in the majors and the past five with the same team, I had the right to veto any deal. One proposed trade had me going to the Tigers in exchange for outfielder Kirk Gibson. Another had me headed to the Blue Jays for reigning American League MVP George Bell.

I brushed off the chatter and let it be known I intended to remain a Yankee. I didn't explain why I hadn't asked for a trade a long time ago—or why I wouldn't accept one now. A lot of players would have done anything to get away, but I wasn't going to let George run me off. It was a choice between fight or flight, and I chose to fight. The speculation about my future and the allegations about my past could wait. I had a wedding to prepare for.

Tonya and I had kept our engagement under wraps, sharing news only with our closest friends and immediate family. We didn't want our once-in-a-lifetime experience to be marred by gawkers or reporters. When we booked the ballroom at the Royal Sonesta New Orleans, we told the staff that Tonya's mother and father would be reaffirming their vows there.

It all turned out beautifully. Tonya looked radiant at the altar. My mother, though fighting a losing battle with cancer, wore a smile throughout the entire ceremony. It was uplifting to be surrounded by so many people who had helped shape my life. My brother, Steve, was my best man. My former teammate Don Baylor, my agent Jeff Klein, and childhood best friend, JD, served as ushers.

My father and I were on the outs at the time. He wasn't invited. I wouldn't see him again until my mother's funeral.

In Robert Turner, I was gaining a father-in-law who embodied the loyalty, consistency, and sense of family that I aspired to emulate. After returning from World War II, Mr. Turner went to work for the railroad and was active in the union. His stories about fighting for workers' rights over more than 30 years inspired me to continue doing the same in my profession.

Our honeymoon would have to wait. Just four days after saying "I do" at the Lawless Memorial Chapel at Dillard University, I reported—right on time—for spring training.

•

I was entering what could be my final year with the Yankees. After the season, Steinbrenner had the option to buy out the last two years of my 10-year contract for around $2 million.

Unlike past springs, when I could ease into the demands of an upcoming season, I stepped into a pressure cooker as soon as I arrived in Fort Lauderdale.

At first, the silence was deafening—maybe because everyone working for or covering the Yankees seemed to have their heads buried in a book—my book, advance copies of which had been shipped down to Florida.

I was happy with the cover of *Winfield: A Player's Life*—a close-up portrait, my face half in shadow with a slight smile, and eyes that hinted I'd seen some things. The clothes looked nice too—in a very late-1980s kind of way: a red collared shirt under a black zip-up jacket with blue stripes. On the back, I was pictured in uniform, sprinting out of the batter's box after hitting the ball.

I was happy with the book's contents too. There wasn't a great deal of Yankees material in it, but I felt good about what there was—and I was ready to defend my shots at Steinbrenner over his leadership style and refusal to pay my foundation the money he'd promised.

I waited for the spring training "book club" to do its assigned reading—and for the only review that really mattered. As he floated around camp, I watched George for any sign he'd finished the book. But behind his big sunglasses, he wore a poker face.

On a road trip to West Palm Beach to play the Expos, I spotted him sitting with Donald Trump, who had recently bought a little place in the area called Mar-a-Lago. Trump was on the bestseller list at the time with his book, *The Art of the Deal*. I hoped to join him on the list soon.

Not surprisingly, George didn't like my book—at all. He was particularly upset about a passage in which I wrote what teammate Willie Randolph had told me soon after I joined the Yankees. Speaking about the organization's view on race, Willie commented that Black players could be "good" Yankees—but never seen as "true" ones.

I hadn't meant to put Willie in an awkward position, but I should've known the quote would be red meat for reporters—especially with Willie being the team captain. When asked for comment, he denied ever saying it, explaining that what I wrote was just my interpretation of something he'd said a long time ago.

I've always known Willie as a man of honesty and integrity, and I don't think he distanced himself from the quote to save face with Steinbrenner—I think he genuinely didn't remember the conversation. He'd seen and heard a lot since joining the Yankees in 1976, after all.

Billy Martin, now back for a *fifth* stint as manager, backed George.

"I just want to make it clear that I'm behind George one hundred percent," Billy said. "I'm loyal to George."

Given Billy's employment history with the Yankees, it was hard to miss the irony of his comment.

Steinbrenner capitalized on Willie's hedge and Billy's support.

"I think we're beginning to see the unraveling of what has been a very carefully plotted PR campaign over the years concerning Dave and the Winfield Foundation," Steinbrenner told reporters. "First, there was the common-law wife and the child out of wedlock. Now, the team captain is saying Winfield lied."

Steinbrenner realized he could get more mileage out of labeling me a bad teammate than a bad employee, so he also targeted a few paragraphs of the book about a team party in Detroit in 1984—an angle he hoped would turn my teammates against me.

The party was funny as heck—just a way for players to blow off steam after hours. I didn't break rank by naming names or going into too much detail. I just described the scene: the Yankees in a hotel penthouse surrounded by a crowd of eager women and plenty of booze. I'd played an important role in the festivities. A guy I knew who ran the best Creole restaurant in Detroit supplied the food.

It was your typical party—until midnight, when a naked dance routine took center stage. But the dancers weren't hired. They weren't women, either. They were two of my teammates—unidentifiable because they were covered head to toe in shaving cream.

If a Yankee wife or girlfriend suspected their guy had been there, all he had to do was say, "No way, honey. I ordered room service and went to bed early." If she chose not to believe him, that was his problem, not mine. I had enough problems of my own on that front.

To their credit, a couple of high-profile teammates came to my defense over the book. Don Mattingly said I was a good person who commanded a level of respect in the clubhouse that would surprise those who only knew me from what they read in the papers. Rickey Henderson called me a friend and said my book wasn't going to hurt team chemistry.

Many of my teammates chose to say nothing—and kept their distance. I didn't blame them. Some were probably angry about what I'd written, but most were just toeing the company line. None of them wanted to be in Steinbrenner's crosshairs.

In some ways, my closest confidant in the clubhouse was our assistant athletic trainer, Steve Donahue. As he taped me up, stretched me out, twisted my torso, and got my arm ready to throw, we'd shoot the breeze about things great and small.

"How's it going today, Dave?" he'd ask.

"Domestically or internationally?" I'd reply, which became a running joke.

When we talked baseball, he got a kick out of my euphemisms for a hitting slump: "statistically acceptable variation" and "period of adjustment."

A trainer knows the inner workings of a player's body and mind better than anyone else in the clubhouse—including the manager—and I appreciated that Steve respected me, both as a person and a player.

One day, during spring training, I opened up my playbook to him.

"Watch what happens today, Steve," I said. "They're going to attack me."

I wasn't guessing—I had moles inside the team's public relations office who occasionally tipped me off about stories they knew were coming.

"So what are you gonna do?" Steve asked.

"Well, you've got three options: defense, counterpunch, and offense. Today's going to be a counterpunch. That vein in George's neck is going to explode."

The best thing about Steve was that he never repeated anything said to him in the sanctity of the training room. His skill—combined with his discretion—goes a long way toward explaining how he worked his way up the ladder and, as of 2026, was still with the Yankees organization.

George and I weren't going to duel it out. This wasn't Burr and Hamilton's New York. But that didn't mean I couldn't land a few blows just doing my job.

One day, at spring training, he put on a glove during batting practice and stood in the shallow part of left field—out of harm's way as long as guys were trying to launch balls over the wall.

When my turn came, I decided to practice hitting line drives. George just happened to be standing in the spot I was aiming for. After getting warmed up, I hit three scorching liners right at him. He might as well have been wearing an oven mitt—he had no chance of fielding them.

He moved over to shallow right field, so I started rocketing the ball in that direction. After nearly getting hit right in the ass, he scurried off the field. I was more than satisfied with my display of situational hitting.

I obviously wasn't looking for a repeat of what happened with the bird in Toronto, but I wouldn't have minded if Steinbrenner left the field with a baseball-shaped welt or two.

I made the rounds promoting my book on interview shows like CNN's *Larry King Live*. My friend Mario Casciano, with his ties to John Lennon's family, got me booked on the NBC show *Friday Night Videos*—where I appeared alongside Lennon's son, Sean, who was helping promote *Moonwalk*, a new book by his friend Michael Jackson.

But Steinbrenner might have been my best publicist. Every time George accused me of being a "me-first" guy by promoting the book, he was only helping me sell copies. Despite—or perhaps because of—his protestations, my book landed on the *New York Times* bestseller list, alongside novels like *The Bonfire of the Vanities* and nonfiction titles like *The Art of the Deal* and *Citizen Cohn*, a biography of the late Roy Cohn—who had died of complications from AIDS in 1986.

The success of the book led George to intensify his attacks.

He fed Howard Cosell information for a *Daily News* column suggesting he was planning to go to court to prove my foundation had misused and misappropriated funds—and that I was under investigation by the IRS and various prosecutors' offices.

Cosell, a "journalist" who sat in Steinbrenner's box at games, also wrote that George had evidence that someone close to me had fabricated the death threats I'd received during the 1981 World Series.

I assume he was referring to Al Frohman. As I sit here today, I don't know whether there's any truth to that allegation. Other Yankees players had also received threats around this time. Does that mean Al was the mastermind behind those too?

It was getting ugly.

I didn't know where the road ahead would take me. I just knew there was no turning back—the bridge behind me was already up in flames.

Amid the turmoil, I seemed to be holding my own in the court of public opinion. At the Yankees' annual "welcome home" dinner at the Waldorf-Astoria, fans greeted me with an ovation, chanting, "No trade! No trade!"

When Steinbrenner was introduced, the crowd booed.

At times, it felt like George and I were political opponents. That year, the *Daily News* published a poll ranking the "biggest BS artists" in New York—68 percent of respondents said George was full of you-know-what. I, on the other hand, topped a related list of "most trusted" public figures, edging out Governor Mario Cuomo.

A Yankees fan named Ken Rader eloquently captured the essence of Steinbrenner in a 1988 letter to *The New York Times*:

> On a conscious level, Steinbrenner may seek victory, but time and time again he has shown that he is controlled by an unconscious need to be the most famous Yankee of them all: a need that can be satisfied only by staging those disruptive, self-defeating melodramas in which he plays the leading role. The team and its fans suffer endlessly, but Steinbrenner eternally stars.

Well put, Ken.

That's not to say that George didn't have his share of supporters in the bleachers. Take Jack Scarangella from New Rochelle, who wrote to the *Times*:

> I think Steinbrenner is getting a bad rap simply because he is not a wimp and has the courage to speak his mind. If he were less assertive, he would

> blend into the background like so many other owners and wouldn't be the focus of so much attention. Steinbrenner is a decent man with strong convictions. He exerts many leadership qualities. Maybe those people—fans and players—who dislike Steinbrenner are wimps.

For the record, I've never considered myself a wimp. But there are ways to push my buttons. If Steinbrenner was trying to get under my skin by commenting on my personal life, he succeeded.

Renfro's lawyers had begun interviewing witnesses in her case against me. One of the first people deposed was my mother, who couldn't leave home due to her illness, so the lawyers came to her condo in Minneapolis to question her.

The last thing she needed was that kind of stress, but she sat for hours answering their questions, making it clear that her son wasn't married to Sandra and never claimed to be—to her or anyone else. Their badgering of her really irritated me. So did their argument that the condo I'd bought for Ma wasn't really hers—that it was "community property" that Sandra and I would have to fight over if she prevailed.

My phone hardly stopped ringing during those months. There were reporters—of course—interested in talking about Steinbrenner and the book. Old friends reached out after hearing about Ma's cancer diagnosis. Business advisors checked in to see if I had any needs now that Al Frohman was gone.

And then there was Howie Spira—calling just to send my blood pressure a little higher, perhaps? I didn't return his call. It had been several years since I told him to take a hike, to stop calling and showing up at the foundation offices. With one exception—a phone call at the end of 1986, supposedly to congratulate me on the opening of my new restaurant—he'd stuck to those terms.

The conversation in '86 went something like this:

"Chriiist almighty—Howard Spira."

"How are you, Dave? I'm calling because I'm hoping we can have a reinvolvement. Al told me you'd look out for me."

"I don't know what you're talking about, Howie."

"Well, with everything you've got going on, I think I can help you."

"I don't need your help, Howie."

"I know a lot of things, Dave—things that can help you . . . and things that can maybe hurt you."

"What's that supposed to mean?"

"Please, Dave. Please. You have to help me. I need a job."

"You're almost begging, Howie. I'm gonna hang up on your ass in a minute."

"Don't bother," Howie said, hanging up on me.

I'd called Al to let him know that Howie was back again and had dropped his name. He said Howie told him he'd rejected an offer to join the FBI witness protection program for information he'd provided about New York mobsters.

"I thought maybe you had something for him at the foundation," Al said. "He owes a lot of people a lot of money."

Yeah, a compulsive gambling mob informant—*exactly* the kind of person I wanted hanging around my charitable organization.

The Winfield protection program doesn't have any room for him, I told Al.

I'd later learn that, after I rebuffed him, Howie's next call was to Steinbrenner.

I had an enormous target on my back heading into the 1988 season. Steinbrenner believed there was language in my contract that overrode my rights as a 10-and-5 player who couldn't be traded without his consent. He worked out a three-way trade with Toronto and Houston that would have sent me to the Blue Jays, Jesse Barfield to the Astros, and Kevin Bass to the Yankees.

The deal might have gone through if Lou Piniella hadn't interceded.

After clashing with Steinbrenner the previous season, Lou had been banished to the rubber room for exiled managers—otherwise known as the general manager's office. Billy, meanwhile, was released from the front office and told he could return to the Yankees dugout.

George could push for the trade, but Lou was the one who had to execute it—and he refused. We'd played well during the first month of the season, and I was a big reason why. I was hitting over .400 and leading the league in RBIs.

After Lou told reporters that the trade might hurt team chemistry, Steinbrenner backed out of it. A few weeks later, Lou resigned as GM—but I guess there were no hard feelings, because by August, he was back managing the team after Billy, along with right-hand man Art Fowler, were once again shown the door.

While criticizing my book, Steinbrenner suggested I was a ballplayer in decline—an aging athlete with diminishing skills who might be nearing the end of my career. I appreciated that Lou had the guts to speak truth to power—the truth being that I was a respected team leader, still producing at a high level.

•

There was another phone call I received that May—one that truly tested my mental resolve.

Over Mother's Day weekend, Tonya flew in from Los Angeles for our series against the Rangers—and to spend time with her mom, who had loaded up a van with family on a Friday night for the eight-hour drive from New Orleans. It was going to be a joyous weekend.

Tonya and I started to worry when the group still hadn't arrived by late Saturday. We waited and waited, assuming they'd hit traffic or needed to make extra rest stops. This was before cell phones, before we could send a quick text asking: "Where u at?"

We stayed up all night, hoping they'd pull in.

Early the next morning, I got a call in my hotel room—from the Texas Highway Patrol. There had been an accident.

We flew by helicopter to a hospital in Tyler, Texas, where we got the devastating news: Tonya's nine-year-old niece, Kristen, had been killed in a rollover crash. Everyone else was seriously injured.

The papers said I missed Sunday's game due to a personal matter. Nobody ever knew what had really happened. The tragedy put everything else into perspective—and it deepened my desire to cherish every moment I had with my family.

That summer, I flew my ailing mother to Cincinnati for the All-Star Game, knowing that it might be her last chance to see me play in person. But she wasn't well enough to leave the hotel, so she watched the game on TV with her private nurse. I know it filled her with pride when I scored the winning run in the American League's 2–1 victory.

It broke my heart and made me feel powerless to see Ma grow weaker every day. She was a fighter, though, undergoing treatment in New York and at the Mayo Clinic in Minnesota for a disease that refused to let go.

She was close to the TV again when we played Detroit in the nationally televised NBC Game of the Week in mid-September. My run-scoring double in the seventh inning gave me 100 RBIs for the season and elicited "MVP" chants from the Yankee Stadium faithful.

"That one was for my mom," I said after the game.

After we beat the Orioles on September 27, I got back to the team hotel and found a two-word message from my brother, Steve: "Call me."

"Mom is really declining," he told me. "She might not have much time left."

I found Piniella and explained the situation. He supported my decision to go home. We still had a mathematical chance to catch the Red Sox for the division, but our chances of doing so were slim. And I knew I couldn't live with myself if I didn't get to see Ma one last time.

Tonya and I flew to Minnesota. For several days, I never left Ma's side, sleeping on the floor right next to her each night.

She passed away on October 3—my birthday—at the age of 66.

After her cancer diagnosis, Ma looked to Tonya's mother, Louise, for reassurance that I would still have a mother figure in my life.

"When I'm gone, you have to take care of my boys," Ma told her.

"You know I will," Louise said.

Ma's death left me reeling. She had always been my rock—the one I turned to for love, support, and guidance. Though she stood just five foot two, she was fierce. She inspired me. She was my best friend—and the person I respected most.

I was fortunate to have the entire offseason to cope with the loss.

•

The Yankees chose not to exercise the $2 million buyout clause in my contract, which meant I wouldn't become a free agent. It was clear Steinbrenner didn't believe his own claim that I was a player in decline—at least not enough to just give me away.

Since I'd be sticking around the Bronx, I planned to keep pressing the issue that had helped trigger our battle royale in the first place: his failure to pay the money he'd promised my foundation.

I had already taken him to court twice to compel payment, and both times we settled. But he fell behind on his obligations again, prompting me to file another lawsuit seeking the $450,000 he owed. My complaint alleged that George was deliberately withholding payments because I had refused to accept a trade.

George was ready with the response that Cosell had written about a few months earlier. His suit accused me of failing to make payments of my own to the foundation and of mismanaging funds.

But another allegation stood out: He claimed I'd loaned money to known gamblers.

I laughed out loud when I read that line—but then I remembered the time Al had talked me into loaning money to Howie. What was it—$15,000? When was it—1981? Only three people knew about that: Al, Howie, and me.

So how did George's lawyers find out? Not from me. And Al was dead.

That left Howie.

In the wake of the lawsuits, a couple of teams reached out to the Yankees to ask about my availability—but I made it clear, once again, that I wasn't going anywhere—except on vacation.

But it was hard to get away from it all.

On a trip to Nepal, about as far from New York City as you can get, Tonya and I were watching a royal procession when a voice rang out behind me: "Holy shit, it's Dave Winfield!"

I turned to see a man in a Yankees cap. He told me he was a carpet salesman from New Jersey.

Even in far-flung Kathmandu, I couldn't go unnoticed.

Meanwhile, debates about Steinbrenner and me raged in the papers and on WFAN, New York's new 24-hour, all-sports radio station, which thrived on drama in the local sports scene.

They were about to get more than they could have ever hoped for.

I was right in the eye of Hurricanes George, Sandra, and Howie—and the storms were heading for a collision.

Chapter 14

SPIES, LIES, AND RBIS

If Howie hadn't been so desperate for his 15 minutes of fame, who knows how things would have turned out. But desperation defined him.

Within days of Steinbrenner filing his lawsuit, Howie appeared on WFAN and Channel 9, boasting that he was the source of the information Steinbrenner was using against me. He claimed he was performing a public service—because I was, in his words, "an arrogant SOB."

His message couldn't have been clearer: "Steinbrenner asked me to dig up dirt on Winfield."

And yet, not a single one of the dozens of journalists covering the Yankeeverse—or Major League Baseball itself—questioned the unholy alliance. No one connected the dots until later.

Howie then went on *The Morton Downey Jr. Show*—a popular late-'80s TV show featuring people shouting over each other for an hour—and challenged me to a 4 AM fistfight on a street corner of my choosing.

I'd messed up getting involved with "The Dweeb," as one *Daily News* reporter nicknamed Howie, but so, too, had the most powerful owner in the game. How could that go unpunished?

That question—and the many others swirling around my life—made the acid in my stomach boil again. I went to a gastroenterologist for an upper GI scan, which revealed a small triangle burned into the lining of my stomach.

"You have an ulcer," the doctor told me.

"An ulcer?"

"Eat more fruits and vegetables. And if at all possible, try to reduce your stress levels."

There must've been *Daily News* and *Post* clippings in my medical chart, because he seemed to know the second part would be a tall order.

It didn't help that Howie, after making the rounds on TV and talk radio, showed up unannounced at my lawyer Jeff Klein's office to make his pitch. Jeff listened patiently as Howie railed against me for not giving him a job, for freezing him out, and even for driving him to gamble beyond his means.

"Please have Dave call me," Howie said.

"I'll let him know you stopped by," Jeff replied.

"Will you tell him to call me?"

"I don't think he has anything to say to you."

"Well, tell him I'll put a bullet in him for what he's done to me."

Maybe that was just Howie's version of a sign-off, but I wasn't about to take any chances.

As I tried to soothe the ulcer and avoid Howie, another part of my body turned against me. When I'd experienced discomfort in my back near the end of the previous season, I'd hoped it was just a mild strain and tried to power through it. But pain shot through me every time I swung the bat—which helped explain why I hit only one home run in the final month.

I'd also started carrying around two briefcases, just to keep track of the growing number of documents I needed. The extra weight hadn't done my back any favors.

The team doctor diagnosed me with back spasms and prescribed a regimen of heat and ice therapy along with massage.

•

Steinbrenner—uncharacteristically—had hired a new manager, Dallas Green, with no prior connection to the organization. I liked the move, because I believed the team would benefit from a fresh set of eyes and ideas. By all accounts, Green was a good baseball man—he'd managed the Phillies to a World Series title in 1980 and, as general manager, helped turn the lowly Cubs around.

Green won me over with what he said about me to reporters the week of his hire: "Maybe I have to convince George that his view of Dave Winfield isn't fair. The player I knew, and that a lot of people talk to me about, flat-out busts his rear one hundred percent of the time."

Not knowing Green, I wasn't sure if his statement was heartfelt or just meant for the ears of general managers around the majors—who had long since gotten the memo that I was on the trading block.

One thing I did know was Green's reputation as a no-nonsense, my-way-or-the-highway kind of guy. I wondered how that would play with Steinbrenner. Spoiler alert: He was fired in August after calling George out for meddling in his managerial decisions.

I never played a game for Green. A second opinion on my back led to a far worse diagnosis—a herniated disc—and surgery in March, which caused me to miss the entire 1989 season.

That wasn't easy to swallow. Being on the baseball field had always been my refuge from the turmoil in my life. If I couldn't be there, I wanted to be with Tonya. But now, I couldn't avoid confronting some of that drama head-on.

Being sidelined freed up my schedule for a reckoning in Texas with Sandra Renfro—who, in addition to seeking alimony, was now asking for unspecified damages for the emotional distress caused by my real marriage.

On the one hand, I was dreading it. I wanted to be standing in a batter's box, not sitting in a courtroom responding to baseless allegations. On the other hand, if it meant bringing closure to the whole thing, I was as ready as I'd ever be.

Besides the obvious reason—money—I couldn't for the life of me understand why Sandra was putting us through this. Lauren Shanel was almost seven, old enough to start understanding the public spectacle it was creating. She had recently come to visit me in New York for the first time. Tonya and I did our best to show her a good time, taking her to a diner for milkshakes and FAO Schwarz to pick out toys. In hindsight, letting her watch *The Wizard of Oz* on TV wasn't the best choice. The witches and flying monkeys scared her.

But I was learning.

Sandra was now dating a Texas attorney—and would eventually marry him. I feel like if she truly had our daughter's best interests at heart, she would have just moved on with her life instead of pretending—or talking herself into believing—that we had ever been married. Then, we could have focused on what we really needed, a formal agreement about child support and visitation.

Before my surgery put me out of commission, the judge had set an April trial date that conflicted with the start of the season. He said it was locked in, no chance of postponement, making me wonder if Steinbrenner had a hand in choosing it. Nothing would look worse than missing games because I had to be in court. After my surgery, the judge quietly rescheduled the trial for June.

It was an odd sensation being on trial. Family court doesn't have defendants—only respondents—but I still felt like I was being prosecuted . . . and persecuted.

Outside the Harris County Courthouse, it was so hot I was sweating through my shirt. Inside wasn't much cooler.

I sat at the counsel table, taking in the room. A stuffed animal head—I wasn't sure if it was an ox, a steer, or a bull—was mounted on the wall behind the judge's bench. Nearby hung a Confederate battle flag.

Where am I, and what year is it again?

It appeared the only thing missing from the courtroom was a kangaroo.

I realized I wasn't only going to have to refute Sandra's claims—I'd be fighting the system too.

A guy I'd seen outside the courthouse just a few minutes earlier walked into the room. He looked familiar, but I couldn't place him. He had the unmistakable aura of a New Yorker—that much I could tell. He saw me staring, walked up to the front row of the gallery, and said, "Hi, Dave."

That voice. I'd recognize it anywhere.

I waved the bailiff over.

"Can you frisk this man, please? He's been threatening me."

The bailiff patted down Howie Spira. He was clean.

"What's Spira doing here?" I asked my attorney, Tom Alexander.

"He's on the witness list," he told me.

Maybe Howie wasn't in Texas to physically harm me, but one thing was clear: He was Steinbrenner's guy—and he was there to cause trouble.

Tonya flew in to give me emotional support I badly needed. The whole situation had taken a toll on her. She had to face all the news articles and gossip suggesting that I was married to two women. We were still newlyweds, and the stress of the trial provided the first real test of our marriage. In a gesture that meant a lot, Tonya's parents also came to Texas to stand by me.

All I wanted was a fair shake. But in a case that pitted two Black people against each other, the good ol' boy of a judge set his sights on the one he thought he could knock down a peg or two. During a sidebar, Judge Allen J. Daggett told my lawyer, in no uncertain terms, that he had no use for athletes, especially Black ones. His exact words were: "I don't care anything about no n-word athletes."

To establish we had a common-law marriage, Renfro had to prove three things: that we agreed to be married, that we presented ourselves as married, and that we lived together.

She took the stand and testified that for three offseasons we lived together in the Houston condo I'd bought for her while she was pregnant. In reality, I'd spent only a week or two there during that time.

She described an evening at an airport hotel in Arlington, Texas, in 1982 when I supposedly gave her flowers, popped a bottle of champagne, and told her, "We are as good as married." This had allegedly happened when we were in town playing the Rangers.

When I took the stand, I testified that I'd never stayed at an airport hotel—I always stayed with the team. But, in what became a recurring theme throughout the trial, I couldn't produce any hard evidence to contradict Sandra's version of events.

Her attorney, Earle Lilly, called a parade of friends as witnesses—some testified that we cohabitated and presented ourselves as husband and wife. But several others said the opposite. Tellingly, she couldn't even get all her own friends to back her.

Another witness, who lived in her condo complex, testified that she'd once introduced Renfro and me as a married couple—and that I hadn't corrected her.

Then it got worse.

To this day, I'll never understand why a former employee of my foundation testified—without a shred of evidence—that I'd spent most of those offseasons in Houston with Renfro. It was a flat-out lie. And it's hard not to get conspiratorial about her motivation—though the fact that she'd been fired for incompetence might have had something to do with it.

The reason that *Lifestyles of the Rich and Famous* profiled me wasn't because I spent my offseasons in Houston. It was because I spent them traveling the world.

If I could have claimed Texas residency, I'd have saved a fortune in state taxes compared to New Jersey. I didn't have a bank there. I didn't have a car there either. None of it added up.

I shook my head so many times during her testimony, I thought I might mess up my back again.

To make matters worse, Judge Daggett kept cutting off my lawyer and threatening to remove him from the courtroom. Apparently, the two had a history I didn't know about—my attorney had once investigated Daggett's alleged involvement in the sale of a car in exchange for favorable treatment in a divorce case.

The judge wouldn't allow the deposition of my late mother to be entered into the record. He also barred me from submitting the lease on the Houston condo—an agreement stating that Renfro could stay there rent-free until she started working again. That's not the kind of document you draw up when you're actually living together.

Adding to the sinking feeling, I found out the Yankees traded my good friend Rickey Henderson to the A's while I was stuck in the courtroom.

Howie was never called to testify, depriving me of the comic relief that would've come from him claiming he knew anything at all about my personal life. But just having him there for the duration of the proceedings was unsettling.

After three days of testimony, the jury went back to deliberate. It's a harrowing feeling having your fate in the hands of 12 strangers. Still, I felt confident that the jurors would weigh what they'd heard and see through Renfro's scheme.

A juror interviewed after the verdict said the panel had leaned heavily in my favor on the first day of deliberations. Most believed there was no evidence that I had agreed to marry Renfro.

But in his jury instructions, the judge included a provision that allowed them to bypass that question and move on to whether we had lived together and presented ourselves as a married couple.

On the second day of deliberations, the jurors decided that both of those conditions had been satisfied—even though the evidence for either was shaky at best.

Immediately after the verdict, the judge ordered me to make temporary monthly payments of $10,000 in alimony and $3,500 in child support. He also ordered me to pay $210,000 toward Renfro's legal expenses.

And that was only the beginning—the judge still had to determine what portion of my earnings Renfro was entitled to.

My legal team got blindsided by how Renfro presented her case. They hadn't come prepared to account for every day of my life during the period she claimed we were married—but as it turned out, that's exactly what they needed to do.

I didn't waste any time filing an appeal.

Fortunately, I'd get a second crack at presenting a stronger case—this time with the evidence to expose Sandra's lies, shady lawyering, and Howie Spira's part in the whole sordid mess.

The Texas courtroom massacre continued in New York, where Renfro took a victory lap. She flew north to appear on Channel 9's *People Are Talking*. Then she hit the *Phil Donahue Show* to talk even more about the psychological damage I'd supposedly inflicted on her. It was an aggressive campaign aimed at convincing the judge that she deserved a large chunk of my net worth.

I countered by appearing on Arsenio's Hall late-night show. It was a welcome change to be interviewed by a Black man who understood the pitfalls of fame and success. Talking to Arsenio felt a little like lying on a therapist's couch—only with millions of people watching from home.

Adding to my anxiety was the uncertainty of my recovery. What if the surgery didn't take? What if I couldn't play at a high level again—or at all? And if this was the end, how would my career be remembered? What would my legacy be?

I returned to New York in a darker headspace than I'd ever been. I wasn't planning on staying long. Being with Tonya in Los Angeles—where I'd had the surgery at the Kerlan-Jobe Orthopedic Clinic—felt like the only place for me at that moment. There, I could recuperate and try to get perspective on all that was unraveling in my life.

Even if I was only going to be in New York for a couple of months, I knew I couldn't take anything for granted—not even my safety. The city seemed to be conspiring against me. I felt watched. And not in the way I was used to.

Media reports surfaced that Steinbrenner had hired two private investigation firms to dig into my personal life. My childhood friend Jerry

Douglas told the television show *Inside Edition* that someone—who didn't identify themselves—had called him, offering cash for damaging information about me.

When I spotted an unfamiliar car parked near my house late at night, I wondered if it was one of Steinbrenner's operatives. Were raccoons rifling through my trash—or was I being surveilled? Maybe the Gordon Gekko–looking stockbroker I passed in Manhattan wasn't a stockbroker at all. Maybe he was another of Steinbrenner's spies.

I couldn't even trust the people who approached me on the street or in restaurants to talk baseball. What if they reached for a pen—and then *bang!* I'm dead. I avoided Yankee Stadium entirely, afraid Steinbrenner might try to have drugs planted on me—the main reason I refused to rehab my back at the team's spring training facility.

Beyond all that, I had no idea what the consequences of the verdict in Texas might be. Back when things seemed simpler—before anybody had heard of Sandra Renfro—there was a woman going around pretending to be my wife. Her name was Betty Anne, and she went so far as to have a checkbook printed with the name "Mrs. Winfield." She wrote bad checks all around Manhattan—one of which got flagged at Bloomingdale's, alerting me to her.

A few months later, Betty Anne surfaced in Georgia, still claiming to be my wife, this time trying to buy a car. When the police showed me a photo of her, I realized I'd seen her at Yankee Stadium on several occasions. I managed to shrug it off—even though she fit the textbook profile of a stalker.

Now, with my name all over the news because of the Renfro trial, I had to face the reality that there might be hundreds of Betty Annes out there—people who might want to buy more than cars or handbags. People who might want to hurt me.

One of the few times I felt at ease that summer was when my foundation employee—and de facto security detail—Rick Scott and I went to Harlem to watch Spike Lee's new movie, *Do the Right Thing*. Maybe it was the makeup of the audience, or maybe it was because Spike's movies are so absorbing, but for a couple of hours, I was out of my own head and fully immersed in the streets of Brooklyn.

Afterward, the movie's rhythmic language got me thinking about my own situation—how the Yankees preached pride but trafficked in snide; how I wanted candor but got rancor; how confidence was mistaken for arrogance and assertiveness for belligerence; how I needed support, not court; fun, not "you're done"; smiles, not denial.

My friend Mario noticed I was fidgety, distracted, and staring off into space a lot—something he'd never seen me do. He joked that the post-trial beard I'd grown was making a statement, kind of like when Paul McCartney grew one before the Beatles broke up. In truth, it was more of a thinly veiled disguise.

One night, he drove me home to Teaneck and noticed two handguns tucked inside one of my kitchen cabinets.

His eyes grew wide. As someone who knew John Lennon personally, he didn't like being around guns.

I told him about Spira's threat, my suspicion that Steinbrenner might resort to setting me up with drugs, and my lingering unease about what had happened in Texas.

I was still in a daze when my lawyer, Jeff Klein, called to say he'd reached a settlement with Steinbrenner's lawyers regarding my foundation. George and I would each contribute a significant amount—with him covering a much larger share—and I'd reimburse the foundation for a much smaller sum flagged by an audit as questionable spending.

Bill Madden of the *Daily News* called the settlement "unquestionably a victory for Steinbrenner" and "strike three for Winfield," citing the rough year I was having with injury and personal turmoil. I wasn't surprised. Madden had always been a Steinbrenner guy. George even trusted him to write his biography, which would come out shortly before his death.

Steinbrenner called a press conference to announce the terms, and Jeff suggested I attend. The last thing I expected to be doing before heading back to Los Angeles was standing next to George at a public peace settlement, but I agreed to go.

If George wanted to spin this as a victory, which I assumed he did, I had a few things I wanted to say.

So, for the first time since my introductory press conference in 1980, George and I stepped up to a podium together.

"It's difficult for a man to admit he's made mistakes, but David is doing that, and that makes him a bigger man in my eyes," Steinbrenner said. "I will be most happy to have him back with the Yankees next season. I am calling him Mr. May, June, July, August, September, and October—because that's how much we've missed his bat."

Listening to George's statement made me feel like a POW trotted out for a photo op. I think my facial expression that day said it all—a knowing half smile that seemed to say, "I don't know exactly what's going on here, but this isn't going to be the last word."

As the press conference drew to a close, I shuffled toward the microphone, hoping to say a few words about how I felt. But a wall of attorneys blocked my path and escorted George and me off the podium.

I didn't trust Steinbrenner. My instincts told me there was more to his make-nice gesture than met the eye.

But at least he'd acknowledged that the Yankees were a lesser team without me in the lineup.

While I recuperated from surgery, they stumbled to their worst record since 1967, marking the first time in history that the team went an entire decade without winning a World Series. Meanwhile, the rumor mill was churning with reports that George was planning to bring back Billy Martin yet again, this time to replace Bucky Dent.

I didn't like missing a season of baseball, but I didn't miss the Yankees. Watching them struggle, I was glad I wasn't there to be the scapegoat. Getting a respite for a year turned out to be not such a bad thing.

On the eve of a new decade, the Yankees had plenty of baseball questions to answer. I fully intended to return for the 1990 season to help with that. The time had also come to blow the lid off a scandal that was about more than just me and Steinbrenner. The 1980s should have been a triumphant decade for Yankees baseball, but instead, the organization became a model of dysfunction. George's actions hadn't just hurt me—they'd hurt the team too.

The media and the commissioner had somehow missed the most explosive part of the story. But I knew someone who could help connect the dots—and fortunately, he was already one step ahead.

Chapter 15

GOING UNDERCOVER

Steinbrenner and I weren't through with each other yet—not by a long shot—but at least the Berlin Wall had come down. The real one, not the one between us.

Our settlement required me to contribute $229,000 to my foundation, while Steinbrenner would kick in $600,000. I also had to reimburse $30,000 for expenses an audit found were inappropriate—a far cry from the six-figure sum Steinbrenner had claimed.

I played 81 games a season on the road and spent a large portion of every offseason traveling, leaving long stretches when others at the foundation were in charge. And no one was scrutinizing every expense or making sure we didn't spend too much on overhead.

I was happy to correct the books and set up safeguards so that wouldn't happen again. I'd helped blaze a trail when I started my foundation, and part of being one of the first to do something is learning best practices along the way.

It angered me that all the noise Steinbrenner had made about the foundation threatened to overshadow the great work we were doing.

Another example of the mark we were making came when our anti-drug initiatives caught the attention of Senator Joe Biden, who invited me to

Washington, DC, on Halloween Day in 1989 to testify before the Senate Judiciary Committee about drug prevention. I sat in Room 206 of the Dirksen Senate Office Building, speaking about our "Turn It Around" antidrug program. It was a welcome change from testifying in a dusty Texas courtroom that felt stuck in another era—though Senator Strom Thurmond of South Carolina gave off some serious antebellum-South vibes.

I needed to snap out of my funk so I could focus on getting to the bottom of what was going on between Steinbrenner, Spira, and Sandra Renfro's attorney.

My future—and my mental health—depended on it.

As much as I was looking forward to being in Los Angeles for the off-season, there was only so much digging I could do from there. But my friend Mario knew the situation well enough to understand the urgency.

"Do you have Spira's number?" Mario asked, as he drove me to the Newark airport.

"I could get it," I said.

"Thanks."

I considered asking him why he wanted it, but the look on his face told me not to. I pulled out my car phone and called the foundation, knowing that Howie had left more messages for me than I could count. Sure enough, they had his number. I jotted it down on a slip of paper and handed it to Mario.

"Good luck," I said. "Keep me posted."

With that, Mario was deputized.

Over the next several months, Mario called me every so often to share updates about his budding relationship with Spira, one that proved the adage: "Keep your friends close but your enemies closer."

Mario's friendship with John Lennon had inspired him to imagine a world with everyone living life in peace. But Howie didn't know Mario was such a pacifist. So in his first interaction with Howie, Mario leaned into being "Mario from Brooklyn" and tried to sound intimidating enough to make Howie crawl under a rock and hide.

"I'm a friend of David's," Mario told Spira on the phone. "I heard you've been bothering him. You need to stop."

That didn't work. If anything, it just emboldened Howie that someone in Dave Winfield's universe had actually contacted him. Ever since Al Frohman's passing, he'd been looking for a way back in. And he wasn't about to be deterred by Mario telling him to go away.

If the New York mob couldn't shake itself loose of Howie, I suppose it was unrealistic to think Mario would fare any better.

Howie kept calling, complaining that I'd done him wrong. But, according to Mario, I wasn't the main target of his anger anymore—Steinbrenner was. George had also failed to come through for Howie—at least that's how Howie saw it.

Sensing an opportunity to find out more about Howie and George's relationship, Mario switched up his strategy. One thing was already clear: Howie loved to talk—and Mario was going to give him his ear.

He invited Howie to come to the public relations firm on 42nd Street where he worked. Howie wouldn't stop yammering at that meeting about George and me, but Mario quickly picked up on something else: Howie saw himself as the real star of the story.

"The guy's nuts," he told me. "He's got diarrhea of the mouth. Anybody who talks to him immediately becomes his best friend."

"So you're his best friend now?"

"Yup . . . did I mention he told me he tapes all his phone calls?"

"Interesting. Let's see what he's got."

The next time they met, Mario pitched Howie an idea.

"You really have an amazing story, Howie," he said. "I think we should do a book together."

Howie's eyes lit up at the suggestion, Mario said.

His PR firm was going through a merger, so Mario had nearly an entire floor of the office to himself. As luck would have it, he also had access to a secretary who could take notes—and make copies of audiotapes.

"I'm ready to start when you are," Mario said.

So as not to blow his cover—which, given Howie's level of excitement, probably wasn't even a risk—Mario patiently listened to Howie talk about his dysfunctional family and growing up in the Bronx.

Howie also spoke of the obscene amounts of money he'd wagered on credit—and lost—on sports. He'd once dropped $150,000 on a football game. He liked betting on baseball too.

"I couldn't help feeling sorry for the guy," he told me.

"Don't go soft on me now," I said, laughing.

"No chance of that. Just showing a little heart."

It was at their next meetup that everything started to come into focus. Mario found out that after I'd brushed off Howie when he called me begging for a job in December 1986, he had almost immediately called Steinbrenner.

Howie let Mario listen to recordings of both conversations.

"I want to get even with him," Spira said on the call with Steinbrenner. "If anybody can use what I have, it's you."

Without missing a beat, Steinbrenner said he'd found a court record of my old snowblower theft case in Minnesota. He indicated he was going to try to use it against me—and that he was interested in hearing more of what Howie had to say.

He flew Howie to Tampa for a meeting, where Howie laid out what he had—or at least claimed to have—on me. They discussed the death threats I received during the 1981 World Series and what Howie supposedly knew about the inner workings of my foundation. Also in the room at the headquarters of George's shipbuilding company was Steinbrenner's security chief, Phil McNiff, a former head of the FBI's field office in Tampa.

All of Howie's information ended up in the lawsuit Steinbrenner filed against my foundation, in Howard Cosell's column, or in the hands of Sandra Renfro's attorney.

"And what exactly did Howie expect to get from all this?" I asked Mario during one of our debriefs.

"A lot," Mario said. "He says Steinbrenner promised him $150,000, a job, and a waterfront place in Florida."

"And what did he get?"

"None of the above. And he's pissed off. He's been harassing Steinbrenner for months."

It strengthened me to know that the truth was beginning to reveal itself.

•

As Tonya and I prepared for Christmas in Beverly Hills, I tried to strip my mind of all the destructive energy in my life. For the first time in years, I felt a sense of calm. I was living with my wife in a city that seemed a million miles away from the people and places I'd come to associate with grief and anguish. The trials and tribulations of the past year could easily have torn us apart. Instead, they brought us closer.

I spent time with Tonya and friends like Earvin Johnson. He understood what it meant to live in a fishbowl—though, as a member of the "Showtime" Lakers, he'd never had to endure being treated like anything less than a superstar. He had a hard time wrapping his head around what I'd been through in New York, but in addition to being a great ball handler, he was a great listener too.

On the day after Christmas, I got an early-morning call from Mario, who was usually good about respecting the time difference and not waking me up.

"You hear about Billy?"

"Billy? No, what?" I said, still half-asleep.

"He died last night in a car accident."

"Who—Billy Martin?"

"Yeah, Billy Martin."

"Oh wow, no, I didn't know that."

"Anyway, I'll let you go, but I'm putting something in the mail to you. Call it a late Christmas gift."

I downed a cup of coffee and went out to buy a copy of the *Los Angeles Times*. I sat in my car and read that Billy had been riding in a Ford pickup near his farm in upstate New York when the truck skidded off the road and plunged 300 feet into a ravine. His friend, a bar owner from Detroit, survived—and was charged with DUI. It later came out that he and Billy had been drinking all day.

Billy had lived a hard 61 years, but his death still came as a shock. He was one of those guys who got knocked down but was nearly impossible to finish off. His managerial history with the Yankees was proof of that.

Billy's death cut to the heart of the difference between a "true" Yankee and a "good" one. No reporters called to get my reaction. And I didn't attend his funeral—as many "true" Yankees did—because I couldn't bring myself to reenter the New York media circus.

Steinbrenner helped wheel Billy's coffin into a packed St. Patrick's Cathedral. Willie Randolph, Don Mattingly, and Ron Guidry came to represent the teams of the 1980s. Yogi Berra, Whitey Ford, and Mickey Mantle were among Billy's former teammates who attended. Even Richard Nixon showed up to pay his respects.

Reggie Jackson and I were noticeably absent. I stayed behind in Los Angeles, remembering Billy in my own way—and opening Mario's late Christmas gift.

It was an unmarked cassette tape. My curiosity was piqued. I popped it into my Sony Walkman and hit play. A conversation between two men came through my headphones. I recognized Howie's voice immediately. The other voice—inflected with a Southern accent—I couldn't place right away.

"Sandra was as married to Dave . . ." Spira said.

"As you or I," the other speaker finished the sentence.

I rewound the tape and listened to the exchange probably five times. Then I called Mario.

"Is that who I think it is talking to Howie?"

"Well, if you think it's Sandra's lawyer, then you'd be correct."

Hearing the exchange between Howie and Earle Lilly incensed me—and bolstered my suspicion that Steinbrenner had meddled in my Texas case. I hoped the day would come when I'd have the chance to use Lilly's words against him.

During the first week of 1990, Mario went silent. I didn't know what to make of it, but I trusted that he'd get in touch once he had something new to report.

Finally, on January 8, he called.

"You sitting down?" he asked.

"Yeah, by the pool."

"So, Howie went to Steinbrenner asking for his money."

"And?"

"And I'll tell you."

Mario proceeded to recount the events of the previous week. Speaking to Howie as a *friend*—a role I have no doubt Mario played convincingly—he felt there was only one thing he could do: encourage him to go get what he was owed.

So, over a lunch of corned beef and cabbage at a local bar, Howie decided to take Mario's advice.

"As soon as you get the money, call me," Mario told him—not believing he'd really get anything, but wanting to keep his confidence up.

A couple of days later, Howie called Mario, sounding dejected.

"I didn't get what he promised me."

"Well, you tried."

"I need more than what he gave me."

"What did you get?"

"Forty thousand."

Mario nearly dropped the phone. And so did I when he relayed the news to me.

It was bad enough that Steinbrenner had used Howie as an unpaid informant. A baseball owner shouldn't be involved with a gambler, even if no money is exchanging hands. That was a particularly sensitive subject at the time—a few months earlier, Pete Rose had been banned for life for betting on games.

But once Steinbrenner paid Howie, things went to a whole other level. Now they were officially in business together—a baseball owner paying a high-stakes gambler to help bring down one of his players.

Mario assumed Howie had been paid in cash, but then came the next surprise.

George had cut him two checks—one for $30,500 and the other for $9,500. Included with the payments was a nondisclosure agreement drafted by Steinbrenner and signed by Spira stating that Howie would not "seek or create any publicity, or make any public statement with respect to the nature or substance of this matter."

Good luck with that. Anyone who knew Howie knew that document wasn't worth the paper it was written on.

"Can I see the checks?" Mario asked him. "They'd make a perfect cover for the book."

And just like that, Mario was in possession of the smoking guns.

"I need some time to process this," I told Mario.

"Me too."

Mario told me he couldn't shake the feeling that he was somehow being set up. Why would Steinbrenner leave such an obvious paper trail? It didn't make sense—in fact, it was just plain stupid.

Mario's detective work didn't give me all the answers—it just reinforced what I already knew: Steinbrenner had no scruples.

It didn't comfort me to think this might help me "win" our battle, because there were no winners in any of this. My goal was never to bring Steinbrenner down—it was to keep him from tarnishing my name. But somewhere along the way, everything got turned on its head.

As spring training approached, I was able to stand up straight for the first time in over a year. There were flecks of gray in my hair now, but my body felt great—a small scar on my lower back the only trace of my surgery. If the 1990 season was going to be my final act in New York, I was going to be ready.

I still considered myself the best right fielder in the game, but I said I'd be willing to move to left or take on the designated hitter role so that Jesse Barfield—one of the few bright spots on the '89 team—could stay in right.

George, blissfully unaware that his professional life might soon come crashing down, praised me to reporters as a team player. But if he truly believed in me, he would have made sure my name appeared on the 1990 All-Star ballot. Instead, the Yankees submitted the names of Barfield, Roberto Kelly, and Mel Hall, claiming they didn't know if I'd be healthy enough to play that season.

Mario, meanwhile, let Murray Chass of *The New York Times* know that a major story might be coming down the pike—and to be ready. He was vague on the details. We felt the best course of action was first to go directly to Commissioner Fay Vincent's office with what we now knew about Steinbrenner's dealings with Spira. That way, it would be Major League Baseball—not me—confirming the story.

But Howie, not surprisingly, had an agenda of his own. And so did Steinbrenner. In a sly act of journalism, the *Daily News* blew the lid off the whole situation—using both as sources and playing them off each other in a story that not only exposed Steinbrenner's payments but also revealed that the FBI was investigating Spira for extorting Steinbrenner—and had already searched his Bronx home.

Howie tipped Mario off to the story the day before it was published. I was on East 49th Street in New York at the time, meeting with the Players Association about a lockout that had delayed the start of spring training.

A throng of reporters was staking out the building, waiting for me to leave. But I slipped out a back exit, where Mario was waiting in his little Volvo, ready to take me to the airport. As we sat in traffic on the Queensboro Bridge, windows rolled down, the story was all anyone was talking about on WFAN. The media would have to settle for a "not available for comment" from me—but some of the other drivers on the bridge caught a glimpse of me enjoying every moment of what I was hearing on the radio.

In defending his actions, George claimed he paid Spira the $40,000 purely out of the goodness of his heart—no other reason. He said he was just trying to help a troubled young man straighten out his life. But then he admitted he was worried Howie might reveal embarrassing information about former Yankees employees. How Howie got that information in the first place was a mystery. It later came out that George was particularly concerned that Howie might peddle dirt on former Yankees player and manager Lou Piniella.

In explaining himself, George couldn't bring himself to say my name.

I knew it wasn't going to be business as usual when camp finally opened. How could it be? Still, I resolved to focus on playing baseball.

I arrived at spring training a day late because the judge in my family court case had summoned me to Houston for a post-trial hearing.

In Fort Lauderdale, I was greeted by all the reporters I'd dodged in New York—and then some. It was almost a year to the day since I'd left spring training to undergo back surgery. A lot had happened in the meantime.

Manager Bucky Dent and our hitting coach, Champ Summers, liked what they saw from me in the batting cage. And more importantly, I felt no pain when I took my cuts.

I hadn't planned what I was going to say to George if I ran into him at camp. I figured I'd just play it by ear. Funny thing, though, he was nowhere to be found when I arrived. I guess he was off somewhere waiting for the next shoe to drop.

Two days later, it did.

While I was preparing for the opening of the exhibition season on Florida's southeast coast, a grand jury across the state charged Spira with making physical threats against Steinbrenner and me—and with trying to extort George. Once the indictment was handed down, the FBI swooped in and arrested him at his Bronx apartment.

I hadn't expected things to move so quickly. But when your head of security is ex-FBI, I guess the agency has a way of speeding up investigations.

I didn't shed any tears for Howie. No, no, no. But the more that came out in the press about his relationship with George, the more I realized he was taking the fall for the actions of a powerful man who should've known better than to get involved in such unethical behavior.

At the end of the day, it was George's own fault that a pit bull had latched on to his wallet and wouldn't let go.

It came out that Howie spoke on the phone to Steinbrenner and McNiff hundreds of times. McNiff even wrote him a heartfelt card for his 30th birthday. They strung Howie along to get to me—and then dropped him like a hot potato.

Several of Howie's letters were attached to the indictment. In one to McNiff, he warned that George and I would need to "hire a lot of extra security" if the stress he was under worsened his mother's failing health.

Using his one phone call from the Metropolitan Correctional Center,

Howie called the *Times* to accuse George of trying to set me up—and frame him.

Against this backdrop, the hand that Steinbrenner extended to me in the spring training clubhouse felt more like a desperate gesture than a real peace offering.

With each new wrinkle to the story, *Pride of the Yankees* was turning into *Days of Our Lives*. But baseball has always been a pretty good soap opera all on its own—as the 1990 Yankees proved beyond a doubt.

Would Don Mattingly get a new contract and remain a Yankee? Yes. A good one.

Could Deion Sanders establish himself as a two-sport star in the Bronx? No, but he gave it a good run, and I would have liked to play alongside him.

Was Pascual Pérez really going to be the savior of the Yankees starting rotation? Not even close. His career ended due to injury after pitching just 17 games for the team.

And me? I was Dave Winfield, No. 31, coming off a 1-for-29 spring, fighting to regain a spot in the starting lineup, and keeping an eye on the sand slipping through the hourglass.

Chapter 16

•

BRONX EXIT

You've got to hand it to Yankees fans—they can go from nostalgic to hostile in a New York minute.

Take Opening Day 1990, which began with a solemn tribute to Billy Martin, narrated by legendary public address announcer Bob Sheppard. It featured a video montage of Billy through the years—from his days as a scrappy player to his time as a fiery, dirt-kicking manager.

Bucky Dent penciled me in as designated hitter that day, batting cleanup. The crowd's roar for Don Mattingly—who was hitting third—kept rolling when Sheppard got to my name. I'd become the highest-paid player in baseball in 1980. Now, after some public squabbles with Steinbrenner, Donnie had inherited that title in 1990.

Not bad for a guy who, as a rookie, couldn't even find someone to play ping-pong with him in the clubhouse.

But not everyone came to reminisce and cheer that day. There were growing calls for Steinbrenner to sell the team, and the game had to be delayed twice to clear a swarm of "George Must Go" balloons that someone released in the stadium. There was also a sign in the stands that read: "It Ain't Over 'til the Fat Man Sells."

And who might he sell it to? From the left-field upper deck, a group of fans started chanting: "We want Trump! We want Trump!"

Just imagine how differently American history might have played out if that had happened.

My nightmare in Texas had left me with a strong dislike for the Lone Star State. Just stepping foot there riled me up. But it was in Texas where I got right in April 1990, hitting two home runs in a game and gaining a vote of confidence from my manager.

But I knew Steinbrenner was just waiting for my next slump—sorry, "period of adjustment"—to take out his frustration on me. The balloons, the chants, the commissioner's investigation . . . it all had to be wearing on him.

Sure enough, after I went hitless for a few games, George traded for outfielder Claudell Washington, who had left the Yankees after the 1988 season. His return tightened the competition for playing time. I was 0 for my last 20 when the Yankees traded for Claudell, and I was facing the possibility of being relegated to pinch-hitting duties.

That's when we left on a fateful West Coast swing to play the Angels, A's, and Mariners.

I tried to focus on regaining my rhythm out west, but at each stop, someone different approached me to ask how I'd feel about a trade.

Reggie Jackson—retired and broadcasting Angels games that season—walked up during pregame stretching in Anaheim and asked where I'd be willing to go.

I liked and respected Reggie, but I didn't appreciate him doing George's bidding.

"Nowhere, Reggie," I told him. "Now get the fuck outta here."

In Oakland, it was general manager Pete Peterson's turn to persuade me to accept a trade. He spoke in ominous terms, warning that if I stayed with the Yankees, I'd be riding the bench.

I told him basically the same thing I told Reggie.

It's perfectly normal to wonder why I wanted to stay. I'd reached the tipping point in my relationship with the Yankees a long time ago. From a baseball standpoint, the opportunity to go somewhere I could play every day would help boost my value as a free agent.

The main reason I wouldn't go quietly is that I had promised myself I would only leave on my own terms, in a deal that made sense for me. But there was another reason, one I didn't fully realize at the time.

My time in Yankee pinstripes had in some ways conditioned me to the drama-filled culture Steinbrenner had built. George and I had become almost dependent on each other for conflict, motivation, and maybe even validation.

That resulted in a frustrating decade for both the team and me.

Despite missing the 1989 season, I ranked among the major league leaders in home runs and RBIs for the decade. But I didn't have a ring. The Yankees won more games than any other team in the '80s, but we couldn't turn that sustained success into division titles. According to the "Steinbrenner Doctrine"—which held that anything short of a championship was a failure—we had failed.

I went into the last leg of the road trip in Seattle hitting just .213. It was so bad that Bucky had me come out early to take batting practice with the reserves. If that's the way it was going to be, I'd accept it and bide my time until they had to put me back in the lineup.

After I finished taking my cuts, he called me into his small office in the visitors' clubhouse.

"Take your uniform off," he said. "You're no longer a Yankee."

Bucky told me they'd just traded me to the Angels. The words hit me like a shock wave. I hadn't expected to find out about a deal *after* it had already been made. It wasn't supposed to happen this way. As a 10-and-5 player, it was my right to approve or reject any trade.

Twenty minutes later, the Yankees convened a shotgun press conference in the same glorified broom closet where Dent had broken the news to me.

A group of beleaguered beat writers—worn down by the road trip as much as the nonstop stream of headlines over the past year—gathered around Dent and Peterson, who told them I was going to the Angels for pitcher Mike Witt.

Suddenly, an uninvited guest appeared in the back of the room—me.

"I'm not going anywhere!" I blurted out. "I'll make the choice when and where and how I go. I guess I'm going to be in limbo. Can I catch a cab to limbo?"

Instead, I caught a cab back to the hotel, where Tonya was just returning from Pike Place Market with Dungeness crab and fresh fruit for what was supposed to be a postgame dinner.

"What are you doing here?" she asked.

"They traded me," I told her.

She looked almost relieved.

"But I'm going to fight it," I added.

I called my agent, Jeff Klein, and let him know I'd be returning to New York the next morning to talk strategy.

When the Yankees got back home after the Seattle series, I was in the clubhouse waiting for them, ready to suit up for that night's game against the Twins. But a few hours before first pitch, Commissioner Fay Vincent ruled I couldn't play, because, technically, I was no longer a Yankee. The contract I signed in 1980 included a list of seven teams that I could be traded to—and the Angels were one of them.

But the players' union saw it differently, encouraging me to assert the rights it had collectively bargained for veteran players like me.

As my case moved to arbitration, Steinbrenner tried to distance himself from the trade, telling reporters that Dent and Peterson had been the ones pushing for it.

"It was handled about as poorly as we could handle it," he said.

On a phone call with Jeff and me, he apologized for what was happening. He said he couldn't rescind the trade, but if the arbitrator ruled in my favor, he'd be happy to have me back in a Yankees uniform—and that I'd even get my right-field job back.

Before security could boot me from the clubhouse, I called over some reporters and told them exactly what George had said.

Given the history of our relationship, George's position made no sense. There was only one plausible explanation: He was scared. The commissioner held his fate in his hands, and he was trying to play nice before that ruling came down—and maybe even convince me to testify against Howie Spira.

The arbitrator never made a ruling.

A day after my meeting with George, Angels owner Gene Autry—a former actor and musician known as "The Singing Cowboy"—rode in on horseback and ended the standoff by offering me a three-year, $9.1 million contract extension with generous buyout provisions.

Even though only one of those years was guaranteed, it was an offer I couldn't refuse.

I quickly wrote a farewell note to New York:

> My love affair with metropolitan New York and its people started in 1981 and will continue and deepen for as long as I live . . . My first regret is to leave at all, and a larger regret is to leave with my Yankee dream of a world championship for baseball's greatest fans unfulfilled and unaccomplished.

I ended the letter by reaffirming my commitment to continuing the work of my foundation in the New York area.

After I faxed the letter to reporters, Mario picked me up in Manhattan for a final drive to the airport. So much had happened in the six months since our last airport run. A few conversations with Spira had resulted in the whole house of cards crashing down.

We didn't say much on the ride. I knew we'd talk again soon. I looked out the window at the passing parade of people on West 43rd Street—knowing I was headed for Disneyland and feeling elated about it.

But first, it was off to Milwaukee to meet my new team. I caught a flight out of Newark and arrived just in time to pinch-hit against the Brewers that night.

•

I was leaving behind a team that was 13–18 and already six games out of first place—and joining a club that was in an even deeper hole. It was something of a Padres reunion for me. Manager Doug Rader—he of the tone-deaf comment about *Roots* that almost got him popped in the face—had been a teammate of mine in San Diego. And Mike Port, Anaheim's general manager, had been the Padres' minor league director during the mid-'70s.

Rader welcomed me to the team with a handshake and a warm hug—proof we'd have no trouble putting the past issues behind us.

When we got back to California from the road trip, I got to meet Autry—the man who deserved a medal for breaking the impasse between the Yankees and me. Over lunch, he welcomed me to the team and told me how much he admired my philanthropy. At 83, he'd largely handed day-to-day control of the team over to his wife, Jackie, but he was still deeply invested in the franchise he had owned since its inception in 1961.

"So tell me about George," he said with a grin.

It wasn't his first go-around with an exiled Yankee—he'd signed Reggie after the 1981 season.

"What's there to say?" I replied. "I think you and I are going to get along a whole lot better than he and I did."

"Yeah, he's a first-class SOB, ain't he?"

I almost spat out my iced tea.

Someone once summed up the difference between Gene and George in the following way: Autry lived by the Cowboy Code, Steinbrenner adhered to the Win-or-Else Code.

I wasn't quite ready to ride off into the sunset—but for the first time in a while, the trail ahead looked wide open.

The pieces were already in place for the Angels to succeed—just as they had been the season before when they won 91 games.

I wanted to make it clear to Rader that no one on the coaching staff needed to treat me with kid gloves. I hadn't come to the West Coast just to . . . coast. I was there to put in the work to become the hitter I still knew I could be.

But, first, I had to have a conversation with the team's young pitching ace, Chuck Finley, about the No. 31 jersey he was wearing. It was the number I'd worn since college, and I hoped to continue that tradition.

"Hey, Chuck, man—what's it gonna take for me to get thirty-one?" I asked, unsure of what I'd be willing to offer.

It didn't come to that.

"Nah, Winny, thirty-one is my number," he replied. "That's what I like."

So I got fitted for a No. 32 jersey—the number worn by my good friends Magic Johnson and Kirby Puckett—and got ready to go to work.

Fifteen years earlier with the Padres, I'd made a major adjustment to my hitting style by standing farther from the plate. This change allowed me to extend my arms and drive the ball more effectively. Then, during my first spring training with the Yankees in 1981, I made a second adjustment: cocking my front leg, shifting my weight back, and striding forward with my hands set further behind me. This helped me cover more of the plate.

Regardless of where I stood in the box or how I positioned myself, I'd always had a lot of movement in my hands before swinging. That worked when my reflexes were at their peak, but as I got older, that little bit of extra motion could mean the difference between making contact and being late on a pitch.

Rader and his hitting coaches had an idea for improving my reaction time. Instead of hitting off a pitching machine from the usual 60 feet six inches away, I faced pitches from just 50 feet away. The shorter distance forced me to keep my hands still—a habit I planned to carry with me onto the field.

When it came to daily motivation and staying sharp mentally, I wanted to be my own best coach—so I turned to a video I'd made of myself deep beneath Yankee Stadium, where I had set up a camera on a tripod and filmed my own swings.

Equal parts pep talk and instructional video, the VHS tape also included clips of 15 or 20 at-bats, each illustrating the approach to hitting that I tried to emulate every time I came to the plate. The video featured verbal reminders of the routine I needed to follow—everything from scanning the defense for clues about how I'd be pitched to displaying the kind of body language that told the pitcher I was ready to inflict damage on the baseball.

I leaned on those mental reminders as I embarked on the next chapter of my career.

•

Anaheim was a lot like San Diego when it came to press coverage of the hometown team. *The Orange County Register* was the paper of record, while the *Los Angeles Times* assigned a reporter to the team—but saved most of its resources for the Dodgers. That didn't mean *Register* writers lacked bite. One referred to me as a "Yankees castoff" and warned that the trade might prove to be "an unsuccessful reach."

I had my skeptics, but I was happy to be there. Recovering from surgery in Los Angeles had reminded me what I'd always liked about Southern California: the weather, the water, the laid-back pace of life.

I was a bicoastal media darling now. A few times a week, an Angels media rep would tell me a reporter from New York wanted a comment on MLB's investigation of Steinbrenner. I always returned the calls, but in most cases, I didn't have anything to say for attribution. They were looking for quotes—but in the days before there was easy access to online news, I was the one relying on them to keep up to date on what was happening back in New York. I pumped them for as much information as they had.

The Steinbrenner probe was being led by John Dowd, the same lawyer whose investigation had resulted in Pete Rose's lifetime ban from baseball. In early June 1990, Dowd submitted his confidential report to Commissioner Vincent. Now it was up to the commissioner to hold a hearing and decide if Steinbrenner had violated any clauses of the collective bargaining agreement. I wasn't an expert on every article and subsection of the CBA, but I had enough common sense to know George's actions were wrong—and that he needed to be held accountable.

On the same day Spira pleaded not guilty in federal court to charges of extorting Steinbrenner and threatening both of us, George sat before Vincent. It all came down to one question: Had he violated "the best interests of baseball" rule, which gives the commissioner broad authority to mete out punishment?

Before their meeting was even over, Vincent issued a separate ruling. He found Steinbrenner had committed tampering by meeting with me after the trade. Vincent said that George's promise to give me my right-field job had forced the Angels to sweeten their offer. He fined him $25,000 and ordered the Yankees to pay $200,000 to the Angels.

I didn't take the time to read the transcript of George's entire testimony. I didn't need to—I'd already lived it, either directly or vicariously. *SportsCenter* reports that played in the Angels' clubhouse confirmed what I suspected he would say. His main defense was that he was scared of Spira and paid him in the hope that he'd go away. But George also claimed the money was well spent, because Howie had provided him with accurate information about me. Why, George asked, wasn't the league office questioning me the same way they were questioning him?

It was a last-ditch attempt to discredit me.

The next day, Claire Smith of *The New York Times* helped put his question to rest.

"There is no reason to look at Dave Winfield any further than we did," Vincent told her.

As fate would have it, I was with family and friends in Minnesota, playing a night game against the Twins when Vincent announced his decision: Steinbrenner was barred for life from running the Yankees.

In the clubhouse after the game, I saw a clip of fans at Yankee Stadium erupting in cheers at the news.

I hadn't yet heard the details of Vincent's ruling, so when reporters flocked to my locker for reaction, I kept it simple.

"I'm vindicated," I said.

In the days that followed, I found out more.

The best line in the ruling was that George had demonstrated "a pattern of behavior that borders on the bizarre."

Even more bizarre was that Vincent had been prepared to give him a two-year suspension—but George opted instead for the lifetime ban. He'd already been suspended once by Major League Baseball—in 1974, after the conviction for making illegal contributions to Richard Nixon—and apparently preferred what he considered the softer language of the sanction he accepted. The reality of it was that he could no longer sit in the owner's box and had his ownership stake reduced from general partner to limited partner.

But what about any of this *wasn't* bizarre?

Nowhere in these pages have I tried to explain George's motivations. That's a task best left to others—preferably those with advanced degrees in psychology. He was complex—or at least hard to figure out. That much I can say.

Maybe George was in denial, or maybe he believed a lifetime ban wasn't really a lifetime ban.

I also knew him well enough to recognize he was a showman. This was a guy who once kept the Mets off the front cover of the *New York Post* by grabbing a rake and helping the grounds crew get the field ready for a game. George loved nothing more than seeing a Yankees headline dominate the newspapers. And what better way to get front-page headlines than to sacrifice himself at the altar of Fay Vincent. Suspensions are for suckers. Real men get lifetime bans.

I'll throw out one more possibility: Maybe, just maybe, he did some soul-searching and realized that everyone, himself included, would be better off if he stepped aside. Maybe he finally understood that the spotlight should be on the players the fans came to see—not on a loud, controversial owner.

Coincidentally—or not—after the commissioner's ruling, I went on an absolute tear at the plate. I was seeing the ball well, squaring it up, and helping to lead a suddenly potent Angels offense.

I didn't have my return to the Bronx circled on the calendar—but that doesn't mean our three-game set against the Yankees starting on Labor Day was just another series. Playing your former team—especially after a bad breakup—is like being stuck in a house with your ex for three days. Not that the house was particularly crowded. Many Yankees fans had already checked out on the season.

As we wrapped up warmups, Rader walked over to me.

"Hey, Winny, you wanna bring out the lineup card?"

I hadn't realized players could be part of that ritual, but I appreciated the gesture. Doug knew what I'd been through in New York and wanted me to have that moment.

The crowd gave me a nice round of applause when I handed the card to the home-plate umpire.

When I stepped to the plate in the first inning, someone about 20 rows up unfurled a white sheet with bold black letters: "Dave Come Home."

My eyes kept climbing, past the sign, up toward the owner's box. It was empty. The succession plan hadn't gone as expected. George's son, Hank, had declined the opportunity, and the newly named successor, Robert Nederlander, hadn't been approved by the league yet.

The informal welcoming-back ceremony culminated with a standing ovation when I took my spot in right field in the bottom of the first.

I went 0-for-4 with a run scored in the first game of the series—a 7–0 win for the Angels. Taking two out of three in New York put us over .500. We weren't going to catch the A's for the division title, but after a dismal start to the season, we'd worked our way back to respectability.

A couple of weeks later, we hosted the Mariners, whose outfield included my former teammate Ken Griffey and his son Junior, who I hadn't seen up close since he was a 13-year-old hanging around the Yankees' clubhouse.

It turned out to be a special night. In the first inning, the Griffeys hit back-to-back home runs to almost identical spots in left-center field. No father and son had ever homered in the same game before—let alone one right after the other.

It choked me up, thinking back to when Billy Martin had banned Junior from sitting in the Yankees dugout with his dad. Now, "The Kid" was the fastest rising star in baseball.

But I was only so sentimental. The Griffeys had their moment, and then I had mine. In the third inning, I hit a three-run home run to give us the lead. And after the Mariners tied it up, I went deep again in the seventh to seal the win.

In 112 games with the Angels that season, I hit .275 with 19 home runs and 72 RBIs, becoming the active major league leader in RBIs—and putting to rest any doubts about the health of my back.

The Yankees may have thought they were exiling me when they traded me—but in reality, they had done me a tremendous favor, right down to the fact that I was now a short drive up the 405 from my Los Angeles home. In recognition of my performance in Anaheim, the writers at *The Sporting News* named me Comeback Player of the Year.

Meanwhile, back in New York, the ship had run aground.

In one of his final acts as general partner, Steinbrenner fired Bucky Dent. Mattingly missed a large portion of the season with a back injury. Deion Sanders left the team in July to return to the NFL. And Mike Witt—the guy they traded me for—got injured too. Over three seasons with the Yankees, he won only eight games before arm trouble prematurely ended his career.

When all was said and done, the Yankees experienced their worst season in nearly 80 years, losing 95 games. On top of that, Lou Piniella, who George had fired as manager after the 1988 season, won the World Series with the Reds that year.

But George seemed to cope with all the chaos just fine. To prove that he could laugh at himself, I guess, he agreed to host *Saturday Night Live*.

Ironically, the musical guest that night was Morris Day and the Time—a funk band that shared my Minnesota roots. I could only imagine what Morris and George might have talked about in the green room.

I can't say whether George was actually funny—I didn't watch the show. But one thing was for sure: He wasn't going to just fade away.

And neither was I.

I wasn't long for the Angels, but I'll always credit them with revitalizing my career and helping me rediscover a sense of happiness, relief, and comfort—feelings I hadn't felt in a sustained way in a long time. I also admire the organization for being one of the first to employ a mental strength coach. Recognizing and embracing the psychological elements of the game was an important step forward.

Tonya couldn't help but notice that I seemed relaxed during a baseball season for the first time since she'd met me. My game-day wardrobe sent that message loud and clear: loose-fitting Zubaz pants—the kind rapper MC Hammer made famous—and a pair of flip-flops.

I gave off a casual vibe, but the fire in my belly still burned. Pushing 40, I didn't know how many more shots I'd have at a dream season. So I made myself a promise: my comeback wasn't over—on the field . . . or in a court of law.

Chapter 17

I WILL GET BY

I was feeling whole again on the baseball field—and I wanted to bring that same sense of calm and balance to my personal life. Marrying Tonya was the best decision I ever made—and 38 years later, it still is. But the shadow of my court case in Texas continued to hang over me, preventing me from fully enjoying that happiness.

I needed to find a way to reveal just how unfair the ruling in that case had been. And because everything in my life was connected, that path led straight to Steinbrenner's favorite tipster, Howie Spira.

Steinbrenner wasn't the only person Howie had tried to extort. He'd also got his hooks into Sandra Renfro's attorney, Earle Lilly, threatening to expose scores of taped phone calls between them. That led to two more counts of extortion being filed against him.

The cassette that my friend Mario sent me at Christmastime the year before said it all. On it, Lilly agreed with Spira that his client's claim of being married to me was nonsense. I sought to have the verdict against me overturned based on Lilly's own words, along with other evidence I'd begun to gather showing Sandra and I weren't even close to being legally married.

Opening Day of the 1991 baseball season coincided with the opening of Spira's trial in US District Court in Manhattan. Happily, I was 3,000 miles away in Seattle for games against the Mariners—this time fully enjoying the Dungeness crab from Pike Place Market that had tasted bitter on the day the Yankees traded me.

Mario had been subpoenaed as a potential witness by both the defense and prosecution. As a neutral—but still interested—party whose name was bouncing around the courtroom, I asked him to keep me posted on the testimony.

Spira's defense was that Steinbrenner paid him for information he believed he could use against me—not out of the goodness of his heart, and not because of threats.

According to Howie, his demand for more money was a dispute over payment for services rendered—not extortion. Spira's lawyer quipped that Steinbrenner's shifting explanations for why he paid Howie matched the number of managers he'd fired.

The prosecution introduced Spira's letters and phone calls to Steinbrenner and his associate Phil McNiff to show that Howie's threats to reveal damaging information about the Yankees then crossed the line into physical threats—including against me.

"I'm afraid I'm gonna lose control and kill Dave and then myself," he said in one of the calls played for the jury.

Thankfully, I was alive and well, doing my best to stay relevant beyond the tawdry details of the Spira trial. I got off to a blistering start to the '91 season—including a game in Minnesota where I smacked three home runs, which helped earn me American League Player of the Week honors.

The Angels' media department pounced on my success, featuring me and teammate Dave Parker on the cover of a game program with a photo of a lightning storm and the headline "Daves of Thunder"—a nod to the hit Tom Cruise movie *Days of Thunder*.

Parker and I were the same age, the same size, and had broken into the majors around the same time. I used to envy him for having Willie Stargell in the Pirates' clubhouse to mentor him. Now, he and I were the OGs in

Anaheim, sharing stories with the young bucks about playing ball in the 1970s—when some of them were still learning their ABCs.

There was an overall sense of camaraderie in the Angels' clubhouse that stood in contrast to the atmosphere with the Yankees, where everyone always seemed to be walking on eggshells. I'd had teammates in New York whom I'd considered friends—Don Baylor, Willie Randolph, and Rickey Henderson, to name a few—but I wouldn't say we ever experienced anything close to true team unity.

In New York, players' wives had to wait in a parking lot to meet their husbands after games. With the Angels, a family lounge allowed Tonya to get to know my teammates' significant others.

In Anaheim, the social dynamics flowed more freely. One time, in Detroit, pitcher Mark Langston asked if I wanted to join him and some of the guys for a Grateful Dead concert. My style was more fur and leather than tie-dye and flannel—but I thought, *Why not?*

I asked Langston to name some of the band's songs. When he did, I didn't recognize any of the titles. Then he popped a cassette into his Walkman, handed me his headphones, and a song about getting by and surviving filled my ears.

"Not bad," I said, taking off the headphones. "Sounds like a white guy's version of a Gloria Gaynor song."

"It's called 'Touch of Grey,'" Langston said. "Could be your new theme song, Winny."

We laughed.

We stood out in the crowd, a bunch of clean-cut ballplayers who probably looked like undercover cops. I didn't know any of the songs they played that night—except for a 25-minute psychedelic cover of Chuck Berry's "Johnny B. Goode." At least I think that's what it was—but I had a great time.

When we got back to the hotel, Langston invited a friend who was in town to play a few tunes in the hotel bar. So there we sat, drinking beer and listening to Bruce Hornsby—who was performing with the Dead at the time—play piano until the wee hours of the morning. Still high—on music—we went out the next day on barely any sleep and beat the Tigers.

Mario, who had become my personal Court TV correspondent, called me early one morning with an update on the Spira trial, which was wrapping up after four weeks. Despite knowing more about the allegations than anyone, he wasn't called to testify, but he hung around to listen to the other witnesses—including Steinbrenner, who nearly broke down in tears, lamenting how the ordeal with Spira had ruined his good name.

As the case was about to go to the jury, Mario came face-to-face with George in the witness room. It was the first time the two had met. Mario's work had been in the shadows—his name or picture had never appeared in the papers. Even Steinbrenner's investigators probably had no idea how much he'd done to help expose everything.

But George was a savvy guy—he knew Mario was somebody.

"Hi, I'm George," he said, extending his hand. "I hear you do good work."

Mario shook it.

"Hi, George. I'm Mario. I work for the Winfield Foundation."

I don't know what George was expecting to get out of the conversation, but the mere mention of the words "Winfield Foundation" hit him like kryptonite. Without saying another word, he packed up his briefcase and walked away.

Spira was found guilty—and later sentenced to 2½ years in federal prison.

Steinbrenner tried to spin the verdict as a rejection of the fairness of his lifetime ban from baseball, but Commissioner Vincent threw cold water on that idea, making it clear that the criminal case against Spira and the baseball investigation of Steinbrenner were separate matters.

We were at home playing the Yankees when the Spira verdict came in. I tripled and homered in the series, letting my bat shape the narrative—and reducing the number of "What about George?" and "What about Howie?" questions I had to answer.

The arc of my life and career called for glances back to the past, but as long as I continued to put on a uniform, I was intent on keeping both eyes locked on the future.

I used the occasion of the Spira verdict to shift the conversation toward what I still hoped to accomplish. Another five years in the majors felt like a real possibility. Without uttering their names, I delivered a clear message: George was out of baseball, Howie was headed to prison . . . but I was still going strong.

In June, I became the oldest player in major league history to hit for the cycle. Then in August, I hit my 400th career home run. In fact, I hit more homers that season than I had since 1983. It wasn't all roses, though—I also struck out more than I ever had in a season, and my on-base percentage dropped to a career low.

We got great pitching from Langston, Chuck Finley, and Jim Abbott—whose performance on the mound with only one hand was nothing short of awe-inspiring. But as a team, we just didn't hit, finishing near the bottom of the American League in home runs, RBIs, and runs scored.

After a miserable July and rough start to August, Doug Rader was fired as manager. Dave Parker was released in September. The team struggled to reach .500. All signs pointed to the Angels entering rebuild mode—and to them declining the option years on my contract.

On October 3, I woke up to the realization that I was now officially 40 years old. The team had just returned from Toronto and had an off day before the final series of the season. Tonya and I planned a nice dinner out to celebrate the big 4-0.

We enjoyed a relaxing morning at our LA home, drinking coffee and reading the paper. But it was a little too quiet. No one—not even my brother, Steve—called to wish me a happy birthday. So I called him—but got no answer. I tried to reach a few friends, but no one picked up. It made me wonder if Pacific Bell was having some kind of outage.

This was before Facebook reminded everyone of your birthday, so I figured people were just going about their business on a fall Thursday and would check in when they had time.

By the time Tonya and I were ready to head to the restaurant, I still hadn't heard from anyone. She could see I was sulking.

"I need to make a quick stop at the clubhouse before we go," she said, referring to the building in our new Bel-Air community where people hosted events. "Sid and Ethel are celebrating their 60th anniversary. I said we'd drop by to say hello."

It was a ruse, of course. When we walked into the darkened clubhouse, the lights flipped on and dozens of people jumped out and shouted, "Surprise!"

The first faces I saw were Gene and Jackie Autry, who came over to hug me. Steve was there, along with my childhood friend JD—and 15 or 20 of my Angels teammates and their partners. It was a special evening, equal parts birthday celebration and going-away party. The Autrys were among the last to leave, sharing co-hosting duties with Tonya, mingling with everyone, and even showing off their moves on a makeshift dance floor.

About a week later, I got a belated birthday present: an appeals court ruling that overturned the verdict in my family court case in Texas. I was in Maine with Tonya, enjoying the fall colors and eating lobster when the news came through.

The court confirmed what my legal team had suspected all along—that the trial judge's improper jury instructions had influenced the jury to rule in Sandra Renfro's favor. The ruling gave me another bite at the apple—and this time, I was going to make it count.

One by one, my nemeses were facing the music. My career felt back on track—even with the uncertainty of where I'd be playing next. Tonya and I had survived a test to our marriage—and emerged stronger.

Things were falling into place.

•

It ended up being a mutual—and amicable—parting of ways between the Angels and me. The new manager Buck Rodgers let me know I wouldn't be in line for much playing time, and I let him know I'd be happy to go elsewhere.

In December 1991, I signed a one-year contract with the Blue Jays, a team coming off an American League East title the year before.

In a nice twist, the Blue Jays had signed pitcher Jack Morris to a free-agent deal just a day earlier—a move the Yankees had declined to make after the 1986 season due to collusion. Five years later, Morris was still at the top of his game, having just helped lead the Twins to a championship.

I missed the last 10 games of Blue Jays' spring training with a sore left hamstring but proved on the last day of camp that I was physically ready for the regular season. It wasn't because of anything I did on the field.

It seemed Sandra's lawyers, who were preparing for a new trial, had sent a process server to Dunedin, Florida, to hand me a summons for the next hearing in Texas. The guy was milling around the complex, asking my coaches and teammates where I could be found. I guess he wasn't much of a baseball fan, because he couldn't tell me from Joe Carter, Devon White, or any of the other Black players on the team. But I knew what *he* looked like, and I spent a few days evading him.

On the last day of camp, he boldly walked onto the team bus looking for me—but I hadn't boarded yet.

"Where's Dave Winfield?" he asked. "I've got papers for him."

The glares he got from my teammates let him know he needed to get his ass off the bus.

He waited on the sidewalk for a few minutes and then decided to look for me inside the stadium, where I was gathering the last of my things.

I was crossing the outfield when I saw him, with nowhere really to go except for the clubhouse—where I knew he'd have me cornered. I was about ready to give myself up when I saw an equipment truck rolling across the field, loaded with gear and headed for the airport.

He was maybe a few hundred feet away and closing fast—or as fast as a chubby guy in khakis and a dress shirt could close.

I banged on the driver's door.

"Open up the back, man!"

"What? I can't do that!"

"Do it! And hurry!"

My adversary broke into a jog as the driver reluctantly unlocked the back of the truck. I jumped in and wedged myself among the bats, gloves, and pitching machines.

"Now close it back up, and let's get the hell out of here!" I shouted.

We cleared the walls of the stadium, and a few minutes later, we were on the grounds of the Clearwater airport.

Sandra's lawyers would hear from me when I was ready—and that time was drawing near.

Chapter 18

WINFIELD WANTS NOISE

Goodbye, sunny California. Hello, the Great White North—or more accurately, hello to a temperature-controlled domed stadium in Canada's largest city. At least the seagulls weren't in danger anymore. I moved into a waterfront apartment on Queens Quay—close enough to walk to the ballpark—and started getting excited for the season ahead.

The acquisitions of veterans like Jack Morris and me helped bolster an already talented team. I had no doubt we could compete for a division title—but I wasn't there just to win a division or a pennant. I was there to win it all.

My manager was my friend and former Padres teammate Cito Gaston. The general manager was Pat Gillick, who had been trying to acquire me for years. I knew both men believed in me and trusted me as a leader, so I took it upon myself to help build a championship-level culture in the Blue Jays' clubhouse.

That meant coming on stronger than I ever had before.

On Opening Day in Detroit, I laid out my goals to the team—short and sweet.

"Alright, you MF's," I said with a smile, immediately getting everyone's attention. "We're going to kick some ass and win it all this year! I don't know about you, but I'm starting things off right. Get your asses on base and I'll drive you in. Let's go out there and begin our road to the World Series!"

I got three hits, Morris pitched a complete game, and we won the first of six straight to open the season.

But I'd been through enough 162-game grinds to know that divisions, pennants, and World Series titles aren't won in April. To get where we wanted, we needed to stay locked in.

One day, I was sitting on the bench with Cito before a game. First pitch was 15 minutes away. I looked around and noticed it was just me, him, and a few guys.

"Where is everyone?" I asked.

Being the laid-back guy he was, Cito just shrugged.

"I'll be back," I told him.

I walked to the clubhouse and saw about five or six guys goofing off—some still half-dressed, a few scarfing down Egg McMuffins from McDonald's. One of them was David Wells, the former "Winfield Kid" who used to sit in the right-field pavilion at Padres games.

I grabbed the food and threw it in the trash.

Then I told everyone to get their uniforms on and their asses out there before the national anthem started playing. Or else.

They looked like a bunch of kids caught sneaking cigarettes and girlie magazines. But they got their asses where they belonged. Nothing like that happened again for the rest of the season.

I made sure I was always around to keep guys honest. When Candy Maldonado blared his Puerto Rican pop music in the clubhouse or David Cone showed up late for the anthems, they were hauled in front of the team's kangaroo court.

If I wanted to effectively motivate my teammates, I knew I needed to lead by example. No one was going to listen to a guy who couldn't hit his weight just because he'd been around a long time.

It helped that I was batting .303 with 14 home runs and 47 RBIs at the

All-Star break—more than enough production in most years to earn a trip to the Midsummer Classic. But in the final days of voting, I fell from third to fourth place among American League outfielders, which meant AL manager Tom Kelly would have to choose me as a reserve.

Instead, he picked my teammate Joe Carter. I was disappointed by the snub—especially since the game was being played in San Diego—but the three days off were a blessing in disguise. They allowed me to recharge for the second half of the season, which turned out to be tremendous. I set a Blue Jays record with 32 RBIs in August.

From late May on, we never relinquished first place—becoming the first team in major league history to draw four million fans in a season.

We clinched the division at home on the second-to-last day of the season. When the sellout crowd realized the celebration fell on my 41st birthday, they serenaded me with "Happy Birthday." That brought tears to my eyes.

Leading the team in games played, I turned in one of the best statistical seasons of my career—26 home runs, 108 RBIs, and a .290 average. I came in fifth in American League MVP voting.

The connection I felt to the team and community inspired me to revive my foundation by sponsoring a breakfast program in Ontario schools called "Win With Winfield."

In my only previous postseason appearance—with the Yankees during the strike-shortened 1981 season—we knew as early as August that we were headed to the playoffs, regardless of how we played down the stretch.

This time felt different. We'd played well all year and finished strong, going on a tear in September to fend off the Brewers. Clinching the division in Game 161 meant we entered the American League Championship Series against Oakland with real momentum.

The franchise and I both had demons to exorcise.

My struggles in the 1981 World Series had haunted me throughout my time in New York. The Blue Jays, meanwhile, had come up empty in three recent trips to the ALCS.

I didn't feel the need to deliver another fiery speech to the team, because I was confident by then that this Blue Jays group wasn't going to settle for anything less than a championship.

The A's were a stacked team, led by Mark McGwire, José Canseco, and my old friend Rickey Henderson. After winning two of the first three games of the series, we trailed 6–1 heading into the eighth inning of Game 4. A three-run rally in the eighth pulled us closer, and then in the ninth, Robbie Alomar took A's closer Dennis Eckersley deep for a two-run, game-tying homer. We went on to win the game—and the series, four games to two.

I hit two home runs in the series, both in losing efforts, but my seven runs scored led the team. One of my homers sailed directly over a sign in left field that read "Winfield for PM"—a flattering sentiment, even if I wasn't exactly prime minister material . . . or Canadian. I was feeling the love.

For the first time since signing with the Yankees nearly 12 years earlier, I appeared on the cover of *Sports Illustrated*, sliding into second base in a game against the A's. I hoped to grace it again if we beat the Braves in the World Series.

The Braves were looking to avenge a World Series loss the previous season. They weren't pushovers by any stretch, but man for man, I knew we were the better team. It was more than that, though. We *needed* to win. It felt like destiny.

After splitting the first two games in Atlanta, we returned to Toronto for the next three.

All season long, we'd been drawing capacity crowds of 50,000, but somehow they managed to squeeze in a few thousand more for the first-ever World Series game played outside the United States.

Back in September, I'd told reporters that, despite all the fans we drew, SkyDome was still a lot quieter than a lot of other stadiums. Maybe it was Canadian restraint that kept Blue Jays fans from screaming their heads off. But I felt I needed to challenge them to be louder. My words touched a nerve, because the very next day, a young fan showed up to a game with a sign that read: "WINFIELD WANTS NOISE!"

The Blue Jays' PR team liked the slogan, and before long, it was flashing on the scoreboard during pivotal moments of games.

Our fans rose to the challenge. For Game 3, SkyDome was loud—louder than anywhere I'd ever played.

It was a tight battle throughout. We scored a run in the fourth inning, but the Braves answered with a run in the sixth. In the eighth, we traded runs, setting the stage for a dramatic finish.

The crowd let out a collective exhale when the Braves were retired in the top of the ninth. Now we had a chance to reward those fans—to show them that we'd heard them.

The decibel level climbed even higher after Alomar started the bottom of the ninth with a single and then stole second, prompting the Braves to intentionally walk Joe Carter with first base now open.

That brought me to the plate.

I understood the move. Joe was a dangerous hitter, and putting him on gave the Braves a better chance at turning a double play. Still, it's hard not to take it personally when a team essentially says, "We'd rather face you." I wasn't used to that.

So with the game on the line—and a "Winfield of Dreams" sign hanging from a facade down the third-base line—I strode to the plate to face right-handed rookie Mark Wohlers, exuding the don't-mess-with-me swagger I'd projected my whole career. With towels and miniature Canadian flags waving in the stands, I kicked at the dirt around home plate, did a few deep-knee bends, took some vicious practice swings, and glanced down at third-base coach Rich Hacker, who gave me the sign to swing away.

And then I squared and laid down a bunt—just like I was taught all those years ago on a rain-soaked day at Oxford Playground.

The Braves' defense was caught off guard by my sacrifice. The ball bounced past the pitcher and was fielded by the first baseman, giving the runners on first and second plenty of time to move up a base. With one out, the winning run was 90 feet away.

Later that inning—with the bases now loaded—Maldonado lifted a ball over a drawn-in outfield to bring Alomar home.

That night, the Puerto Rican music blared—kangaroo court wasn't in session.

The next day, I called my youth coach Bill Peterson.

"How'd you like that bunt?"

He reeled off a string of superlatives that almost brought me to tears.

"You taught me well, Bill."

After pulling out another tight win in Game 4, we had champagne on ice, but we dropped Game 5 at home and had to board a flight back to Atlanta to try to finish off the Braves.

For most of the season, Cito had used me as the designated hitter. With no DH in National League ballparks back then, he decided to get creative, putting me in right field, moving Joe Carter to first base, and sending John Olerud—who'd been swinging a hot bat—to the bench.

I wanted to reward his belief in me.

Game 6 gave me the ultimate opportunity to prove what I already knew—but hadn't had a chance to show in more than a decade: I didn't shrink from career-defining moments.

Top of the 11th. Two outs. Two runners on base. Tie game.

I stepped to the plate 4-for-21 in the series, with no extra-base hits and just one RBI. I was either going to meet the moment—or come up short on baseball's biggest stage. But, like I said, I felt destiny was on my side.

I knew I'd had success against Braves pitcher Charlie Leibrandt back when we were both in the American League. He threw a lot of off-speed stuff, and as long as I didn't chase the pitches that fluttered out of the strike zone, I believed I had the edge.

It was almost a year to the day that my friend Kirby Puckett had crushed a hanging Leibrandt changeup over the center field wall for a walk-off homer in Game 6 of the 1991 World Series. I was hoping he'd make the same mistake with me.

I took a pitch outside, swung through one out of the zone, took another in the dirt, looked at a low strike, and laid off a curveball low and away. The count ran full.

Leibrandt didn't want to walk me to load the bases—so I sat on his changeup, got one I liked, and rocketed it down the left-field line, past third baseman Terry Pendleton, who wasn't guarding the line.

Devon White and Robbie Alomar both came around to score as I pulled into second base standing up. Most players will tell you that hitting a home run—especially in a critical moment of a big game—is a sensation that can't be topped. I won't argue with that, but I'll also put in a plug for the feeling of ripping a go-ahead double and standing in the middle of the field as 50,000 fans go from tomahawk chopping to dead silence. That's a vantage point from which you can really admire your handiwork. I looked up and smiled at the small band of Blue Jays fans who had made the trip to Atlanta. They were easy to spot—they were the only ones still making noise.

We needed both of those runs, because the Braves got one back in the bottom of the 11th to cut our lead to 4–3. With a runner on third base and two outs, Otis Nixon of the Braves tried to bunt for a hit—but he couldn't leg it out.

We were World Series champs.

Back in Toronto, a packed SkyDome crowd celebrated right along with us.

With four gritty one-run wins, we'd reached the top of the mountain. But that's the kind of team we were, mentally tough and at our best when the game was on the line. Our manager wasn't scared of losing his job after every three-game losing streak. Our players didn't have to worry about being called out in the papers after a couple of bad games. Quite simply, we had a culture and atmosphere that was conducive to winning.

I was on cloud nine. What made the moment even sweeter was the fact that Cito became the first Black manager to win a World Series.

A few days later, I appeared on *Charlie Rose.* His producers identified me on screen as "Former New York Yankee" Dave Winfield. Charlie tried hard to get me to talk about what winning it all meant to me considering my history with Steinbrenner—but I wouldn't bite. Living well felt like the best revenge, and I was World Series champion Dave Winfield.

"If I don't play another day, I'd say I had a hell of a career," I told Rose.

But I was having too much fun in the twilight of my career to just walk away.

And wouldn't you know it, "former New York Yankee" George Steinbrenner wasn't done yet, either.

Chapter 19

•

HOMECOMING

My final trip to the SkyDome as a Blue Jay was magical. Around 250,000 people gathered along our victory parade route that led to the stadium. The cars we rode in crawled through the crowd, stopping occasionally so that we could high-five and chat with our jubilant fans. It was an up-close-and-personal celebration befitting a city that didn't get the credit it deserved for its love of baseball.

Another 50,000 people rose to their feet as we rolled into the stadium. When it came my turn to address the crowd, I delivered our rallying cry one last time: "Winfield wants some noise!" They didn't need the reminder.

Dressed in a mustard-colored sports jacket, I directed everyone's attention to the roof of the stadium, where the World Series banner was being unfurled.

I soaked it all in, realizing my time in Toronto was winding down. The Blue Jays and I hadn't discussed a new contract, and I knew they didn't plan on making me one of the 15 players they could protect from being selected by the Rockies or Marlins in the upcoming expansion draft.

I debated whether to attend the White House ceremony honoring the Blue Jays, but I decided to decline the invitation since I was on the verge of signing with another team. It meant a lot to me, though, to hear that I was singled out for praise by outgoing President George H. W. Bush, who said, "It was Old Man River's eleventh-inning double in Game Six that put this series in the record books. And that hit, by a forty-one-year-old veteran, showed baseball isn't about country; it's about courage and stamina and grit. After twenty-one years in the majors, Dave Winfield finally has the World Series ring."

After I declared for free agency, my agent, Jeff Klein, fielded several offers—but there was one team I was holding out for: my hometown Twins. My former teammate Chili Davis had just left Minnesota, which meant they'd be looking for a new designated hitter. I called Twins general manager Andy MacPhail and made a pitch for why he should sign me.

"I heard you need a hard-hitting DH," I told him.

MacPhail spoke with owner Carl Pohlad and then came back with an offer I couldn't turn down.

It was a two-year deal—which, at 41, I definitely appreciated. And there were other reasons I didn't hesitate to sign. My good friend Kirby Puckett had just signed a five-year extension with the Twins, a team that had won more than 90 games in each of the past two seasons. But most importantly, it gave me the chance to come home. And home is where I wanted to be as I approached the biggest personal milestone of my career—my 3,000th hit.

It turned out the 1993 season was also a homecoming of sorts for George Steinbrenner. As one of his last acts as commissioner, Fay Vincent removed George's "lifetime ban," allowing him to return to the Yankees with no restrictions. All he had to do was agree to drop the lawsuits he had filed against Major League Baseball. He also pledged not to violate the "best interests of baseball" clause again.

Nobody in the commissioner's office gave me a heads-up about the decision. But it didn't come as a surprise—Major League Baseball had always looked out for the owners.

I didn't have to worry about George anymore. It wasn't like he could do anything to me. He wasn't going to channel Max Cady—the Robert De

Niro character from *Cape Fear*—and come after those he blamed for getting him banned. No, he was more like the guy in the Napoleon costume, posing on horseback for a *Sports Illustrated* cover story about his reinstatement. Silly, theatrical, and harmless—at least to me.

Still, there was principle at play. Jeff Klein and I insisted that the commissioner's office let us review all the materials that had led to George's so-called lifetime ban. They agreed.

We weren't allowed to make copies or take anything with us, but seeing all the documents laid out on a table reassured me that I hadn't imagined it all. I already knew most of what was there, but a few internal memos between Yankees officials confirmed what I'd thought for a long time: There had been an orchestrated scheme to discredit me.

George's return came at a time when Major League Baseball was dealing with another ownership scandal, this one involving Marge Schott of the Cincinnati Reds. It had come to light that she'd directed the n-word at her players—calling Dave Parker her "million-dollar n-----"—and routinely tossed around anti-Semitic slurs. Her punishment: a year away from baseball for violating the league's "best interests" rule. It wouldn't be the last time she faced sanctions. A few years later, she was suspended again—this time for publicly praising Adolf Hitler.

By comparison, George suddenly looked sane and reasonable.

•

Coming off a World Series title in which I'd played a key role, I felt a sense of validation—one that insulated me from this outside noise. Being back home in Minnesota only added to my comfort level. I didn't have to hunt for an apartment, I had family and friends all around me, and I was playing for the team I'd grown up rooting for. It was the closest thing you can come to in baseball to living in a bubble.

Before the season, I even picked up a side gig writing a weekly column for the *St. Paul Pioneer Press* called "Ask Dave." It gave me a small taste of life as a working journalist—one of the paths I was considering after retiring from baseball.

Playing for the Twins was comfortable—if not particularly exciting. In the dugout, it felt like I was back in St. Paul, sitting on the front porch, shooting the breeze with friends. One day, we were blowing out my former team, the Blue Jays, and having some fun at the expense of their starting pitcher, Todd Stottlemyre. With each successive hit, Kirby, Shane Mack, and I let out a bemused, drawn-out "Geeeez!"

Thanks to the Metrodome's acoustics, no conversation there ever stayed private. Anything louder than a whisper in the dugout could carry out to the field. We were having a good old time, laughing it up—but Stottlemyre didn't take kindly to the razzing. He turned red as a beet and stalked off the mound toward our dugout, ready to take us all on. Fortunately for him, he was held back by teammates.

One of the best parts of that season was getting to play alongside Kirby. I'd gotten to know him as an opponent, but now I had the pleasure of seeing him every day. He brought light and sunshine with him everywhere he went—there's no other way to put it. Just looking at him brought a smile to my face, especially when he launched into his pregame ritual of stuffing his face with Mike and Ike candies.

On off days, he introduced me to the pleasures of bass fishing at one of the state's 10,000 lakes. We'd sit out on the water, drinking beer, waiting for the fish to bite, just talking about life. I returned the favor by introducing him and his wife to the joys of island cruises.

On one cruise, Kirby and I squared off against a couple of other passengers in a two-on-two basketball game. The guy guarding Kirby had about a foot on him, so Kirby had to really fight for every rebound. Midway through the game, he went up for a board and caught the big guy in the face with a flying elbow—accidentally breaking his nose. Blood went everywhere.

Kirby felt terrible. But after getting bandaged up, the guy came over and apologized *to Kirby* for going after the rebound too aggressively. That's how much people liked Kirby.

And, man, that little bowling ball of a guy could really hit a baseball too!

Despite our strong team chemistry, we just couldn't find a rhythm that season. So—like with my batting race against Don Mattingly in 1984—the countdown to my 3,000th hit started to draw much of the attention. I'd gotten off to a slow start at the plate, which put me behind the pace I needed to reach the milestone, but manager Tom Kelly kept putting me in the lineup almost every day. Eventually, I found my groove.

I'd played enough times in New York since leaving the Yankees for it to feel like just another road game. But our June trip to the Bronx that season took on another dimension, because it was the first time I'd returned there since Steinbrenner had been reinstated.

After starting the series with a pair of two-hit games, I got a surprise in the third game. As I stepped to the plate in the first inning, public address announcer Bob Sheppard, breaking from his normal introduction, said, "Attention, ladies and gentlemen: Twenty years ago today, Dave Winfield made his major league debut for the San Diego Padres." The fans rose and gave me a standing ovation.

I went 1-for-4 that day with an infield single—the exact stat line I'd had in my very first game. Talk about symmetry.

I don't know if Steinbrenner signed off on that introduction, or whether Sheppard—or someone else in the organization—went rogue. But if, in his return, George really had come to praise me—and not bury me—he gave me a very special moment.

In some ways, it would have been poetic for me to get my historic hit in the state of Texas—the scene of so much personal anguish for me. I went into a September series against the Rangers just four hits shy of 3,000, with an outside chance of reaching that rarefied air in style—against one of the greatest pitchers of all time: Nolan Ryan.

Nolan was retiring at the end of the season and making his final home start against us. To mark the occasion, the Rangers planned a night of festivities in his honor.

For most of our careers, we'd played in different leagues, but I always relished doing battle with him. He usually got the better of me—I was 3-for-26 against him lifetime. But one of those hits had come a couple of years earlier when I broke up his bid for a record eighth no-hitter in the eighth inning. And, of course, there was the other kind of "hit"—when I connected on a right hook to his head in 1980 after he threw a few too many brushback pitches.

A final confrontation would've made for great theater.

But not on Nolan's special night—and with a block of home games on deck for us, the Twins and I agreed it made more sense to celebrate the milestone in Minnesota. So Tom Kelly sat me for the final two games of the Arlington series.

Nolan and I ended up posing for photos before the game—two future Hall of Famers who, as baseball's first million-dollar men, had set the bar for players who would soon come along and make that figure seem old-fashioned. We were never friends, but we had the utmost respect for each other.

•

With its springy turf, inflatable roof, and an outfield wall that looked like it was made of garbage bags, the Metrodome resembled a bounce house at a kids' birthday party—just bigger. It wasn't my favorite place to play, not by a long shot, but there was nowhere I'd rather have been a few nights later.

My 3,000th hit came on a ninth-inning single off Dennis Eckersley of the A's. My teammates had planned to run onto the field to congratulate me, but one look at Eck—who had just given up the tying run—and they decided against it. The whole night had a *This Is Your Life* feel that stirred some deep emotions. As joyful as it was to see so many of my friends and family gathered together, it also hurt not to have my mother there.

Tonya sensed that this defining moment had made me introspective, so to shake me out of it—and to celebrate—she threw a party that weekend. The Blue Jays happened to be in town, so many of my former teammates were able to attend, including Rickey Henderson, who had recently joined Toronto in a trade.

Over the years, more than a few people have asked me what it was like to experience Joe Carter's walk-off home run against the Phillies—the one that brought the Blue Jays back-to-back World Series. I wasn't on the team, of course, but a surprising number of people swear I was. I believe this is what they call the "Mandela effect." In reality, the Jays brought in another St. Paul native—and future member of the 3,000-hit club—to play DH that year: Paul Molitor.

As for my actual team, the 1993 season was a disappointment. After consecutive winning seasons, the Twins lost 91 games. Almost everyone on the team—including me—took a step back from the season before. But my numbers were respectable enough to quiet any talk that I was finished. Appearing in 143 games showed I could still be counted on to play nearly every day, and my 21 home runs proved I still had some pop.

Speaking of pop . . .

One day the following spring in Fort Myers, Tonya came in all exasperated. She told me she'd found a baby rattle in our car and didn't know how it got there. Earlier that day, a rookie pitcher for the Expos had hit me in the side with a fastball, and I wasn't exactly in the mood to solve the mystery of the rattle. I thought about joking that it maybe belonged to one of my young teammates.

Tonya handed it to me. I looked at it for a couple of seconds—and then it hit me. We were expecting!

I hugged her and broke down in tears. We'd been trying to have a baby for a while, and now it was really happening. The next day, we went to the obstetrician for an ultrasound. Maybe I was seeing double, but it looked like there were two small beans on the screen.

Tonya was pregnant with twins!

At this stage in my life, I was ready for the joys and challenges of fatherhood—a role I hadn't been able to embrace with my daughter in

Texas—though I still held out hope that one day, we'd be able to build a true father-daughter bond.

•

My post-baseball future was starting to come into view, but I still had games left to play.

My days of competing in the All-Star Game were behind me, but the invitation I received to the 1994 game wasn't about performance—it was to recognize my accomplishments off the field. Receiving that year's Roberto Clemente Award—given to the player who best represents the game of baseball through character and community service—felt especially meaningful, because the game was played in Pittsburgh. That's where Clemente had starred for the Pirates and dedicated his offseasons to humanitarian work in Latin America. He died in a plane crash on New Year's Eve 1972 while on a relief mission to Nicaragua.

Before the game, American League president Bobby Brown took me aside to congratulate me. "I don't know why it took so long for you to be recognized for all you've done," he said.

I had a pretty good idea why: To be considered for the award, you had to be nominated by your team. And during the years that my foundation was doing its most impactful work, I wasn't getting nominated. But it was never about winning awards—it was about the work. That point was driven home when I met Roberto's children and talked with them about their father. Being there for the official unveiling of his statue outside Three Rivers Stadium was a humbling experience.

It turned out I didn't have as many games left to play as I'd expected, because a little more than halfway through the 1994 season, there was a players' strike.

Several issues had prevented owners and the union from reaching a new collective bargaining agreement—the biggest being the owners' proposal for a salary cap, which had come up in previous negotiations and remained a nonstarter for the union.

With each passing day of the strike, I knew my career drew that much closer to an end. But I stood squarely with the union—just as I had during lockouts in 1973 and 1976 and work stoppages in 1981, 1985, and 1990. That was despite having a 10-year contract with the Yankees that guaranteed me financial stability—as long as we were playing. I didn't waver in my support of the union, because I knew I wouldn't have enjoyed all the benefits of my career if the players before me had broken rank. It was my duty to pay that forward—and to make that part of my legacy.

So I continued to fight for the principles that I learned from men like Marvin Miller, the first executive director of the Major League Baseball Players Association. Marvin built the players' union into one of the strongest in the country by driving home the fact that players couldn't simply rely on the benevolence of team owners or the commissioner, who worked for those owners. We needed representation.

Fighting Steinbrenner over cost-of-living raises and other parts of my contract taught me something I carried with me long after I stopped playing. Those disputes weren't just about money—they were about power. It was an owner, speaking for all the others, making sure a player knew his place. The message was clear: We're in charge. You're just a temporary hire, a well-compensated employee—but an employee just the same.

Of all the compliments I've ever been paid, this one from Players Association associate general counsel Gene Orza during the 1994 strike might be the most meaningful: "If the union movement was composed exclusively of Dave Winfields, the distribution of wealth in this country would be substantially different than it is right now," he said. "Dave Winfield is the premier union member in my personal book."

On September 14, Commissioner Bud Selig canceled the remainder of the season. For the first time in 90 years, there would be no World Series.

The only silver lining of the strike was that it gave me more time to support Tonya during her pregnancy. We were staying in the Minneapolis condo I'd bought for my mother in the early 1980s, and I could still feel her presence there with us. Being in Minnesota also meant we had the added support of friends and family. Tonya's mother, Louise Turner, came up from New Orleans to lend a hand as well. At one point, she joked, "Ain't that something! He waited until he was out of work to be having some children!"

As Tonya and I brainstormed names for the twins, Kirby chimed in with a suggestion.

"How 'bout Beulah and Hercules?" he said.

"Thanks, Kirby, we'll consider that," I said, laughing.

In October, I was in the delivery room with two cameras in hand—one to photograph, the other to videotape. Arielle and David Winfield—true Minnesota Twins—entered the world by cesarean section, healthy and full of life.

•

Whether they've played two years or 20, every professional athlete faces the dilemma of knowing when it's time to walk away. I'd accomplished everything I could have dreamed of and didn't want to risk tarnishing my legacy by staying in the game too long.

But I also knew that once I walked away, that was it—no more legging out a double, no more clubhouse camaraderie, no more cheers of the crowd. I'd never experience those thrills again.

Three factors weighed heavily in my decision to return for the 1995 season. First, I didn't want my career to end because of a strike. Second, there was a team—the Cleveland Indians—that seemed to really want me. And third, that team just happened to be one of the best in baseball.

The Indians had acquired me at the 1994 trade deadline, hoping that I could help them make a playoff push if the strike ended. In return, the Twins were supposed to receive a player to be named later. But when the rest of the season was canceled, the teams weren't permitted to finalize the deal.

So, as legend has it, a few folks in the Indians front office treated some of their Twins' counterparts to dinner at a steakhouse. Instead of being traded for a player to be named later, I went to Cleveland for a filet mignon.

When the strike finally ended, the Indians brought me back for another year. I got fitted for a No. 31 jersey so I could go out wearing the number I came in with.

I knew in my heart that this would be my last season and came into it with realistic expectations about playing time. The team was full of young stars—including Kenny Lofton, Manny Ramírez, Jim Thome, and Albert Belle. And Cleveland already had a seasoned vet in switch-hitting Eddie Murray, who was expected to handle most of the DH duties.

As the strike dragged on, Eddie and I attended a Players Association meeting in New York that brought together several players nearing major milestones—or the end of their careers. Eddie was fewer than a hundred hits away from 3,000. Cal Ripken Jr. needed to play about a hundred more consecutive games to break Lou Gehrig's record.

Eddie, long known for being gruff and tight-lipped around reporters, delivered a fiery speech to his baseball brothers. I then spoke with such passion that Eddie stood up and shouted, "Thank you, Reverend Winfield!"

The strike finally ended in early April 1995—not because the two sides had reached an agreement, but because a federal court issued an injunction requiring the owners to abide by terms of the previous collective bargaining agreement. At 232 days, it was the longest work stoppage in MLB history.

By that time, owners had already brought "replacement players" to spring training, anticipating the strike would stretch deep into the season. The court's decision spared everyone the nightmare scenario of watching baseball move forward with such an anti-player stance.

With the real players back, Major League Baseball announced an abbreviated spring training that would be followed by a 144-game season.

Tonya, the babies, and I set up shop in the Cleveland suburb of Westlake. Our new neighbors greeted us with a basket filled with meats, cheeses, and baked goods. We hired a nanny to help with David and Arielle.

I'd been in the majors a long time. The clubhouse music was proof of that.

"This Is How We Do It" by Montell Jordan—a catchy tune blending jazz, funk, rap, and R&B—became our unofficial anthem that season. *Stevie who*? *Marvin who*? *Smokey who*? As a public service, I introduced the younger guys to those OGs.

Eddie didn't need a lesson on the sounds of the '70s. Like me, he'd lived them. He could still play too—nearly a month into the season, he was batting over .400.

I wasn't so fortunate.

In 21 seasons, I'd only landed on the disabled list a couple of times, a run of durability I attribute to healthy living, smart workout habits, and a good dose of luck. At some point, however, the body breaks down. For all the sliding, swinging, and diving I'd done, it was the simple act of running the bases that tore the rotator cuff in my left shoulder in 1995. It felt like I'd been shot.

At that stage of my career, in-season surgery wasn't an option. Instead, I did daily exercises to improve my range of motion and keep the pain at bay. But the constant throbbing, day and night, eventually forced me onto the disabled list twice.

Once I was well enough to play again, I passed on the opportunity to do a rehab assignment at Triple-A. It might sound vain, but I just didn't want that on my résumé. I'd never played a day in the minor leagues—and I wasn't about to start now.

I wanted to play myself back into game shape at the major league level, but that only led to frustration. Once, Mike Hargrove, the nineteenth manager of my career, called on me to pinch-hit, but when the other team countered with a right-handed reliever, he pulled me back before I even stepped in.

Like many people, Mike was scared of my temperamental—and extremely talented—teammate Albert Belle. Sometimes he'd ask me to be a go-between and deliver messages to Albert. After the pinch-hitting slight, I told him I wouldn't do it anymore.

"You're the manager, Mike. That's on you now," I said.

Tonya, too, had made her mark in Cleveland, becoming something of a fixer among the players' wives.

When the wives decided to auction off a quilt for charity, they collected signatures from every player to include in each square. As the day of the auction approached, only one signature was missing: Eddie Murray's. No one on the committee—including Eddie's wife—wanted to be the one to approach him.

Tonya, who was working on another aspect of the event, spoke up.

"Give me that goddang quilt," she said, reaching across the table. "And hand me a pen."

From there, she and two other wives marched from the conference room down to the clubhouse. By the time they reached the bottom of the stairs, Tonya was alone.

She opened the clubhouse door a crack and shouted, "Eddie Murray! Get over here!"

Eddie looked up with a scowl on his face.

"What do you want, woman?!" he barked.

"Get over here and sign this goddang thing! We're waiting on you and you're holding the whole thing up."

We all waited to see how Eddie would react. After a few seconds, he got up, went to the door, took the pen from Tonya's hand, and signed the quilt.

"You happy now?"

"Yes, thank you very much, Eddie," Tonya said with a smile that could charm anyone.

Hargrove put me in as a pinch-hitter in the final game of the year. In what turned out to be my last major league at-bat, I grounded out sharply to second base, running full speed to first. The crowd gave me a standing ovation as I trotted back to the dugout.

We ran away with the newly formed American League Central, finishing with one of the best winning percentages in baseball history. We beat the wild-card Red Sox in the inaugural Division Series, topped the Mariners in the Championship Series, and advanced to the World Series against the Braves.

I watched it all from the bench, having been left off the team's postseason roster. I understood the decision—even if I couldn't quite come to accept it. I'd been injured, but I still felt I could help the team. What made it even harder to swallow was that the final roster spot went to a pinch-running specialist.

I traveled with the team—my teammates wouldn't have had it any other way. A Braves fan doing the tomahawk chop in our hotel groaned when he saw me.

In Game 6, with the Braves one win away from clinching the title, we trailed 1–0 in the top of the eighth inning. I would've loved the chance to come off the bench to face Tom Glavine for the first time in my career, but my replacement on the roster batted instead, grounding out to end the inning.

In a classic case of great pitching beating great hitting, the Braves held on to win the game—and the World Series.

It wasn't the fairy-tale ending I'd hoped for. My unofficial farewell tour just sort of faded out. No final heroics. No standing ovations during my last visits to each ballpark. No big announcement. Just a quiet ending.

But the kid from St. Paul—who earned his stripes in San Diego, went to battle every day in New York, resurrected his career in California, reached the pinnacle in Toronto, made history back home in Minnesota, and came back for one last hurrah in Cleveland—was calling it a day.

Chapter 20

MOVING ON

For the first time in 23 years, I didn't have to get ready for spring training. Out of habit, I kept up my workouts and watched what I ate. But without a new season to focus on, I finally had the mental space to deal with my Texas court case, which had been dragging on for over a decade.

I'd lost the case in 1989, because my lawyers couldn't refute Renfro's claims that we'd lived together in Houston.

After the verdict was overturned on appeal, I hired new lawyers in case we went to trial again. But I knew they weren't going to be the ones to save the day. To finally get out from under this mess, I had to prove that I hadn't been in the places Sandra claimed I'd been. That meant combing through personal calendars, credit card bills, foundation records, newspaper clippings, airline tickets, and other documents to conduct a forensic analysis of my every movement from 1982 to 1985.

In the pre-internet, paper-only era, it felt like putting a very complicated jigsaw puzzle together. Thankfully, friends, family, and business associates helped fill in some of the missing pieces by sharing their memories of where I was and what I was doing on specific days and weeks.

When all the detective work was done, I determined I'd spent no more than 27 days in the state of Texas over that three-year period—and most of those came during games at Arlington Stadium, not with Sandra. Only nine of the days were with her and our daughter—a far cry from her claim that I'd spent most of my offseasons in Houston.

To discredit her case, I referred my attorneys to that day in Texas in April 1982 when Sandra claimed I gave her flowers, popped a bottle of champagne, and said, "We're as good as married." I now had evidence it never happened—because I wasn't even in Texas. I was in New York, playing a doubleheader that had been scheduled to make up for a snowed-out season opener. We hadn't arrived in Texas until the next day, and I didn't see Sandra on that visit.

This new evidence tore holes in the argument that we'd agreed to be married and had lived together—two of the three elements required to prove a common-law marriage.

We hadn't represented ourselves as married either, but that was almost beside the point. I now had more than enough ammunition to take back to court. During Sandra's deposition, her lawyer instructed her not to answer all but two of the 40 questions we'd prepared.

Once they saw what we had—and were prepared to present to a jury—her lawyer asked to take the case to mediation. At first, I declined the offer, because I wanted vindication in a courtroom—just like I had suffered defamation in one. But ultimately, I decided that mediation could still be a win for me. And it was.

A consent decree dismissing the case read, "No marriage, whether ceremonial, informal, or common law, has ever existed between Sandra Renfro and David Winfield at any time."

As part of the settlement, I agreed to continue paying $3,500 in child support for Lauren Shanel, who was now 13 years old. But Sandra wasn't getting any other of my earnings or property.

Her lawyer—a real Yankees killer, who later represented Alex Rodriguez's then wife in her divorce—asked that the settlement include a clause preventing me from suing either of them for their conduct. I found that unusual but accepted it because I just wanted the whole thing to end once and for all.

The agreement allowed me to start moving past the acrimony and toward a relationship with my older daughter, who had become a bargaining chip instead of a child.

It was a time for new beginnings—in both my life and my career.

•

Officially, I was a free agent, which meant I wasn't retiring as a member of a specific team. There was never any doubt in my mind where I would publicly share the news—in New York. It just wasn't going to be anywhere near Yankee Stadium.

I said I was announcing it at a Manhattan hotel near the Major League Baseball Players Association's East 49th Street headquarters because I happened to be in town on business, but there was more to it than that. I wasn't trying to stick it to the Yankees—it just felt right for the February 1996 announcement to take place with a group of people that had always had my back and whose mission I supported with every ounce of my being.

Tonya and our 15-month-old twins came to offer moral support. My father and brother flew in for the occasion too. Nearly the entire staff of the Players Association, including top dogs Marvin Miller and Don Fehr, were also there.

Fifteen years earlier, when my signing with the Yankees was announced at Jimmy Weston's Restaurant & Jazz Club, I was all business, dressed in a gray suit and red tie. This time, a few blocks away and many years removed from that moment, I wore a striped navy suit and a tan turtleneck that reflected my more relaxed state of mind.

George Steinbrenner didn't attend my farewell, nor did I expect him to, but he did issue a statement saying he considered me a friend. He also extended an open invitation for me to participate in future Yankees Old-Timers' Day events.

"Dave Winfield was one of the standout players of his era, and a certain first-ballot Hall of Famer," he said.

I appreciated his words, but in the end, they were just words. And they came a little too late.

Some reporters there—looking for one last juicy headline—asked me whose cap I'd be wearing when I got inducted into the Hall of Fame.

Nearly a decade of dealing with the New York media had made me pretty good at sidestepping questions I didn't want to answer. This time, I flicked it aside by saying I wouldn't comment on something that wasn't going to happen for at least another five years—even though everyone in the room knew that 3,000 hits and 465 home runs practically guaranteed enshrinement in Cooperstown.

"I'm not taking anything for granted," I said. "And I won't speculate about the cap."

The truth was, I didn't know how I'd feel when the call came. My more immediate concern was how I'd adjust to life after baseball.

The game had meant too much to me to leave it behind completely. I wanted to stay involved—whether that meant in a front-office job, a position with the union, or sitting behind a microphone. The 162-game grind of working as a manager or hitting instructor didn't appeal to me, especially if it meant paying dues in the minor leagues. I'd never played in the minors, and I didn't plan to manage there, either. Besides, I felt I could make a bigger impact on the game in a different role.

My new agent, Randy Grossman—a wonderful guy I'd known since he was just a kid in San Diego—thought it was time to rekindle my relationship with the Padres. Amazingly, I hadn't been back to San Diego since leaving the team in 1980 and playing exclusively in the American League.

Randy reached out and let the team know I was interested in making a visit. That led to me throwing out the first pitch at a game and spending an evening with owner John Moores in his box.

"You oughta come down more often," John told me as we said our goodbyes.

"You should give him a reason to," Randy said, smiling.

"Maybe I will."

For the time being, a broadcasting job seemed ideal. So after Randy laid the groundwork, I accepted a gig with Fox as a pregame host during the network's Saturday *Game of the Week* and postseason coverage, which included the World Series. It was the perfect way to keep talking baseball—without having to leave Los Angeles or my family.

Perfect in every way but one: I didn't enjoy it as much as I thought I would.

In these pages, I've had ample space to explore the nuances of the game and reflect on the ups and downs of a major league career. But on a 30-minute studio show—where you're limited to carefully scripted sound bites and have to compete with others for airtime—it's a lot harder to offer real insight.

I liked to talk. I liked to talk to other people. And I figured I'd enjoy sitting around discussing baseball. But alongside Chip Caray and fellow analyst Steve Lyons—a former major leaguer best known for once accidentally pulling his pants down during a game—I struggled to find a rhythm.

The Yankees reached the World Series for the first time since 1981—a season I was more than qualified to discuss. But it also put my producers and me in the awkward position of deciding just how candid I should be about my time in a Yankees uniform.

Ultimately, it was a no-brainer: I was there to provide expert opinion and to be a cheerleader for a sport trying to win back fans still angry about the 1994 strike—not to sound like a guy with a case of sour grapes.

It helped that I admired that Yankees team. I'd known their manager, Joe Torre, since his playing days. His first year at the helm in New York showed he knew how to manage both young and veteran talent—and handle the pressure of working for a guy who hadn't magically turned into a model of patience during his exile from baseball.

Torre's hiring had come after George tried to rehire the manager he'd just fired—Buck Showalter. After signing a two-year contract, Joe asked Steinbrenner whether he should rent or buy a home; George told him to rent.

I also had a soft spot for that Yankees team because of the guy who helped build it: my former teammate Bob Watson, who had taken over as general manager before the season.

Since the early '90s, the Yankees had done a superb job of drafting and developing their stars of tomorrow. At the top of that list was Derek Jeter—the kid who once had a poster of me hanging in his Michigan bedroom—who would go on to win Rookie of the Year in 1996. Andy Pettitte, a 21-game winner in just his second big-league season, was another major reason for the team's success that year—and for years to come.

Bob took that core of young talent and masterfully added to it. He acquired veterans like Dwight Gooden, Darryl Strawberry, Tim Raines, Cecil Fielder, and Jimmy Key. Without those players, I'm not sure the Yankees dynasty of the late 1990s would have taken off—at least not as quickly.

I was still bothered by a Dodger executive's comment a decade earlier about Black people lacking "the necessities" to be successful managers and general managers.

The truth was simple: The only necessity for minorities to succeed was opportunity.

I'd been proud to be with the Blue Jays when Cito Gaston broke through the glass ceiling for managers, winning not one but two World Series, and I knew how significant it would be if Bob could do the same for general managers.

It felt a little unreal being back at Yankee Stadium in my new role. Our broadcast set was out in left field, within earshot of dozens of fans who had gathered nearby. When it came time to predict who I thought would win—the Yankees or the Braves—I had a choice: be diplomatic or be honest. I chose honesty, saying I thought the Braves would prevail because of their outstanding pitching.

The Yankee faithful around us erupted in boos and shouts of "Traitor!" But it was all in good fun—at least I think it was.

It looked like my prediction was accurate after the Yankees dropped the first two games at home, by a combined score of 16–1. This came on the heels of Atlanta's dominant play at the end of the National League Championship Series, which included wins by scores of 15–0 and 16–0.

We learned that Steinbrenner had met with Torre after Game 1 to emphasize the importance of winning the next game. Joe had to be feeling the heat after losing that one too. But he and the team didn't retreat. They stormed back to win the next three games in Atlanta, returning to Yankee Stadium with a chance to clinch.

Fox assigned me a pregame interview with Torre, which I enjoyed doing—though, in hindsight, interviewing Watson would have felt more on point for me. Most of the best banter that night happened in the control truck, where I sat with some Fox colleagues and *Bull Durham* actor Robert Wuhl, who cracked jokes throughout the game. At one point, he asked whether George had invited me to throw out the ceremonial first pitch. I responded with a "Ha!" and a quick bit of profanity.

I was in the truck when Yankees third baseman Charlie Hayes squeezed the final out, setting off a massive celebration in the Bronx. My work was done for the night. I made my way through a sea of people and slipped into a car bound for my hotel. The Yankees' World Series drought was over—and, as it turned out, so was my time with Fox. We parted ways after the season.

It would be years before I took another shot at broadcasting—but the result was largely the same. I was a *Baseball Tonight* analyst at ESPN's studio in Bristol, Connecticut. I'd leave LAX on a Saturday, connect through

Chicago, New York, or DC, and eventually land in Hartford, where I'd grab a car to Bristol.

At some point during my trip, a producer would call to go over what we'd be discussing on Sunday night. I had to get up to speed—not just on what had happened while I was in transit, but also on the specifics of the teams we'd be covering. Unlike their fans who watched them every night, I dropped in once a week and was still expected to sound like I knew what I was talking about.

John Kruk, Karl Ravech, Tim Kurkjian, and I didn't quite have the chemistry that's helped make NBA pregame shows with Ernie Johnson, Charles Barkley, and Kenny Johnson almost more entertaining than the games themselves. In our case, there was no camaraderie, no postshow get-togethers, no late-night meals. It all felt very clinical—and not as much fun as I thought it would be.

When I left Fox, baseball was entering a new era—one that would seriously damage the integrity of the game. By the time I got to ESPN, that era was, thankfully, coming to an end. In the years in between, steroids and other performance-enhancing drugs (PEDs) forced me—and everyone else connected to the game—to do a lot of soul-searching.

It was a problem that spun out of control because owners and players didn't agree on a testing program for PEDs until the early 2000s. There's plenty of blame to go around for that.

The cheating cast a shadow over everything. Baseball is a game built on statistics, and the steroid era shattered the sanctity of many records—especially when it came to home runs.

Hank Aaron's 715 career home runs didn't include a single season in which he hit 50 or more. In the late '90s and early 2000s, we saw players with half his talent hitting 50-plus homers.

I'm another example of how PEDs distorted statistics. My 465 career homers came without ever hitting 40 in a season. When I retired, I ranked 19th on the all-time home run list—a number that reflected nearly a century of baseball history. As of the 2026 season, I'd dropped all the way to 36th.

Not all 17 players who passed me were using performance enhancers—but some were.

I take the conversation seriously, because it's impacted my legacy and the legacies of many others.

Based on what came out after I retired, there were almost certainly players injecting steroids when I played—but I never witnessed it firsthand or even heard about it. Some players openly popped amphetamines—"greenies"—like they were aspirin. And of course, the clubhouses were always littered with empty bottles and cans that doubled as spittoons for chewing tobacco. That's what I actually saw.

But I stayed clear of all that stuff. In my view, even in the twilight of my career, I had a clear advantage over most of the pitchers I faced. I didn't need an edge—I already had one.

I have no idea how many players cheated just to keep up with the Joneses. But the baseball culture of that era most definitely had an "if you can't beat them, join them" attitude. Borderline major leaguers got the boost they needed to stick around. And established All-Stars who went down that path? They were chasing records, endorsement deals, and accolades. Sure, they got all of that—but in the process, they embarrassed themselves and the game.

I don't know how history will treat these players. With the passage of time, the response to their actions might soften or even be completely glossed over. The same question applies to Pete Rose, who was posthumously reinstated to the game in 2025 after receiving a "lifetime ban" in 1989 for gambling while managing the Reds.

Does Pete deserve to be in the Hall? He's the all-time hits leader, a champion, and a guy who played the game with incredible passion. But baseball has always been clear about its two biggest taboos: drugs and gambling. I expect the Hall of Fame will establish a committee to review Pete's candidacy—and who knows, I might be on it. For that reason, I won't express a firm opinion here, because that might mean having to recuse myself from the vote.

While Mark McGwire and Sammy Sosa chased the single-season home

run mark—a record McGwire would hold until Barry Bonds shattered it a few years later—I was taking a break from the game.

The time was right. Baseball needed time to figure things out—and so did I. I planned to get involved again, but at that point I'd had enough of watching muscle-bound hitters sending pitches into the upper decks of stadiums.

The hiatus gave me an opportunity to bond with my twins—who were at that adorable preschool age—and pursue other interests.

The friendship I started with Robert Wuhl in the Fox control truck during the World Series led to a couple of appearances as myself on his HBO show *Arli$$*, where he played a wheeling-and-dealing sports agent. After living in that world for so many years, it was fun to step into a fictional version of it. Those appearances even helped me earn my SAG-AFTRA card.

Having summers off was something I had to get used to, but spending a few weeks on Martha's Vineyard with Tonya and the kids helped with the learning curve.

I felt good. I felt recharged—so much so that I felt inspired to give George a call. Maybe I'd just been in the sun too long.

Chapter 21

•

GLORY AND GRIEF

I had an excellent chance of getting into the Hall of Fame in my first year on the ballot—2001—and I planned to be ready when the call came. That meant deciding what cap I was going to wear on my plaque.

George and I hadn't seen each other in years. It seemed like the right time to reach out.

The Yankees were riding high, having recently won their second World Series in three years. I'd thrown out the first pitch at one of the games of that year's American League Championship Series at Yankee Stadium. I breezed in and out without seeing George, but it still felt like he was extending an olive branch.

In the spring of 1999, we met at a hotel off Park Avenue.

George told me I looked good and joked that he might be able to use my bat in the postseason. I quipped that I could still hit—but with my friend Chili Davis on the team, he already had the next best thing at DH.

He said I'd had a great career, though he admitted he was surprised that it lasted as long as it did—the implication being that he thought I was washed up when he traded me in 1990.

"I don't know how things ended up the way they did with us," he said. "I wish I'd done things differently."

That left a lot to the imagination. I didn't press him on what exactly he would have done differently. We didn't get into the details of the whole ordeal with Howie Spira or why he'd tried to smear me and discredit my foundation.

I just know I left lunch feeling somewhat placated—even if his statement of regret was delivered to an audience of one, and not publicly.

We didn't talk about the Hall of Fame or what kind of relationship I'd have with the organization going forward. But we agreed to stay in touch.

That summer, I participated in my first Yankees Old-Timers' Game. That fall, George invited me to be a part of the team's World Series victory parade. Then, about a year later, he called my agent with a question: How would I feel about a "Dave Winfield Day" at Yankee Stadium? I told Jeff I liked the idea.

Looking back, I can see that this was all part of a campaign to convince me to pledge loyalty to the Yankees by entering Cooperstown in pinstripes. At the time, it gave me a lot to think about.

I was confident my phone would ring on the January day the Hall of Fame announced its Class of 2001, but it was still a thrill to get the call from the head of the Baseball Writers' Association of America at my home in Los Angeles.

In that moment, my life flashed before me. As with every milestone, I thought of my mother and the enormous role she played in everything I had accomplished.

I also thought of my father, who had passed away the year before from complications following a car accident. He had become a better grandfather to my kids than he had ever been a father to me and my brother, Steve. I wish we'd had more time to continue building our relationship.

My day got even better when I found out that my man Kirby Puckett had been voted in too—on his first try. Kirby had scored on my 3,000th hit, and I was ecstatic to share another once-in-a-lifetime experience with one of my closest friends.

He was short and stout; I was tall and sleek. Side by side we looked like a fireplug standing next to a flagpole—a contrast almost as striking as when my former agent Al Frohman and I used to go around together. But it just goes to show: Great baseball players come in all shapes and sizes. There's no telling how much more Kirby might have accomplished if his career hadn't been cut short by glaucoma at age 35.

Pirates legend Bill Mazeroski and Negro Leagues star Hilton Smith also got the call to Cooperstown that year by the Veterans Committee.

Every reporter who interviewed me the day of the announcement wanted to know which team's cap I'd be wearing in Cooperstown. I knew it would be harder to dodge the question now that I was officially in, but I wasn't going to give them an answer right then and there—because I didn't know it myself. Not yet.

I could have chosen to enter the Hall without a team affiliation—a route taken by players like Catfish Hunter and, later, Greg Maddux—who had standout seasons with multiple clubs. But wearing a blank cap didn't feel right.

So I carefully weighed my options.

Most of my success had come in San Diego and New York, but my career wouldn't have been what it was without the stops I made in the early and mid-'90s.

My favorite year—for obvious reasons—came in Toronto. Returning home to Minnesota to collect my 3,000th hit made my time with the Twins unforgettable. Getting a chance to jump-start my career in California left me with warm feelings about the Angels. And Cleveland—well, I just wish I'd had the chance to leave more of a mark there.

The Hall of Fame had a say in the final decision, and they made it clear that I should only be choosing between the Padres and Yankees.

I'd played roughly the same number of games for both teams, hit for a little more power in New York, stole a few more bases in San Diego—but the decision wasn't going to come down to statistics. I had to listen to my heart . . . and my head.

I wasn't the first player to be in this position. Despite his up-and-down relationship with Steinbrenner—and the fact that his most productive years were in Oakland—Reggie chose to go in as a Yankee. I think the sentiment around baseball was that I'd ultimately make the same decision.

No one had ever been inducted as a Padre. With Tony Gwynn finishing up his spectacular 20-year career in his hometown, that wouldn't be the case much longer. But I had a chance to give the organization something to be proud of a little sooner. I'd recently joined the team's board of directors—and had a great relationship with owner John Moores. Still, some people in the media—and probably within the organization—felt that honor should belong to Gwynn.

Back in New York, George continued his charm offensive, which took me back to the days of our courtship in 1980, when he'd wooed me with meals, flowers, and Broadway tickets. The Yankees had scheduled "Dave Winfield Day" to take place a couple of weeks after my induction. Over breakfast the day after the season opener, he hinted that they might even retire my No. 31 at the event. I wasn't sure if it was contrition or calculation on his part.

From a business standpoint, wearing a Yankees cap also had its advantages. Having just won their fourth World Series in five years, they were once again the dominant organization in baseball. By being eternally linked to the Yankees, I might get another shot at the endorsement deals that had eluded me during my playing days. Who knows—maybe George and I would even go on Letterman or do a Miller Lite ad together.

It was a close call—one that could've gone either way. But I reached down deep, threw caution to the wind, and let the Hall of Fame know that I'd made my decision.

It would be the Padres.

I realized that San Diego was more than just where I got my start. It's where I learned to play—and where I began to understand who I was outside the lines. I was the first player ever named team captain. It's where I launched my foundation. And it was the organization I could more clearly see myself connected to in the years ahead.

The day after I picked the Padres, a story by Bill Madden in the New

York *Daily News* claimed that they'd offered me a $1 million package to represent them in Cooperstown. It quoted an anonymous source who said that, before announcing my decision, I gave the Yankees a chance to match that offer. It also quoted Steinbrenner by name as saying, "If you want to go in the Hall of Fame as a Yankee, then go in as a Yankee. We're not paying you."

My friend Mario called me, irate, when he saw the story. Distrustful of George, he'd sat at the next table during our breakfast earlier that month, paying close attention to everything that was said.

"I spoke with Madden," he said. "I told him his source sucks—and always has."

Mario was hot, but I couldn't work up the energy to match his outrage.

"I guess some things never change," I said, feeling more certain than ever that I'd made the right decision not to let my career be defined by my time with the New York Yankees.

I believed my next role in baseball should be with a major league team. Serving on the Padres' board of directors had given me a glimpse into the inner workings of a team, and I knew I had the vision and skill to take on a more hands-on role—whether with the Padres or another organization. But let me be clear: There was no quid pro quo involved in my conversations with the Padres.

I'm convinced they still would've wanted me in their front office even if I'd gone into the Hall as a Yankee. I didn't need the gift of a ceremonial, no-show job. The way I saw it, the Padres wouldn't be doing me any favors by hiring me—they'd be lucky to have me helping shape their future.

The previous summer, the Padres had announced they were going to retire my No. 31 before a game the following season, so I timed my Hall decision to give everyone a little something extra to celebrate that night.

It was a nice ceremony—but one that stirred up more conspiracy theories. As part of the evening at Qualcomm Stadium—the name the park had taken on a few years earlier—the team had me ride around the field in a luxury Mercedes-Benz. The car was mine to keep. There you had it, some claimed—proof that the Padres had bought Winfield off. Fortunately, my former teammate—1976 Cy Young Award–winner Randy Jones—poured cold water on that idea, explaining that the team had given him a red Corvette when it retired his number in 1997. And he wasn't even going into the Hall of Fame.

I put a lot of time into crafting my induction speech—so much so that it ended up running around 25 minutes. But with my 50th birthday just a few months away, I had a lot to reflect on, including the contributions of all the people—family, friends, coaches, teammates—who'd helped me get there. I won't list them here—they're well represented throughout these pages—but without their support, I know I wouldn't have been able to accomplish all that I did. Being honored that day and joining the ranks of the all-time greats was very emotional for me.

I also gave a special shout-out to the thousand or so fans who'd gathered at Qualcomm to watch a simulcast of the ceremony.

And, yes, I thanked George, who didn't make it to Cooperstown for the occasion. Much like my stint as a studio analyst with Fox, it wasn't the time or place to air grievances. And because, as one *New York Post* columnist put it, I was reaching out to just about everyone in the Manhattan phone book, it would've seemed strange not to acknowledge George's role in my journey.

"To George Steinbrenner, I want to thank you for bringing me to the New York Yankees," I said—a line that drew laughter from the crowd and forced me to clarify that I meant it. "I'm serious. It was an experience that changed my life in a positive way."

For good measure, I added, "I'm glad time, distance, and clear minds have brought about a respect and a friendship we didn't have at one time."

Calling it a friendship might've been a stretch, but I wanted to show I was the bigger man. And what better time to do that than on my biggest day?

In less than two weeks, I'd be at Yankee Stadium for "Dave Winfield Day." It would be up to George to show whether he could rise above it all by retiring my uniform number. No Yankee had been assigned No. 31 for the 2001 season, so the possibility felt real.

But it didn't happen.

The day started off on an uplifting note. As I made my way to the stadium, I marveled at the economic development taking shape in the Bronx. They had torn down an old jail and were building a massive shopping center called the Bronx Terminal Market.

But, despite the signs of progress outside, things inside the stadium were as deflating as I remembered. Instead of No. 31 being displayed forever in Monument Park, it was temporarily painted along the first- and third-base foul lines. And for the second time in as many weeks, George didn't show up to a ceremony honoring me.

I did get another car, though—this one a Dodge Viper that was driven onto the field by my former teammate Don Mattingly, whose No. 23 was retired in 1997. His call to the Hall of Fame still hasn't come. My number being retired by the Yankees probably never will.

And that's okay, because there are far more important things in life. Sometimes we get reminders of that.

I was going back and forth between the East Coast and West Coast that summer, making a series of personal appearances and treating myself to some special experiences before starting my job as an executive vice president of the Padres. Knowing what a big music fan I am, my agent, Randy Grossman, suggested we check out a September concert at Madison Square Garden celebrating Michael Jackson's 30th year in the music industry.

The show exceeded all expectations. It was a who's who of the music industry—Dionne Warwick, Gladys Knight, Usher, Al Jarreau, and dozens more—performing Michael's hits.

Then the man himself took the stage to perform an encore that included a version of "Beat It," featuring the heavy-metal stylings of Guns N' Roses guitarist Slash.

Afterward, Randy and I hung out in the VIP room with the likes of Chris Tucker and Lenny Kravitz, basking in the glow of the performances and wishing the night would never end.

But it had to. We had an early-morning flight back to San Diego that we couldn't miss.

It was a beautiful morning, and as we took off from JFK at around 8:40 AM, we caught a panoramic view of the Manhattan skyline. No matter how many times I saw it, it never got old. A bit bleary-eyed from the night before, Randy and I settled into our seats and waited for breakfast to be served. After that, the plan was to sleep the rest of the way to California.

But right after the flight attendants brought the meal, they hurried back down the aisle to collect the trays. Then the pilot came over the intercom system and told us we'd be making an emergency landing in Indianapolis. You could hear murmurs throughout the cabin, but he assured us that nothing was wrong with the plane.

I figured someone must be sick or maybe had gone into labor.

Of course, that wasn't what was happening at all.

When we landed in Indianapolis and people regained use of their cell phones, we received the grim news of what had just occurred in Manhattan.

The first thing I did when I got into the terminal was call Tonya. She started to cry as soon as she heard my voice. The details of the terrorist attacks were still trickling in, and she had feared my plane might be in trouble.

When I called, she was already on the other line with American Airlines, trying to get more information. I told her I loved her and that I'd be home as soon as I could.

I joined dozens of passengers huddled around a TV in the concourse tuned to CNN. We watched replays of the planes slamming into the towers and let out collective moans. It seemed like everyone had a hand over their mouth, murmuring, "Oh my God!" as the footage played on the screen.

Randy and I spent the next few days in Indianapolis, holed up in hotel rooms, watching the news until we couldn't take it anymore. When commercial flights resumed, we made our way back home.

Usually, after returning from a trip, I slept well, comforted by familiar surroundings. But this time was different. I couldn't relax, the unimaginable tragedies of September 11 playing over and over in my mind.

I didn't go into the Hall of Fame as a Yankee—though maybe I would have decided differently if my induction had come a year later—but New York was part of me, and always would be.

I felt compelled to go back. As it happened, I had a speaking engagement in New York at the end of September.

A guy at the NYPD I'd known since my Yankees days helped arrange for me to visit the area around Ground Zero, where recovery crews were working around the clock, clearing debris, and searching for remains.

I had to experience it for myself, even if the smell of death and destruction—and the sight of ashen, sullen faces of the workers picking through the broken rubble—would stay with me forever.

It filled me with so many emotions—anger, sorrow, and, above all, heartache for those who lost loved ones in the attacks. I didn't know any of the victims personally, but in a place like New York, everyone is connected by only a few degrees of separation.

The afternoon before the attacks, I had attended a reception at the 21 Club on West 52nd Street, where I spent a couple of hours shaking hands, posing for photos, and chatting with guests.

About a year later, I received a letter from a woman whose husband had been there that night. He'd called her from the event, excitedly telling her about meeting me and getting an autographed bat. She said good night, knowing he was spending the night in Manhattan because he had an early-morning meeting in the South Tower of the World Trade Center.

As I read her letter, I could almost feel the tears she'd shed while writing it. Enclosed was a photo of her husband and me, taken at the 21 Club.

I still take it out from time to time and look at it.

Epilogue

For me, life has always been about staying connected, giving back, and moving forward—even when the world around you sometimes feels like it's moving backward.

I'd said I'd never become a baseball coach, but sometimes you don't realize you have an itch until it's time to scratch it.

So there I was, on a perfect summer day in 2007, sitting in the dugout before a game, filling out the lineup card and asking my players what they knew about the opposing pitcher.

I felt good about our chances that day. Our starting pitcher was already showing flashes of Cy Young–caliber talent, and I knew I could count on the rest of the team to play hard.

"Okay, guys, let's go out there and play good, smart baseball," I intoned. "If we do, we . . . "

My pep talk was cut off mid-sentence by the sight of a visitor stepping into the dugout. She was technically one of my many bosses. I didn't mind the occasional pregame check-in, but right before first pitch? That's when the dugout becomes sacred ground, a place where focus is paramount and distractions are unwelcome. I had to draw the line—even if, in this case, the intruder was a mom carrying a tray full of Starbucks Frappuccinos for her son and his friends.

"Beat it! This is a dugout," I said, smiling.

And with that, the West Los Angeles Little League team that included my son, David Winfield II, ran onto the field.

All in all, I think I made a pretty good coach. Everyone on the team got a chance to play, and I preached the importance of having fun. If kids love the game, they'll want to keep playing. And in a youth sports landscape with so many options, that was always my number one goal: keep them playing.

That outstanding pitcher I had? That was Lucas Giolito. He kept playing—and went on to enjoy a successful major league career.

Occasionally, I bump into some of the other "kids" around Los Angeles. Once I was pumping gas in Westwood when a guy peeked around the other pump and called out, "Coach Winfield!"

It was a kid I used to call "the Blade" because he was thin like a blade of grass. As we filled our tanks, he told me he'd just earned a baseball scholarship to Georgia Tech.

Another time, I was working out at my health club when one of my former players came over to say hello. He was built like an oak tree and now on the rowing team at Cornell.

Dedicated athletes find their callings. I tried to give my players a foundation for their journey.

In his first Little League at-bat, my son crushed a ball into the trees beyond the left-field wall. So much for the weight of expectations. Growing up, he played baseball, football, and basketball. For him, basketball was the one that stuck. My daughter, Arielle, ran track and played volleyball in high school. It was a joy for me to watch Arielle go up for a spike or David elevate to block a shot. They loved competing, and I loved playing the role of their number one fan.

I never wanted to be one of those "sports parents" who tried to tell coaches how to do their jobs. All I expected from the coaches was that they were committed to teaching kids, not on some kind of power trip or just building their résumé for the next job.

Both twins went on to attend the University of Pennsylvania—making move-in day a whole lot easier for their parents. Arielle played on the volleyball team before switching to track and field. David's promising basketball career was cut short by a knee injury. Still, I was proud to see them competing in Division I athletics while pursuing Ivy League educations they would carry with them for life.

I obviously didn't have the same father-child relationship with Lauren Shanel that I had with the twins. But after my court battles with her mom finally ended, I became determined to do everything I could to make her feel like a part of the family. It helped immensely that Tonya and her parents, before their passing, always treated her like a daughter and granddaughter.

Today, she's a beautiful, smart-as-heck, independent woman. She graduated from Florida A&M University and has worked as a real estate agent. She also brought my first grandchild into the world in 2025. And we're closer than we've ever been.

•

In my work as a vice president for the Padres from 2001 to 2013, I got to play an active role in nearly every facet of the organization's operations—and still got to sleep in my own bed most nights. It gave me a work-life balance I valued. The times I did have to be away from home helped broaden my view of the world—like the time I toured the West African country of Ghana with Padres owner John Moores and former President Jimmy Carter, as part of a larger trip I made with Major League Baseball to help grow the game on the continent and learn about the country's fight against waterborne illnesses.

One of my key initiatives with the Padres was inspired by my longtime friendship with former Negro Leagues player Buck O'Neil. We launched an annual event honoring the Negro Leagues, and I worked with Major

League Baseball to build on that by organizing a special draft that would allow surviving players from the league to symbolically join major league clubs for a day.

It took me a minute to get Commissioner Bud Selig on board with the idea. It wasn't that he didn't want to honor these players—he just had a hard time wrapping his head around the logistics. I assured Bud and MLB's vice president of baseball operations, Jimmie Lee Solomon, that we could pull it off.

I was thrilled for the 17 Negro Leagues players who'd been voted into the Hall of Fame a couple of years earlier—but deeply disappointed that Buck, at 94, wasn't among them. He took it in stride, saying his day would come. But I knew it hurt him to be overlooked.

Buck passed away in October 2006, before we could put the finishing touches on an event honoring him and his peers. In 2008, 30 Negro Leaguers were selected in an honorary draft held alongside the annual first-year player draft. Those players then traveled to the cities of the teams that drafted them for special ceremonies that educated fans and honored the legacy of the Negro Leagues whose statistics MLB officially recognized in 2020.

Buck finally got the posthumous call to Cooperstown in 2022, recognizing his overall contributions to the game. That same year, nineteenth-century Black baseball pioneer Bud Fowler was also inducted. I had the honor of speaking on his behalf that day.

•

I was living the life and raising the family I'd always dreamed of. I was doing meaningful work with the Padres. But 10 years after playing my last game, I was still coming to grips with my history with George Steinbrenner.

The article in the *Daily News* claiming the Padres had essentially bribed me to enter the Hall of Fame wearing their cap left a bitter taste that lingered. After the somewhat halfhearted and very awkward "Dave Winfield Day" at Yankee Stadium, George and I went another five years without speaking.

That's when I went to Tampa to see him, only to find out a lot had changed.

It was clear he wasn't well. He no longer presented himself as the domineering figure I'd known for more than 25 years. His handshake had weakened. He struggled for words and could barely speak above a whisper. I could see he didn't have the strength or clarity to have an in-depth conversation about our past.

So I let it go and kept things light, reminiscing about the time he put on a glove at spring training while I was taking batting practice.

"I had you running all over the field, dodging the ball," I said, laughing.

He seemed to remember the moment.

"I made some pretty good plays out there," he said.

I smiled. The man was stubborn to the end. But he'd probably have said the same about me.

After our meeting in Tampa, I saw George one final time—at the last Old-Timers' Day held at the old Yankee Stadium in 2008. He passed away a couple of years later—just two days after legendary Yankees public address announcer Bob Sheppard also passed away.

As I told *The New York Times* on the day of George's death: "I don't want to have bad feelings about anybody in life, I really don't. He and I went from one extreme to the other, and we're just going to leave it on a good note with him today. He'll be missed as an icon in this sport. The history of the sport is gone. Let's just remember the good things about him."

In an alternate history, I'm an all-time great Yankee, a player who not only carried on the grand tradition of baseball in the Bronx, but who also forged a deep personal relationship with the team owner. In that universe, George and I are giants in the sports and business worlds—together.

If I had led the Yankees to a World Series title in 1981, maybe that version becomes reality. Steinbrenner and I wouldn't have been at each other's throats, wasting valuable energy that I could have used to prevent a guy like Howie Spira from ever getting a foothold in our lives.

In this what-might-have-been scenario, maybe I have a walk-on role—or even a recurring one—on *Seinfeld*, where my office sits next to that of the fictionalized version of Steinbrenner.

As it stands, we're linked—just not in that way. Sometimes my name comes up when a young Yankees prospect is being compared to me—like when Aaron Judge was drafted in 2013. But more often, my place in Yankees history is framed around my feud with George.

So be it. But now you know the whole story.

•

While I've kept both a critical and appreciative eye on the past—my own and the game's—I've also felt driven to stand up for today's players. That's why I left the Padres in 2013 to become an advisor to the executive director of the Major League Baseball Players Association.

By then, the MLBPA was widely recognized as one of the strongest unions in the country, representing major league players whose average annual salary had reached $5 million. Major League Baseball also remained the only major sport in North America without a salary cap—at least for now.

Under the leadership of union head Tony Clark—the first former major leaguer to hold the position—the MLBPA expanded its mission to include minor league players. In 2026, Tony resigned, leaving a legacy of commitment to expanding opportunities for players and expanding their rights.

A major league ballfield is a unique kind of workplace—but it's a workplace nonetheless. I was reminded of that during the negotiations between the players and owners during the COVID-19 shutdown. During a time of extreme uncertainty, standing up for the rights of workers was more important than ever. And we did just that.

I retired from the union in 2025 with a sense of satisfaction that I had helped make a lasting impact on labor relations—and helped ensure that this generation of players wouldn't have to endure the wrath of all-powerful owners like mine did.

But the fight goes on. Players need to know their past, purpose, and power when they act as one.

At a 2025 meeting with Commissioner Rob Manfred, a group of Hall of Famers peppered him with questions about the future of the game—mostly rules changes like an automated strike zone and ways to increase the pace of play.

But I wasn't going to let Manfred leave the room without asking him about the collective bargaining agreement, which is set to expire at the end of 2026. It disturbed me that Manfred had hired a group of distinguished former players to travel around with him trying to sell players on the benefits of a salary cap.

"I hear from different people that you're saying there's going to be a lockout," I said. "Please set the record straight on that."

Manfred dodged the question, but I plan to keep grilling him—and whoever eventually succeeds him as commissioner.

Some say the balance of power has swung too far in the direction of the players and that free-spending teams like the Dodgers are creating a competitive imbalance. But I counter by saying it wasn't that long ago that there was no salary arbitration, player agents, or free agency.

And if spending alone guaranteed success, the Yankees—who still spend plenty themselves—would have a few more World Series titles to show for all of their recent postseason appearances.

The average major league team is worth nearly $3 billion, and I expect the owners will do whatever necessary to get what they want, including fighting dirty and impugning reputations. I know from personal experience how dirty the fight can get.

We must stand strong in defense of our hard-earned rights.

•

When I reflect on the battles I've fought, it's easy to describe them in warlike terms. By sports standards, they were. But there have been moments in my life—and in American history—that put those terms into perspective.

Getting to know the legends of the Negro Leagues showed me what true injustice in baseball really looked like. The terrorist attacks of September 11, 2001, made baseball—and everything else—seem small. Then there was the incident in 2020 that made me question who we are as a nation.

When I first started putting this book together, in the spring of 2020, I was sitting at home like everyone else—trying to stay safe from the coronavirus while watching a tragedy unfold on TV. The fact that it was happening on streets not far from where I grew up made it feel even more personal.

The death of George Floyd at the hands of a Minneapolis police officer became a symbol of racial injustice. The entire world saw a Black man pinned to the ground—an officer's knee pressed into his neck—using his final breaths to cry out, gasp for air, and call for his mother. It was horrific to watch—and a wake-up call for America to finally confront its long, painful history of systemic racism. It hit me even harder knowing it occurred less than a mile from where my twins were born.

After this happened, I got texts from many former associates—people appalled by what they'd seen. One came from Steve Donahue, the former Yankees trainer who had gone on to become the team's director of medical services. He wrote about how sorry he was that racism had once again reared its ugly head, and how it pained him that I—and so many other Black parents—still have to worry about the safety of our kids in ways we shouldn't. He told me he loved me and expressed hope that this incident would force America to change the way it treats people.

The protest movement that followed the deaths of Floyd and other unarmed Black people in 2020 gave me hope during the darkest days of the COVID-19 pandemic. For weeks, people of all colors and backgrounds marched—peacefully, in most cases, despite how some right-wing outlets tried to portray it—demanding change. Both the public and private sectors responded, taking the first meaningful steps toward addressing generations of inequity.

It filled me with pride to see then St. Paul Mayor Melvin Carter emerge as one of the leading voices of the movement. Back in 1997, I had the honor of handing him a Winfield Scholarship award that helped him attend Florida A&M University. Two decades later, in 2018, he made history by becoming my hometown's first Black mayor.

But then reality set in. The protests tapered off, the country opened back up after COVID-19, and most people returned to business as usual.

Within just a few years, a couple of steps forward turned into a few steps back. Words like "diversity," "equity," and "inclusion" became political hot potatoes—or even dirty words to some.

In the early 2000s, I led an effort to diversify the Padres' management structure—and the organization was better off for it. Now, as of this writing, with Donald Trump back in office, the federal government is rolling back key policy reforms, pressuring companies and institutions to dismantle DEI programs—and threatening to drag the country back to the early 1960s.

I had something that George Floyd and so many other Black people didn't—a voice. A chance to speak, to be heard, and to defend myself.

Too many people don't have that chance.

I hope those coming up today keep the pressure on our leaders and stand alongside the "old heads" who have fought through past struggles for equality. I hope they refuse to relent too soon and push tirelessly for real transformation.

•

When I look back at my career, my first thought is, *Did all that really happen?*

I just wish more of my friends were still around to say, "Yeah, Dave, it really did."

Shortly after my last visit with Steinbrenner, in 2006, I was scheduled to attend a charity golf event in Los Angeles with Kirby Puckett. I've never been much of a golfer, but I enjoyed the social side of hitting the ball around with friends—especially when one of those friends was someone like Kirby, who I probably would've enjoyed hanging out with even if we were stuck in line at the DMV.

Kirby was driving up from his home in Phoenix to celebrate his birthday early with me at the golf tournament. I knew seeing him would be the stress reliever it always was.

But Kirby never showed up for our tee time. Concerned, I called his fiancée. She told me he had suffered a massive stroke that morning. He died the next day.

I cried like a baby when I heard the news. Kirby was only 45. He had faced his share of struggles since glaucoma forced him into early retirement, but to me, he was like a little brother, always brightening my day with his smile.

And it wasn't just me. Everyone loved Kirby—teammates, opponents, and fans alike.

In the past decade, I've said goodbye to many of my heroes: Willie McCovey, Hank Aaron, Bob Gibson, and Frank Robinson.

And just since I started working on this book and an accompanying documentary, I've lost two of my closest friends: Rickey Henderson in 2024 and Dave Parker in 2025. Dave passed away just a month before his Hall of Fame induction.

Every July, I make two pilgrimages: one to the Hall of Fame, the other to my hometown.

It nourishes my heart and soul to be in Cooperstown on induction weekend. It's a time to honor the game and reconnect—or connect for the first time—with the best who ever played it. One of my favorite moments in 2025 was posing for a photo with Tim Raines and the newly inducted Ichiro Suzuki—the three of us united by the fact that we all wore No. 31 for the Yankees during our careers.

Not having Rickey and Dave there really hurt. But so did the absence of Ryne Sandberg, someone I never played with or against, except in an All-Star Game, but who became a summer friend in Cooperstown. He passed away from prostate cancer the day after the induction ceremony. That one hit especially close to home for me because of my own battle with the disease.

•

Nearing 60, I was feeling pretty good about life. My health and fitness were solid—I could still dunk a basketball at the sports club in my mid-50s. Retirement from baseball was going well, my family life was positive, and overall, I was very happy.

Then came a reality check.

Up until 2009, my routine physical exams had resulted in only minor things like needing glasses, a hearing aid, and an orthopedic surgery or two. But that year, my doctor noticed something more concerning: a slight but steady rise in my prostate-specific antigen, or PSA, an important marker in prostate cancer screening.

By 2014, the number had climbed too high for Tonya and me to ignore. We sought a second opinion from a highly recommended urologist, Dr. Matthew Bui, who gave us a full picture and explained our options.

The first step was a biopsy, which confirmed I had a malignant tumor. The next step was to remove the prostate.

A lot goes through your mind when you hear the word "cancer." You think about your mortality, your family, what truly matters. You go into fight mode.

Thankfully, we had caught it early. My doctors explained that the most advanced procedures for prostate removal tended to have overwhelmingly positive outcomes. I underwent a robot-assisted radical prostatectomy in Los Angeles and was back at work across the country with the MLBPA within a week.

A few weeks after the surgery, I was told I'd had a more aggressive form of cancer than my PSA scores indicated. It was good that I came in when I did. If I'd waited another six months, I might not be here today.

We continued monitoring everything closely. My PSA, which had dropped to zero after the surgery, stayed there for about five years. Then, during a routine exam in 2019, there was a slight uptick. Further testing showed a reemergence of cancer around the margins.

I underwent a handful of radiation treatments for the next month. The procedure wasn't painful, and I experienced no immediate or short-term side effects.

Today, 16 years after first noticing a problem, I am in deep remission. That means I have essentially beaten this disease.

It's important to understand that prostate cancer is the most commonly diagnosed cancer in men in this country—and a leading cause of cancer-related death. One in eight men will develop prostate cancer. Of that group, one in four will die from it. More than three million men are living with it right now.

Black men are more likely than any other group to develop prostate cancer, and statistically, they are more likely to face more aggressive forms of the disease.

Risk factors include diet, smoking, obesity, and certain environmental exposures.

When prostate cancer is caught early, the chances of dying or becoming disabled from it are very low. My message to all men: Don't be afraid of medical exams, tests, or procedures. Many of us grow up trying to be tough and not taking care of our health the way we should.

I didn't want to be one of those guys who ignored a serious warning sign until it was too late. I didn't want to end up saying, "If only I'd gone for my checkup sooner."

Early diagnosis saves lives. Be your own advocate. That's the reason I'm here today to tell this story.

•

Before heading to Cooperstown for the 2025 festivities, I walked the streets of my old neighborhood in St. Paul, soaking in the memories and reconnecting with the people I've known my whole life.

The construction of Highway 94 back in the 1960s may have displaced dozens of families, but it couldn't destroy the fabric of the community. In the spring of 2026, a statue of me was unveiled at a local baseball field. I'm proud to be part of its history now.

I'm in the seventh inning of life, and I plan on going extra innings for sure. At the most recent Rondo Days festival, I caught up with my brother, Steve, and my first baseball coach, Bill Peterson, who worked together for years on the local Reviving Baseball in Inner Cities program.

As we walked the once-familiar streets one hot afternoon, a rumble of thunder echoed, and the skies opened up. I instinctively glanced down to the curb as the rainwater started to pool. I flashed back to the Popsicle-stick boat races we used to have in that very spot. It's funny how you can leave a place for decades and still feel like the same little kid kneeling in the street and watching those stick boats float down the lane.

So many of our conversations begin with one of us saying, "Remember when . . ."

Later that year, a few days before Christmas, 16 of us gathered at the house my Grandma Jessie used to live in, the first time we'd had such a reunion since the mid-1980s. At the same dining room table where I used to sit growing up, not far from the vestibule where I picked up my sack lunch before school, my brother, my cousins, their kids—and even their kids' kids—sat around, sharing stories over dishes of Italian food.

In these pages, I've taken you from Rondo to San Diego to the Bronx and beyond—not just for nostalgia's sake, but to lay bare my experiences in a way I hope sheds light on pivotal eras in both baseball and American society.

Time comes for all of us, but I take pride in the big swings I've taken—and the connections I've made—in baseball and in life.

Acknowledgments

I feel blessed to have led the life I have—a life that wasn't available to those who came before me. My story exists only because of my ancestors who came from West Africa and endured a harsh existence in America, first in the bonds of slavery and later through the African American diaspora that brought them to Minnesota in the early 1900s. My maternal great-grandmother, Grenia Hunt, was born into slavery in Tennessee and later in life as a free woman entertained shoppers by spinning cotton in the window of a clothing store.

St. Paul was a welcoming place for my grandparents, who laid down roots and set up their children and grandchildren for future success. I remain grateful to all the family, neighbors, teachers, coaches, and friends who helped shape my younger years. I stay in touch with as many of you as possible and love reminiscing about those days. No trip home is complete without a reunion between me; my brother, Steve; and our first baseball coach, Bill Peterson.

This book would not have been possible without the support and guidance of my friend and agent, Randy Grossman, who has been in my corner for nearly 50 years.

Jeff Klein, thank you for your invaluable input across the spectrum of my career and life.

Thank you to Andy Strasberg for sharing your memories of my years in San Diego.

Mario Casciano helped me through some of my darkest times in New York, and his memories of that period were indispensable in writing this book. Thank you, Mario. You are one of a kind.

My story would have looked entirely different without the Major League Baseball Players Association. Starting in 1973 and continuing to this day, leaders like Marvin Miller, Don Fehr, Michael Weiner, and Tony Clark provided unwavering leadership that made it possible for me to step out on a limb and challenge authority. You all were heroic.

I also want to recognize the physicians in my life who have kept me sound in body and mind. Dr. Robert Watkins's surgery on my back helped extend my baseball career by six years. In more recent years, a team of doctors in Los Angeles has kept me upright and active by patching up my knees, shoulders, hip, and back. And I have nothing but gratitude for Dr. Matthew Bui, who helped me wage a winning battle against prostate cancer.

Thank you to my literary agent, Noah Ballard, for believing in this project; to my coauthor, Alan Maimon, for helping me shape this memoir into the story I hoped to tell; and to the team at Matt Holt Books for bringing it to life.

Then there's Ma—Arline Winfield. Without her everyday examples of strength, honesty, dignity, and integrity, I wouldn't be who I am today. She was a guiding light to everyone she touched, and her influence can be felt on every page of this memoir.

Finally, I'd like to thank my wife and children. Tonya, you've been with me half of my life, merged with me and my family, brought me the greatest kids in the world, and made me a whole person. We are stronger together. Our partnership has opened so many doors and taken us so many places.